SECOND TO NONE

SECOND TO NONE

AMERICAN COMPANIES IN JAPAN

ROBERT C. CHRISTOPHER

Crown Publishers, Inc.
New York

Published by Crown Publishers, Inc., 225 Park Avenue South, New York, New York 10003, and represented in Canada by the Canadian MANDA Group

CROWN is a trademark of Crown Publishers, Inc.

Manufactured in the United States of America

Library of Congress Cataloging-in-Publication Data

Christopher, Robert C., 1924–

  Second to none.

  Includes index.

  1. Corporations, American—Japan. I. Title.

HD2907.C45 1986   338.8´8973´052   86-6378

ISBN 0-517-56286-3

10 9 8 7 6 5 4 3 2 1

First Edition

This book is for my parents,
Ruth Adams Christopher
and Gordon Newton Christopher.

Contents

Preface

Some years ago in the preface to an earlier book I suggested that at least for the next two or three decades the way the United States dealt with Japan was likely to affect our national well-being more than our dealings with any other nation except the Soviet Union. Nothing that has happened since has caused me to change that opinion. On the contrary, I have been reinforced in it by the fact that the countries of the Pacific Basin—countries with which the United States now does more trade than it does with all of Europe—have steadily assumed greater importance in world affairs. And in the Pacific Basin, so far as American national interests are concerned, Japan is the key player. As U.S. ambassador to Japan Mike Mansfield tirelessly reminds anyone who will listen: "The next century will be that of the Pacific and what happens then will depend upon the foundations laid down by the United States and Japan in the rest of the present century."

The difficulty, as I see it, is that not enough Americans have yet absorbed Mike Mansfield's message. In the last few years, what has come to be known as "Japan-bashing" has increased both in frequency and virulence in the United States. It has become almost endemic in the Congress as well as in some sectors of American business and the U.S. labor movement. More recently still, it has been taken up by a certain number of influential journalists and other certified intellectuals.

This is a trend which, if it is permitted to develop unchecked, will, in my view, do serious damage to the long-term interests of the United States itself. Yet, since most of the Japan-bashing in which Americans currently indulge is inspired by the belief that the Japanese have taken unfair economic advantage of the United States, there would seem to be only one hope of countering it effectively. That hope, I am persuaded, lies in a dispassionate examination of Japanese-American economic dealings—and, in particular, of the proposition that American business has been systematically denied the possibility of competing successfully in Japanese markets.

There is, of course, a growing library of books that instruct—or purport to instruct—American businessmen on just what procedures they must follow in order to succeed in Japan. This book is not primarily designed to serve as that kind of manual. Instead, it is an attempt to describe as accurately as possible what the past experience of American business in Japan has actually been as opposed to what special pleaders allege that it has been.

Because that experience has been so highly varied, I do not think it is reducible to a neat set of formulas any more than the complex experience of private enterprise in the United States or Europe can be summed up in a few simplistic rules. Nonetheless, in economic life as in politics or diplomacy, there are useful, if not necessarily simple, insights to be gained by studying the past. Accordingly, it is my hope that this account of what U.S. entrepreneurs have already accomplished in Japan will in some modest degree help American business and those who shape American economic policy to lay even stronger foundations for the century of the Pacific.

When I began the research for this book, I was warned that I might have great difficulty in persuading businessmen on the firing line to give me the kind of candid commentary and specific information that I needed. In a few cases that proved true, but a remarkable number of the people who manage U.S. subsidiaries and affiliates in Japan were more generous than I had any right to expect in sharing with me their own experiences and those of their companies. For the most part, these invaluable counselors are clearly identified and extensively quoted in the body of the book and to all of them, Japanese and American, I owe a great debt.

There are, however, some people whose names are not mentioned or mentioned only in passing in my text whose assistance nonetheless was of such great importance that it must be singled out for acknowledgment here. First and foremost among these is Jiro Murase of the New York law firm of Wender, Murase & White with whom I first discussed the concept that underlies the book and who supplied indispensable guidance during the writing of it.

The list of others to whom I am indebted for ideas, information, introduction to sources and/or logistical help fills a whole notebook by itself and is too long to reproduce in its entirety here. Of very special assistance, however, were the following: Dean Jiro Tokuyama of the Nomura School of Advanced Management; Kinji Kawamura and Seiichi Soeda of the Foreign Press Center/Japan; Mikio Kato of International House, Tokyo; Masahisa Naitoh and Mrs. Yoriko Kawaguchi of the Ministry of International Trade and Industry; Shinsaku Sogo, Hiroyuki Wakabayashi, Ms. Junko Kuroda and Hiroaki Sato of JETRO; Kazuo Nukazawa of Keidanren; Tadashi Yamamoto of the Japan Center for International Exchange; Stephan Lesher of IBM and Mark Popiel of Dodwell.

Finally, there are half a dozen people whose psychological and material support I relied upon in shameless degree. My wife, Rita, provided cogent editorial advice while exhibiting extraordinary tolerance for my frequent neglect of family responsibilities. (In the latter, she was joined by our sons, Sandy and Gordon.) Judy McCarthy was both patient and skillful in interpreting my scrawl to her word processor. Tom Mori supplied regular doses of enthusiasm and good company during my stays in Japan. And my agent and mentor, Melanie Jackson, characteristically encouraged me to follow my instincts and concentrate upon this endeavor at a time when I might otherwise have wavered.

Old Lyme, Connecticut
January 15, 1986

SECOND TO NONE

1 Unhonored Profits

In the late winter of 1985, shortly after Americans learned that the U.S. trade deficit with Japan the previous year had soared to what was then an all-time high of $37 billion, I encountered an old acquaintance at a New York club to which we both belong. A distinguished journalist who has spent much of his career abroad, my friend has also served for some years as a member of the U.S. delegation to a major international organization where he had spent much of his time dealing with representatives of Third World countries. Discussing that experience, he admitted that he often found the anti-American posturing of the Third Worlders extremely irritating but added that he felt it was worth putting up with because the nations in question were of great potential importance to the United States and for all their public hostility actually attached considerable value to their relations with the United States.

This struck me as a rather remarkable display of tolerance, but when I was incautious enough to mention that I was working on a book about Japanese-American economic relations my friend's tolerance abruptly vanished. "Tell me, Bob," he said indignantly, "why do we let the Japanese take such advantage of us? How is it that we let them flood this country with their products when they don't let us sell them very much at all?"

At first, I was taken aback by these questions. Here was a man whose sophistication in many areas of international affairs was undeniable, yet he was discussing a central aspect of our country's relations with a vital ally in misinformed and oversimplified terms worthy of the rankest demagogue.

It was, however, foolish of me to be surprised by my friend's reaction. Lacking any particular expertise in economics or the realities of international trade, he understandably enough based his views of Japanese-American commercial relations on those regularly expressed in the media by U.S. businessmen, politicians and governmental "experts" on trade. And for many years now the prevailing message conveyed to the American public by such people has been one summed up with characteristic felicity by Lee Iacocca, that instant folk hero whom a 1985 opinion poll revealed to be even more widely admired by Americans than Dan Rather or Mike Wallace. Speaking to an outing held by the Democratic Caucus of the House of Representatives in April of that year, Mr. Iacocca forthrightly described Japan's trade with the United States as "a rip-off."

It is, in short, a perception of indefensible unfairness and lack of reciprocity that has come to dominate American attitudes concerning our economic dealings with Japan. Less than three weeks after Mr. Iacocca's blast, John Danforth of Missouri, the normally amiable Episcopal priest who chairs the Senate subcommittee on trade, refused to receive two eminent Japanese visitors to Washington with the explanation that "until one of these delegations can produce evidence to show that the Japanese market is open [to U.S. goods], I have no intention of seeing any of them." And a few weeks after that, in an article he wrote for the *New York Times*, Oregon's Senator Bob Packwood, the chairman of the Senate Finance Committee, insisted that "the fury over United States–Japan trade does not reflect resistance to competitive Japanese exports." Rather, he declared, American anger stemmed from the fact that by freezing competitive American products out of its market Japan denies many U.S. industries "the legitimate fruits of their success."

In a vain effort to counter this overwhelming assumption of unfairness, spokesmen for the Japanese government and Japanese industry have repeatedly pointed out that Japan now has the lowest tariffs overall of any industrialized nation and that over the past fifteen years it has also dismantled a wide array of non-tariff barriers such as import quotas, unnecessarily complex customs procedures and unduly onerous testing and certification requirements for foreign products. But confronted with the inescapable fact that U.S. trade deficits have continued to grow, most Americans have come to dismiss Japan's avowed efforts to open its markets as insincere. Along with Senator Packwood, much of the U.S. public believes that the Japanese have "dallied and stalled and lied to us." And even Americans who are prepared to credit the Japanese government with a modicum of sincerity often assert that its trade liberalization efforts are largely vitiated by cultural factors and bureaucratic foot-dragging. This, for example, is the view of Stephen D. Cohen, a professor of international relations at American University and the author of *Uneasy Partnership*, a well-received book on Japanese-American trade. "In formal terms, the Japanese market is open," Professor Cohen told a *New York Times* reporter in April 1985. "In commercial terms, it is impenetrable."

To my way of thinking, Professor Cohen's statement can only be described as astonishing. But it is, of course, of a piece with inflamed rhetoric on Japanese-American trade heard all the way from Pittsburgh to Silicon Valley: like my journalist friend in New York, scores of millions of Americans have come to accept it as an article of faith that U.S. farmers, manufacturers and providers of services do relatively little business in Japan. That belief, however, flies in the face of readily observable reality.

The truth is that a great number of U.S. enterprises have scored remarkable successes in Japan, that the U.S. economic presence in that country is already formidable—and that, given more intelligent behavior on the part of Americans, even greater U.S. penetration of Japanese markets and the Japanese economy is completely feasible.

Undoubtedly the most damaging misperception that bedevils relations between Japan and the United States is the common American impression that our exports to Japan are extremely limited in both size and scope. Because of the disturbing surge in our trade deficits with Japan in recent years, we tend to overlook the fact that Japan consistently buys more U.S. products than any other foreign nation save Canada and is, indeed, one of our fastest-growing export markets. On a worldwide basis, total U.S. exports were actually slightly lower in 1984 ($218 billion) than they had been in 1980 (nearly $221 billion). Throughout those same five years, however, our exports to Japan continued to grow; in 1984 alone they increased by more than 8 percent—which was considerably more than twice that year's increase in our sales to the Common Market nations.

The diversity of American exports to Japan, moreover, is vast, ranging as it does from soybeans to snowmaking machines. Though the fact is seldom reflected in the anguished outcries of U.S. trade negotiators over Japanese beef quotas, or in media reports thereon, Japan buys nearly 70 percent of all the beef exported by the United States. Japan is also by far the biggest foreign market for American citrus fruit and is a major purchaser of U.S.–grown cotton, tobacco, corn, sorghum and food grains. And the appetite of the Japanese for American raw materials is huge as well: in 1984, they bought some $865 million worth of U.S. coal and $1 billion worth of U.S. logs and wood chips.

All this, of course, is scant consolation to the numerous Americans who share Lee Iacocca's concern that by trading manufactured goods for our agricultural products and raw materials, Japan is reducing the United States to the status of a "colony." But this concern hardly squares with the fact that more than half of the $27 billion worth of U.S. exports to Japan in 1984 consisted of manufactured products. Indeed, according to William R. Cline of the Institute for International Economics, the United States sells more manufactured goods in almost all categories to "impenetrable" Japan than it does to West Germany, whose market is generally hailed as an admirably open one.

In a number of manufactured products ranging from photographic supplies to measuring instruments, Japan is actually American industry's best customer. In 1984, for example, Japan was the largest single foreign purchaser of American data processing equipment ($1.17 billion), commercial aircraft and aircraft parts ($979 million), inorganic chemicals ($836 million), pharmaceuticals ($572 million) and broadcasting equipment ($417 million). And by no means all of the American manufactured goods that Japan imports are ones in which the United States possesses any clear technological edge or an inherent competitive advantage: some 70 percent of all the stainless steel razor blades sold in Japan are made in Connecticut by the Schick Division of Warner-Lambert and 50 percent of the paper diapers used by Japanese mothers are imported by Procter & Gamble in finished or partly finished form.

All this, moreover, is only part of the story of U.S. business successes in Japan. What economists call "merchandise trade"— exports of farm products, raw materials and manufactured goods— is far from being a complete measure of the extent to which U.S. business has penetrated the Japanese economy. Though they are not reflected in merchandise trade statistics—which are the only measure of Japanese-American economic relations familiar to most people—the sale of services such as transportation, insurance, financial assistance, TV and movie film rights and the like contribute substantially to the earnings of U.S. companies that deal with Japan. In 1984, in fact, earnings from services were equivalent to well over a third of our merchandise sales to Japan.

Still another substantial source of income to the United States lies in the sale of goods which companies wholly or partially owned by U.S. interests import into Japan from countries other than the United States. Here the most dramatic case in point is that of American oil companies which each year sell more than $20 billion worth of non-American crude oil to Japan. But there are innumerable lesser examples as well: Nike, with the running shoes which it has manufactured in Korea and Taiwan; Warner-Lambert, with candy from Holland; the Loctite Corporation, whose Taiwan-made industrial adhesives help to hold together the engines of Toyota automobiles. The profits from these and many other such enterprises never figure in the bilateral Japanese-American trade balance yet help to fill the pockets of U.S. companies and hence of their stockholders and employees.

Important as they are, however, such "third country" operations are only one aspect of a phenomenon too little appreciated in the United States: the extraordinary extent to which American-owned companies or joint ventures by American and Japanese partners have succeeded in making themselves an integral part of Japan's domestic economy. Any American who has visited Japan can testify to the pervasiveness there of some familiar corporate names: IBM, Coca-Cola, McDonald's, Kentucky Fried Chicken. But even people who know that these companies do big business in Japan are often unaware just how big that business is. Items:

- In terms of total volume, Japanese drink more Coca-Cola than anyone else in the world except Americans and Mexicans—yet Coke accounts for only about half the business done by Coca-Cola Japan; with a line of soft drinks ranging from one flavored with honey to something called Georgia Coffee, the company produces 60 percent of all the carbonated beverages sold in Japan and in 1984 earned an estimated pre-tax profit of well over $100 million.
- IBM Japan, which like Coca-Cola Japan is 100 percent

owned by its American parent, is in one respect less impressive: in 1984, it slipped to No. 3 ranking in the Japanese computer market (behind Fujitsu and Nippon Electric Company). Still, with some 16,000 employees, $2 billion in annual sales in Japan and another $1 billion in exports to some seventy countries, it remains a giant by anyone's standards.

• McDonald's Japan, which is a fifty-fifty partnership between McDonald's USA and a fast-talking Japanese go-getter named Den Fujita, has as its cable address BIG MAC JAPAN and in 1984 the company's nearly five hundred "stores" sold enough of that delicacy—together with Quarter Pounders, Happy Meals, Chicken McNuggets and the rest—to gross over $400 million. (Perhaps the ultimate testimony to McDonald's success, however, is that Japan's Ministry of Education has complained that because of their addiction to hamburgers nearly half the nation's schoolchildren are now clumsy with chopsticks—a development which, as Fujita dryly notes, "may be a big problem for the ministry but is good for me.")

At the opposite pole from such giants as McDonald's are a number of relative midgets, many of which don't even have a parent company in the United States. Between 1980 and 1985 nearly five hundred small companies owned by U.S. citizens were established in Japan. A number of these were involved in things such as the marketing of computer software, a field in which Japan, though steadily gaining ground, still lags somewhat behind the United States. My own favorite among these small enterprises, however, is one that was launched in 1982 by an ex-journalist from Chicago named Lyle Fox. Starting off with just $10,000 in capital, half of it borrowed, Fox began baking "authentic American bagels," a delicacy previously unknown in Japan. By early 1985, Fox's Bagels was selling 2,000 bagels a day and its product had become so trendy in Tokyo that the bakery's institutional customers included the food section of a top department store and the Hotel Okura, arguably Japan's most elegant hostelry.

It is, of course, understandable enough that a firm like Fox's Bagels does not enjoy a high recognition factor with the U.S. public. What is a bit more surprising is that the same holds true for a considerable number of companies which, although their products are partially or wholly manufactured in Japan, are 50 percent or more American-owned and count their annual sales in the hundreds of millions of dollars.

Predictably, some of the most successful of these manufacturing companies are involved in high technology of one sort or another. Some notable examples:

- Yamatake-Honeywell, which is 50 percent owned by Honeywell Inc. of Minneapolis, specializes in automated control systems which it not only sells in Japan but exports to a number of other countries, including the United States. "We're a half-billion-dollar company," says Y-H president Haruo Okinobu.
- Yokogawa-Hewlett-Packard, which is 75 percent owned by California's Hewlett-Packard Company, has sales of nearly $400 million a year in instrumentation and computer products. With justifiable satisfaction, Chairman Kenzo Sasaoka notes that for the four years ending in 1984 his company grew at an annual rate of 27 percent, "which is twice as high as the average for the industry."
- Because it is 100 percent owned by its parent company in Dallas, Texas Instruments Japan does not publish separate earnings figures, but outsiders estimate that in 1983 it sold some $200 million worth of the integrated circuits it manufactures in Japan and earned a pre-tax profit of perhaps 20 percent.

The solid position carved out in Japan by these and other such ventures as Fuji Xerox (annual sales of over $1 billion) has sometimes inspired the assertion that any U.S. company that wishes to operate successfully in Japan must bring some form of high technology to the party. In reality, though, the goods and services produced in Japan by firms with familiar American names include many thoroughly homely ones. Some cases in point:

- Along with pharmaceuticals, diagnostic equipment and other relatively exotic items, Johnson & Johnson's Japanese subsidiaries market locally manufactured Band-Aids, baby oil and other bathroom-cabinet standbys. "We're making pots of money and are very happy," says J&J's top man in Japan, British-born Kneale Ashworth. So they should be: in unit volume, the company's sales in Japan doubled between 1980 and 1984.

• "The other Johnson"—which is to say Johnson Wax Japan—dominates the Japanese market for industrial maintenance products and is at or near the top in consumer sales of wax, polish, glass cleaner and air fresheners. With annual sales of $130 million a year, it is by far the biggest of the forty-five foreign subsidiaries of Wisconsin's S. C. Johnson Company—a fact that tends to crop up early in any conversation with its gregarious, impeccably tailored chairman, Hachiro Koyama. ("My American friends call me 'Buddy.' ")

• With good old Ritz Crackers as one of its standbys, Yamazaki-Nabisco, which is 50 percent owned by Nabisco (and hence, ultimately, by R. J. Reynolds & Company), is a strong No. 2 in the Japanese biscuit market. That fact plus its No. 3 ranking in snack items such as potato chips gives Yamazaki-Nabisco annual sales approaching $200 million.

• The Japan Tupperware Company, 100 percent owned by its American parent, sells Japanese housewives some $100 million worth of storage containers a year—all of them made in Japan. According to its president, Kazunobu Cho, the company's profits increased a tidy 2,739 percent between 1965 and 1985.

• Nearly one Japanese in ten now holds a cancer insurance policy written by the Japan branch of the American Family Life Assurance Company of Columbus, Georgia. Though it did not write its first cancer insurance policy in Japan until late 1974, American Family already boasts annual revenues there of more than $350 million—which is substantially more than its annual revenues in the United States.

American Family, moreover, is not the only U.S. company to do more business in Japan than it does at home. The same is true for Max Factor, which, even though it holds only about 5 percent of the market in Japan, is the biggest foreign-owned cosmetics company in the country and has estimated annual sales on the order of

$150 million. And in at least one of its enterprises, the vast Disney organization also finds Japan a better market than the United States: stimulated in part by the popularity of Tokyo's Disneyland (which regularly attracts more visitors than its California prototype), Japanese now considerably outstrip Americans in total purchases of Mickey Mouse watches, Goofy pencils and other merchandise licensed by Walt Disney Productions. (On a somewhat less upbeat note, there is even one U.S. company, Caterpillar Tractor Company, whose only profitable operation in the entire world in 1984 was its joint venture in Japan with Mitsubishi Heavy Industries.)

What does this all add up to? The honest answer is that nobody knows with absolute accuracy. The companies I have so far mentioned constitute only a sampling of the American business presence in Japan and even Japan's Ministry of International Trade and Industry (MITI), which conducts regular surveys on the subject, is a bit vague as to how big that presence is in total. As of late 1984, however, Shinji Fukukawa, director general of MITI's Industrial Policy Bureau, estimated that there were 1,000 firms in Japan that were either wholly or in substantial part owned by American interests and that amongst them these firms had racked up total sales of more than $55 billion in fiscal 1981. And on the strength of their tax returns, a Japanese research organization calculated that in that same year the thirteen biggest American affiliates alone had earned pre-tax profits in Japan of more than $1.5 billion. Since both the Japanese economy and U.S. participation in it have grown significantly since 1981, the equivalent figures today are obviously even larger.

Back in the 1960s my friend Osborn Elliott, then editor of *Newsweek*, once jokingly posed a mock-ignorant question to a pair of eminent economists. "If you're so smart," he asked, "why ain't you rich?" In a somewhat similar vein, what I have written up to now will certainly prompt some readers to demand: "If so many American companies are making so much money in Japan, why is it that all I hear is how tough it is for Americans to do any business there at all?"

The short answer to that question is that, as so often happens with complex issues, the perception of Japanese economic behavior that currently prevails in the United States has not caught up with changing realities. As late as the 1960s, the Japanese govern-ment by dint of a wide variety of protectionist devices did, in fact, make it very difficult for most foreign companies to do business in Japan and even at times encouraged predatory behavior on the part of Japanese industry. But since then, as I noted earlier, Japan has been steadily dismantling its barriers against foreign products and foreign investments.

I emphatically do not mean to suggest that all such barriers have vanished or that Japanese businessmen are not fierce and some-times unscrupulous competitors. But it is, I believe, fair to say that Japanese businessmen as a whole are no more unscrupulous than U.S. businessmen—or British or French businessmen, for that mat-ter. And according to some of America's leading experts on inter-national trade, essentially the same parity exists when it comes to protectionism. In a study published in mid-1985 by the Institute for International Economics, C. Fred Bergsten and William R. Cline concluded that if Japan were to abandon "all overt and intangible" barriers against American products the U.S. could probably sell an additional $5 billion to $8 billion worth of goods a year in the Japanese market. But by the same token, they esti-mated that the United States excludes about $5 billion worth of Japanese goods from the American market each year through a variety of protectionist devices ranging from "voluntary" quotas to restrictive licensing agreements.

Though their study provoked howls of outrage from Washing-ton officialdom, Bergsten and Cline are by no means alone in believing that U.S. complaints about Japanese restrictions on free trade are not only a case of the pot calling the kettle black but vastly exaggerated to boot. "Non-tariff barriers are not the central problem for U.S. business in Japan," says James C. Abegglen, a much-respected American business consultant based in Tokyo. "By and large, Japanese firms face the same kind of barriers in the United States that U.S. firms face in Japan."

Nonetheless, as Abegglen notes, most Americans, including many if not most American businessmen, cling to "the belief that Japan is still as closed as it was in the sixties." They do so in part because that is the message implicit in nearly every pronouncement U.S. officials make on the subject—pronouncements that most of the time are reported in the U.S. media with a notable lack of the kind of searching skepticism with which contemporary American journalists tend to regard official statements on most other matters.

By so often failing to look behind what might be called "the Washington line" on Japanese-American trade, U.S. journalists inadvertently mislead the public. Not infrequently, says Robert L. Sharp, vice-president of the Manufacturers Hanover Trust in Tokyo and a past president of the American Chamber of Commerce in Japan, the complaints against Japan voiced by U.S. trade negotiators are wrong—"either because the situation has changed or they are just plain misinformed." But even when they are in full possession of the facts, the special trade representatives, Commerce Department officials and assistant secretaries of the Treasury who jet in and out of Tokyo in seemingly endless procession invariably present a highly one-sided picture of Japanese-American economic relations. This, of course, is only natural: like lawyers, the people who conduct America's economic diplomacy are intent on putting their case as strongly as possible. With the trade gap between Japan and the United States steadily widening and some of the most politically potent interest groups in the United States ceaselessly proclaiming that Japanese trade practices are "unfair," Washington's trade negotiators cannot logically be expected to pay much public attention to the considerable steps that Japan has taken to open up its market. Instead, they concentrate almost exclusively on fields in which the Japanese can still legitimately— or at least with some color of legitimacy—be charged with trying to freeze out American suppliers or inhibit the growth of American interests in Japan.

Predictable as such adversarial noises may be from politicians and bureaucrats, it might nonetheless seem surprising at first blush that there are so few countervailing noises from the numerous American enterprises that are prospering in Japan or in trade with Japan. But here again the explanation is a simple one. As Kenichi Ohmae, the managing director of McKinsey & Company's consulting operation in Japan, has noted: "Successful [U.S.] companies in Japan are very quiet; they have no desire to attract competition." And if Ohmae's observation sounds unduly cynical, I can testify from personal experience that it is not unfounded. The head of one well-known U.S. company with interests in Japan made it plain through an intermediary that he would not help me in my research for this book because he was afraid it would encourage other firms in his industry to invade the Japanese market more aggressively. And Victor Harris, the able and engaging Californian who as of early 1985 was president of Max Factor's Japanese subsidiary, was even more open on the subject. "I'm not going to help people compete with me," he said. "When I talk to groups in the States, I always tell them it's impossible to get into the Japanese market. And I think there's a lot of that."

What there's even more of—and, unfortunately, a great deal more of—is anti-Japanese rhetoric emanating from U.S. businessmen and labor leaders who wrap themselves in the banner of national interest but whose overriding concern is actually to perpetuate in their industries pay and profit levels which are not economically justifiable. Predictably, this rhetoric is often not only disingenuous but downright deceptive. In blocking all efforts to repeal the legal ban on export of Alaskan North Slope oil to Japan, for example, spokesmen for a coalition of U.S. maritime unions, shipping lines and pipeline companies argue that such a move would neither improve the U.S. trade balance nor benefit the U.S. consumer. The facts are that selling Alaskan crude to the Japanese would shave many billions of dollars off our trade deficit with Japan and that replacing it with cheaper oil from Mexico or Venezuela would probably reduce our overall trade deficit and would certainly mean lower prices for refined petroleum products on the East Coast. But that is outweighed in the eyes of the anti-export coalition by the fact that the transport of Alaskan oil now employs 90 percent of all American seagoing crews—whose high wages have long since rendered the dwindling American merchant marine uncompetitive internationally.

This, moreover, is far from being an isolated case. In his provocative book *Can America Compete?* Robert Z. Lawrence of the Brookings Institution observes that "the loudest complaints about the closed nature of the Japanese market often come from U.S. industries that have great trouble competing with Japan in the United States and hence are unlikely to benefit from greater access to the Japanese market." What Lawrence might have added is that not infrequently the loudest complainers are quietly playing both ends against the middle. In all of his demands for continuation of auto quotas and denunciations of Japan for flooding the United States with manufactured goods, there was one point that Lee Iacocca until very recently carefully downplayed—the fact that his own Chrysler Corporation has long been one of the half-dozen biggest U.S. importers of Japanese cars.

Even more egregious—though more widely recognized—has been the deception practiced by major U.S. steel producers. With considerable persuasiveness, they argued that they must have protection against imports of lower-cost steel from Japan and other countries overseas in order to amass the capital necessary to modernize American mills and make them competitive again. Yet when they won such protection, they used the resulting profits not primarily to rebuild their steel plants but to buy more lucrative enterprises ranging from shopping centers to oil companies. The result was that employment in the steel industry continued to decline while the price that American consumers paid for products made of steel was inflated by billions of dollars a year.

What has immeasurably aided such special pleaders in their efforts to convince the U.S. public that their problems stem from unfair Japanese competition rather than from their own mismanagement has been the oversimplified terms in which Americans generally discuss our dealings with Japan. Businessmen, labor leaders, politicians, bureaucrats, journalists—all of us tend to talk as though our most pressing international economic concern was our trade deficit with Japan. We do this partly, of course, because the size of that deficit and its consistent upward trend for some years past is genuinely distressing. But we also do it out of a combination of ignorance and intellectual laziness: a trade balance figure is, superficially at least, a handy kind of box score, a readily comprehensible figure that doesn't seem to require the sort of complex and niggling qualification that causes the eyes of newspaper readers to glaze over or the members of a politician's audience to start shuffling restlessly in their seats.

Convenient as it may be, however, many experts believe that to focus exclusively on the merchandise trade balance between one country and another is misleading. As I have already suggested and as anyone with even a cursory acquaintance with economics knows, the trade balance is by no means a complete measure of the economic exchanges between countries. Beyond that, a number of economists argue that the fact that a nation runs a deficit with one or two of its trading partners is not necessarily cause for concern. What is cause for concern is if a nation's overall international balance of payments slips into the red.

That, of course, is precisely the situation into which the United States has now fallen—and in spades. But, ironically, the overriding attention paid to our trade deficit with Japan has served to divert attention somewhat from the deplorable state of our overall international economic position. In 1984, for example, we ran a $23 billion deficit in our trade with Canada. In view of the fact that Canada is not only our largest trading partner but a nation with which we have traditionally run solid trade surpluses, that is a truly ominous portent. Yet we have largely lost sight of it in our preoccupation with Japan. And that kind of selective myopia is only one of the unfortunate consequences of our excessively simplistic approach to our economic relations with Japan.

2 Why Bother?

In early 1985 Stephen R. Levy, the head of a Massachusetts company engaged in the manufacture of switching networks, told Susan Chira of the *New York Times* that he had concluded that it wasn't worthwhile "expending our energies to penetrate the Japanese market right now." The reason for his decision, he explained, was that "the deck is stacked against us there."

Mr. Levy's judgment is one that has been echoed in U.S. executive suites over and over again since the 1950s. However much it might be in the national interest for U.S. companies to try harder in Japan, no corporate manager can be expected to take his products into a market where he sees scant prospect of making money or even one in which it appears to him unduly hard to make money. As Robert Sharp of Manufacturers Hanover Trust in Tokyo says: "If it's easier to get into a market other than Japan, U.S. firms are apt to take the path of least resistance."

On the face of things, that might well seem a prudent reaction. The number of foreign firms that have tried to establish themselves in Japan only to beat an ignominious retreat a few years later is disquietingly large. For a variety of reasons, at least one out of seven foreign firms that enter the Japanese market are so unsuccessful that they eventually withdraw. And among companies without a large domestic base and extensive capital resources, the attrition rate is far higher: according to George Hara, president of Data Control Ltd. of Palo Alto, the predictable failure rate among small American companies seeking to win a niche in Japan runs over 50 percent.

Given these discouraging statistics, it is understandable that an American entrepreneur might ask himself "Why bother with Japan?" It is understandable, too, that he might be puzzled by the attitude of Johnson & Johnson chairman James Burke, who, according to J&J's top Asian hand Kneale Ashworth, "decided some years ago that Japan was the No. 1 geographic priority for our corporation." Why *not* take the path of least resistance and do what the majority of American companies with international interests have done: make your major foreign investments in Western Europe where, both culturally and in terms of business practices, the average American feels more at home than he does in Japan.

The answer to these questions, while obvious, is often given too little weight in American boardrooms. Despite all the achievements of the Common Market, Western Europe is still not truly a single economic unit but a loose confederation of relatively modest national markets separated from each other by trade barriers and differing product standards. It is Japan, ethnically, linguistically and politically unified, that in effective economic terms constitutes the world's single biggest market outside the United States.

Japan's gross national product, in fact, amounts to roughly one-third the combined GNPs of all the world's industrialized nations except the United States—and with higher average earnings than workers in any Common Market country Japanese workers have formidable purchasing power. What's more, this already awesome market is steadily increasing in both size and sophistication. As of mid-1985, the Conference Board, a research organization which maintains a kind of international economic scoreboard, reported that Japan, with a leading index rising at the annual rate of 9 percent, had the fastest-growing economy of any developed nation. (In the United States, where the Reagan boom was still in full swing, the leading index at the time was rising at a rate of only 3 percent.) And an advisory group which the Japanese government convened a few years ago predicted that by the year 2000, even assuming relatively moderate growth, per capita GNP will be 20 percent higher in Japan than in the United States.

Whether or not that prediction is fulfilled, the shorter term prospects in Japan are undeniably pleasing in fields ranging from high technology to the most mundane consumer items. In an interview I had with him early in 1985, Herbert F. Hayde, chairman of the Burroughs subsidiary in Japan, asserted that Japan's computer and telecommunications market, already the second largest in the world, was growing at an annual rate of 20 percent. A few days later, Weldon Johnson, the ruggedly handsome Georgian who heads Coca-Cola Japan, told me: "Growth prospects here appear very bright over the next few years and I see more of that growth shifting to internal consumption as opposed to exports. . . . There are indications that the Japanese may begin to use consumer credit much more liberally than in the past—which should in itself spur domestic consumption."

In short, as Dirk Vaubel of West Germany's Wella once pointed out, foreign businessmen should bear in mind that the Japanese market is "worthy of your efforts even if your market share is small. In absolute terms, for example, a 3 percent share of the Japanese market is equivalent to more than 40 percent of the Swiss market." To put Vaubel's point another way, a company with 3 percent of the Japanese pharmaceutical market would have run up sales of nearly $500 million in 1985 and one with the same tiny share of the cigarette market would have had sales of more than $360 million.

As we have already seen, however, a considerable number of U.S. companies and U.S.–Japanese joint ventures command far more than 3 percent of the Japanese market for some of their products. For such companies, the business they do in Japan can account for a substantial portion of their total turnover worldwide. According to Sam Maugeri, the president of Warner-Lambert Japan, roughly 30 percent of the Schick razor blades sold anywhere in the world are sold in Japan.

Even more to the point, Japanese operations contribute significantly to the profits of many U.S. corporations. As a general rule, the fierce competitiveness of Japanese business tends to keep profit margins in Japan painfully thin. But as Takeo Shiina, the president of IBM Japan, noted in an article in the *Journal of Japanese Trade and Industry*, the profit margins of manufacturing firms operating in Japan but wholly or in large part owned by foreigners runs more than 50 percent higher than those of purely Japanese firms—and in commerce and trade the foreign affiliates enjoy profit margins more than twice as high as their Japanese competitors. One consequence of this is that between 1966 and 1977, according to the American Chamber of Commerce in Japan, the average rate of return on direct U.S. investments overseas was greater in Japan than in any other foreign country.

For most of the American companies that have tried their luck in Japan, the sheer size of the Japanese market and its potential contribution to their profit stream have been motivation enough. But in recent years other factors have increasingly begun to reinforce that basic lure.

One of these new factors is a notable change in the Japanese government's attitude toward foreign investors in Japan. MITI, which for years totally excluded foreign investment in some fields and hedged it about with irksome restrictions in many others, now has a division specifically charged with promoting such investment and as of 1985 it was headed by one of the ministry's rising stars, an incisive woman, with a Yale M.A. in economics, named Yoriko Kawaguchi. As will be evident when we look at the running battle over software copyright law in Japan, MITI is still entirely capable of playing hardball on behalf of what it considers a vulnerable Japanese industry. Moreover, foreign investment in defense-related industries, oil companies and mining—as well as in such politically sensitive areas as agriculture and, for complex historical reasons, the production of leather goods—is still carefully controlled. But in most fields, according to Ms. Kawaguchi, the would-be foreign investor now finds the door open. "All he has to do," she told me, "is give prior notice of his intentions to the Bank of Japan and if no objection is raised within two weeks, he can go ahead." At that point, in fact, MITI's industrial location guidance division, if so requested, will obligingly order its computer to scan a list of some 2,000 industrial sites and come up with a selection of those best suited to the foreigner's particular requirements.

One reason for MITI's change of heart is undoubtedly a desire to take some of the steam out of U.S. complaints about the difficulty of getting into the Japanese market. Another, however, is purely domestic: since the end of World War II there has been a vast exodus of countryfolk into Japan's cities with the result that today half of the entire Japanese population is crammed into the so-called Tokaido megalopolis—a 300-mile-long corridor running along the south coast of the main island of Honshu from Tokyo to Kobe. In an effort to alleviate the social and economic problems created by this situation, Japan's central government has for some time sought to persuade industry to decentralize and establish plants in smaller outlying cities or rural areas. Increasingly, with all the boosterism of any Sun Belt chamber of commerce in the

United States, local politicians and governments in Japan have joined in this campaign. And because it is easier to attract a brand-new enterprise than to persuade an existing one to relocate, they now tend to focus a good deal of attention on prospective foreign investors.

Ironically, one of the most effective of these local boosters, an affable, hard-driving man named Morihiko Hiramatsu, was at one time a senior official in MITI's electronics policy division and in that role kept a very tight rein indeed on foreign companies anxious to establish high-tech operations in Japan. By the early 1980s, however, Hiramatsu had become governor of Oita prefecture on the southern island of Kyushu and, having talked as many Japanese electronics companies as he could reasonably expect into building plants in his fiefdom, he had begun to look on foreigners with a more kindly eye.

Among the foreigners on whom Hiramatsu lavished attention was an American of a temperament very similar to his own—a funny, fast-talking entrepreneur named Sheldon Weinig. A one-time professor of metallurgy at New York University, Dr. Weinig had parlayed a semiconductor-coating process of his own devising into a thriving company called Materials Research Corporation and was bent on supplementing his plant in Orangeburg, New York, with another in Japan. Assisted by Hiramatsu and his men, Weinig found a suitable site in Oita and then, with characteristic insouciance, asked the government-run Japan Development Bank for $1.5 million construction loan. Startled to receive such a request from a foreigner, the Development Bank dragged its feet for months, at one point suggesting that Weinig and his top associates pledge their personal assets as security for the loan. In the end, however, thanks in part to the mediation of a U.S.–educated officer of the Bank of Tokyo, the loan came through and in late 1983 Weinig's Nihon MRC Company plant in Oita began to turn out high-quality machines for coating and etching silicon chips.

For Materials Research Corporation, a prime motive for manufacturing in Japan was to achieve greater access to customers and potential customers there; even though Japan's convoluted distribution processes prevent Nihon MRC from selling its machines directly to Japanese semiconductor producers, the company should gain simply from operating inside the Japanese system. For a growing number of other U.S. companies, however, the establishment of a Japanese subsidiary or joint venture holds an additional attraction: it offers easier access not only to the Japanese market but to the burgeoning markets of the newly industrializing nations of East Asia.

When it comes to doing business in East Asia generally, the advantages that a subsidiary based in Japan and largely staffed by Japanese has over its U.S. parent are not necessarily those which might seem obvious. In a number of industries, geographic proximity to one's customers is of only marginal economic importance. Japanese wages, while lower than U.S. wages, are no longer low compared to those prevailing in Europe and are extremely high by Asian standards. And the strength of the cultural affinity between Japanese and other Asians is often overestimated by Americans. Haruo Okinobu, the president of Yamatake-Honeywell, once assured me that "in China, there's a feeling that sometimes it's nice to be just Orientals together," and that may indeed be the case. But it certainly doesn't hold true in Korea, where affection for the country's former Japanese rulers is minimal, and it is worth bearing in mind that as late as the 1970s a state visit by a Japanese prime minister sparked riots in Southeast Asia.

Often, too, economic differences reinforce the cultural and political differences and help to make Japan nearly as unlike its Asian neighbors as the United States itself is. Even where their tastes in consumer goods coincide—which is not always the case—other Asians are not able to gratify those tastes as freely as the Japanese can. Despite the much-vaunted economic growth of South Korea, for example, per capita GNP there as of 1985 was only about a fifth what it was in Japan.

Yet in some areas of business—particularly high-technology fields—things are otherwise. In the information industry, so Herbert Hayde of Burroughs reported in 1985, "Southeast Asian markets are growing even faster in relative terms than the Japanese market—up to 40 percent a year in some places. And collectively they're growing at a rate of perhaps 25 percent a year. . . . It's to take advantage of that opportunity that major companies in our field are moving significant numbers of people out here."

Even so, I asked him, why make Japan the center of one's Asian efforts? "I think it's important to have engineering capability for Southeast Asia before developing manufacturing capability there," Hayde answered. "And I think it's critical at this time that this engineering capability be in Japan where the cutting edge of technology is being developed."

Clearly, some of Hayde's competitors have arrived at similar conclusions. According to Kenzo Sasaoka, the chairman of Yokogawa-Hewlett-Packard, the reason that Hewlett-Packard increased its share in his company to a controlling 75 percent in 1982 was that it wanted to use Y-H-P as a base for all its Asian operations. And mighty IBM has taken an even bigger step in the same direction. Throughout its long years of operations in Japan, IBM had always kept the number of American faces visible in its Tokyo offices to a negligible few. Then, in mid-1984, the company set Japanese business circles agog by dispatching some two hundred Americans to Tokyo to establish the so-called Asia/Pacific Group, a new echelon in the IBM chain of command whose mission is to supervise all Far Eastern operations. At the same time, President Takeo Shiina of IBM Japan, who had previously reported directly to IBM World Trade headquarters in Mt. Pleasant, New York, began to report instead to George Conrades, the head of Asia/Pacific Group.

To some of my Japanese friends, ever sensitive to matters of status, all this appeared to signal a reduction in the autonomy of IBM Japan. Over an elegantly served but decidedly no-stars, no-martini lunch in an executive dining room at Mt. Pleasant, I suggested as much to Ralph Pfeiffer, the forceful, articulate overseer of IBM's Canadian, Latin American and Far Eastern subsidiaries. His reply was that while superficially it might look as though IBM Japan had been downgraded in importance, that was not really the case at all. Rather, the creation of the Asia/Pacific Group was part of IBM's overall response to a unique problem.

"At the rate we are now growing," Pfeiffer said, "IBM will be doing $100 billion a year in business worldwide before very many years go by. We don't know how to run a $100 billion company because we've never done it. And there isn't any model to follow because nobody else has ever done so either. So we're trying to prepare for the job by making changes in the way we do things, some based on deductive reasoning and some on inductive reasoning."

One of the changes, he continued, was to pursue a policy of judicious decentralization—which was where the establishment of the Asia/Pacific Group came in. "Among other things," he said, "the existence of APG means that decisions affecting IBM Japan can now be taken closer to the scene of action. Now a five-minute taxi ride between the IBM Japan building and the APG office in Tokyo can settle a lot of things that used to require a time-consuming exchange of messages between Japan and the States or a phone call that inevitably came at an awkward hour on one end or the other—or maybe even a twelve-hour plane flight."

That made obvious sense, but it still wasn't clear to me why it had seemed necessary to create a whole new structure. Why not just let IBM Japan oversee all Asian operations? One reason, Pfeiffer answered, was that Japan is not a universal model for all Asian and Pacific countries. "Banking relationships, for example, are totally different in Japan and Australia," he pointed out. "And someone operating in Southeast Asia can encounter marketing problems totally unlike those in Japan."

Nonetheless, Pfeiffer insisted, Tokyo was clearly where IBM's overall Asian headquarters should be. "In transportation terms," he said, "it's the best place from which to cover all Asia. And even though markets in the newly industrializing Asian countries are now growing at a terrific rate because of the time lag in development of the information industries there, Japan still accounts for 60 percent of our Asia/Pacific sales." Then, ringing a change on the theme sounded by Burroughs' Herbert Hayde, Pfeiffer added that where technology was concerned, Japan also had unique resources to offer. In fact, he said, IBM Japan's Fujisawa Research Labs were handling design not only for the Japanese market but for the Chinese, Thai and Korean markets as well and were better equipped to do so than any U.S. facility. The reason: instead of being written with an alphabet, the Chinese, Thai and Korean languages are written with ideographs and/or phonetic syllabaries—a fact that poses problems in computer and computer software design with which the Japanese because of the nature of their own language are painfully familiar.

Because the United States now does more business with Asia than it does with Western Europe, the contribution that possession of a Japanese base can make to a U.S. company's overall Asian strategy is of great importance. But even more than success in Asia can ride on the decision to make—or not to make—a major effort in Japan. "A great many American companies," according to James

Abegglen, "have awakened to find that because they are not in Japan, or are unable to compete in Japan, their profit positions everywhere abroad have become quite insecure."

One American company which believes it has awakened in time to avoid that fate is Eastman Kodak. "We've got a good business in this country," says Dr. Albert L. Sieg, the sandy-haired, soft-spoken president of Kodak Japan. "But we're not the market leader here that we are in almost every other country in the world and that has some unfortunate consequences."

If anything, Sieg understates the case. Though Kodak Japan has sales of about $300 million a year and retains the lion's share of the professional film market, the story is radically different in the much larger amateur film market; there Fuji Photo Film has 70 percent and Kodak only 15 percent.

One reason for this is that for many years Japan imposed extremely high tariffs on imported film. But another reason, Sieg believes, is that "we didn't do the job we should have in the past." Though Kodak has been selling its products in Japan for nearly a century, during most of that time it did all its marketing through agents. Not until 1977 did the company establish its own Japanese subsidiary and only in very recent years has it made a really concerted effort to improve its position in Japan. "For too long," Sieg says, "we granted our Japanese competitors a safe haven. Because we didn't give them any real solid competition in their home market, we allowed them to amass enormous resources that they can use strategically against us in the rest of the world."

True enough, yet even mighty IBM's experience suggests that giving your Japanese competitors a fierce battle on their own turf is no cure-all: it may slow the pace of their march into foreign markets somewhat but is unlikely to forestall or halt it. And, where Kodak is concerned, the cat is out of the bag, in any case; Fuji Photo Film already markets its products worldwide. What then does Kodak hope to achieve by stepping up its efforts in Japan at this already late date?

"We believe we can be a lot stronger No. 2 here," Sieg replies. "But our strategy in Japan isn't just profit motivated. It's also to learn how to do business against our competition in their home territory. We believe that will be a major asset to us as we compete with them in the rest of the world."

Though it was often not part of their conscious purpose in going into Japan originally, many American firms doing business there have experienced precisely the kind of payoff Kodak hopes for. Over time, as things have turned out, there has been a great deal of what might be called reverse flow from Japanese-based companies to their American parents—a development which manifests itself in a variety of ways.

Among the many admirable characteristics of Japanese workers and plant managers is their habit of continually making small changes in the machinery and manufacturing processes used by their company—changes which, incrementally, often add up to major improvements in both worker productivity and product quality. One result of this is that more and more U.S. firms find themselves in the same situation as IBM whose two Japanese plants invariably rank among the top 10 percent of the company's forty-six factories around the world in terms of productivity and product reliability. (Not infrequently, according to Ralph Pfeiffer, they rank first and second.) Time and again, executives of companies ranging from Johnson & Johnson Japan to Yamazaki-Nabisco have boasted to me that their local production facilities were so superior that they have come to serve as models for the parent company's stateside operations. "Nabisco people," says Yamazaki-Nabisco executive director Eiji Irino with quiet pride, "visit our bakeries to study the process modifications we have made in the basic American baking system." And on occasion this kind of reverse flow has proved nothing short of a competitive necessity. When Xerox, for example, was forced to cut manufacturing costs in order to fight back against growing penetration of the U.S. market by Japanese photocopiers, one of its key moves was to send teams of engineers and managers to Fuji Xerox to study the methods of quality control, engineering and procurement practiced by its Japanese offshoot.

Besides improvements in manufacturing technology, the reverse flow to U.S. firms sometimes includes actual product designs or formulations. One of Tupperware's best-selling lines in the United States nowadays consists of containers with square bottoms (for easy stacking) but round tops (for a firmer seal); this particular kind of container was originally designed and first manufactured by Japan Tupperware.

More often, however, the chief contribution that a Japanese manufacturing operation makes to the product line offered by its

U.S. parent lies in supplying the latter with components for use in "American-made" equipment. This process, which was greatly stimulated by the cost advantage that the strong dollar gave to Japan-based producers in the first half of the 1980s, is in a sense simply an international variant on the widespread use that most big Japanese manufacturers make of low-cost subcontractors and it now plays a major role in the economics of some of the biggest U.S. corporations. By one estimate, for example, only about a quarter of the components used in the personal computers that IBM markets in the United States are actually American-made; the other three-quarters are brought in from Japan.

Increasingly, too, U.S. firms with Japanese connections are bringing home from Japan not just components but finished products as well. Thus, while the great bulk of Teledyne Japan's business lies in selling U.S. products to Japanese customers, the firm also ships small Japanese industrial engines to one of Teledyne's countless U.S. manufacturing divisions, an enterprise called Teledyne Total Power. "They're engine-makers themselves and they needed a small engine to fill out their line," explained Peter Katsuno, the thoughtful American-born head of Teledyne Japan. And for very similar reasons, Michigan's Cross & Trecker Corporation decided to offer American machine tool users not only its U.S.–made metal lathes but slower, less sophisticated and cheaper lathes manufactured by a Japanese company in which Cross & Trecker owns a half interest. "That will increase our credibility with the customer and help sell U.S.–made machines," Cross & Trecker chief executive Richard T. Lindgren told a *Wall Street Journal* reporter. "If you don't have the low-price merchandise on your wagon the customer always thinks you are trying to sell him up to get him into your merchandise."

In one of those jargon phrases so dear to American hearts—and to the hearts of American businessmen in particular—a U.S. company that sells at home under its own label products either partially or wholly of foreign manufacture is said to be "sourcing abroad." And like all other aspects of Japanese-American economic relations, sourcing in Japan has been a particularly controversial subject. The ability to source at lower cost in Japan has discouraged some American companies from even trying to manufacture certain items in the United States and has undeniably led a number of others to shut down manufacturing capacity they already had in this country. And this, some people fear, is apt to prove irreversible even if the decline in the value of the U.S. dollar vis-à-vis the yen that began in 1985 significantly reduces—or even eliminates—the cost advantage of manufacturing in Japan for a long time to come. For by now, the argument goes, some U.S. companies have become so dependent upon Japan that they won't be able to start manufacturing in the States again even if they want to do so. In short, the more portentous of the doomsayers insist, sourcing in Japan threatens nothing less than "the deindustrialization of America."

Like so many economic predictions, however, this one may well prove a case of oversimplistic extrapolation from incomplete data. Indeed, the notion that the United States is deindustrializing at all has recently met with vociferous challenge from some economists. In *Can America Compete?* Robert Lawrence offers a great deal of statistical evidence belying that contention, including the fact that the share of manufacturing employment in high-technology industries has actually been increasing faster in the United States than in Japan. And, falling back on an even more basic measure, Robert M. Brown of the American Enterprise Institute found that in 1984 manufacturing output constituted just about the same percentage of the total American gross national product as it had back in the halcyon smokestack days of 1950—and in absolute terms, of course, was far larger.

Beyond all that, critics of foreign sourcing seldom seem to recall that it is not just a one-way street: a considerable number of companies with manufacturing or assembling operations in Japan—companies ranging from Merck in pharmaceuticals to Yokogawa-Hewlett-Packard in computers—do extensive sourcing for the Japanese market in the United States. And for American companies with Japanese affiliates sourcing in Japan is not merely a way of keeping production costs down; it has other advantages that are sometimes overlooked. For one thing, it offers the American parent a more reliable flow of goods and a bigger piece of the action than it would enjoy if it were obliged to buy from wholly Japanese-owned firms. At the same time creative use of a Japanese manufacturing affiliate can provide valuable flexibility in marketing all around the world—a point made to me by President Haruo Okinobu of Yamatake-Honeywell (which itself does some sourcing in the United States).

"Here in Japan," Okinobu said, "Yamatake-Honeywell is a Japanese company with all the local advantages that implies—including access to the Japanese government. Outside Japan, we consider with Honeywell how we should approach a market—whether jointly or independently—and we have the great advantage that we can always market through a Honeywell subsidiary, using Europeans to sell to Europeans, Indonesians to Indonesians, etc. In such situations, Yamatake-Honeywell is in effect a subcontractor. In the eyes of the customers, what they're getting is a Honeywell product—and since our production here is top level both in quality and costwise, that's good for Honeywell."

In a sense, everything I have been discussing in the last few pages can be boiled down to a single statement voiced by IBM's Ralph Pfeiffer: "Much as we Americans tend to think so, not all good ideas originate in the United States." To put it less concisely, it is a commonplace that in acquiring its present competitive strength Japanese industry carefully studied how U.S. industry made, distributed and sold goods in its own home market and then honed those techniques to razor-edge sharpness for application not only in the United States but all around the world. Today, in a kind of jujitsu maneuver, alert and well-managed U.S. companies seek to achieve the same feat in reverse. And that, no less than the profits to be earned there, makes doing business in Japan well worth the bother.

3 Garbage In, Garbage Out

Like the executives of most well-established Japanese companies, the top managers of Max Factor's subsidiary in Japan do not as a rule receive visitors in their own offices. Instead, they meet with them in a large, expensively appointed room that was expressly designed for that purpose and which offers a relaxing atmosphere in which to talk. And during the long conversation that I held with him there in the spring of 1985, the company's president, Victor Harris, mostly reflected the mood of our surroundings. At one point, however, he abruptly turned indignant. "Hundreds of thousands of Americans are out of work because the strong dollar is killing our export business," he complained, "but all anybody ever talks about is Detroit and Pittsburgh."

Mr. Harris's lament was well founded. Because of the undue emphasis we have placed on our trade deficit with Japan and on the alleged indulgence of the Japanese in what Michigan congressman John Dingell has described as "the most outrageous trading practices ever," Americans have frequently failed in recent years to diagnose the causes of our economic difficulties correctly. And, inevitably, wrong diagnosis has led us to consider—and too often to adopt—remedies for our ills that are either irrelevant or actively counterproductive.

Victor Harris was right, too, in pointing to the vexed issue of unemployment in America's steel and auto industries as a classic example of misdiagnosis. To begin with, as Robert Z. Lawrence notes in *Can America Compete?*, unemployment in the auto and primary metals industries, including steel, was never more than a small part of a much larger problem: as of November 1982, in fact, joblessness in those industries accounted for only 4.6 percent of total unemployment in the United States. That, to be sure, was not a statistic likely to offer much comfort to "furloughed" auto workers nor to reconcile them to the imports from Japan which were widely denounced as the prime cause of unemployment among UAW members. Yet, according to Lawrence's research, less than a quarter of the nearly 25 percent decline in the output of the American auto industry between 1973 and 1980 was the result of competition from imports; the great bulk of that decline occurred because increased auto and gasoline prices, compounded after 1979 by high interest rates and a generally depressed economy, simply discouraged Americans from buying as many cars as they had previously.

Lawrence's point in all this is that in the dark hours that Detroit experienced between 1980 and 1982, "Japanese imports exerted little influence on automobile employment." That in turn suggests that what was needed to restore the U.S. auto industry to health was not the "voluntary" curb on Japanese imports that Washington imposed for four successive years. What was really required was a strengthening of the U.S. economy that would stimulate auto buying in general together with a combination of cost-cutting and quality-enhancing measures on the part of Detroit that would boost sales of American cars in particular.

In due course, the first half of that prescription was filled—however temporarily—by the "Reagan recovery." But it is still far from clear how earnestly U.S. automakers are prepared to follow the second half of the prescription. "Sure, they've made progress," a senior executive of one of America's biggest high-tech companies told me in mid-1985. "GM in particular has shown encouraging readiness to learn from the Japanese and to try to prove that good, competitively priced smaller cars can still be made in this country. But, it would have been better for the industry in the long run if it had never gotten the import quotas and had had its feet really held to the fire. As it is, they haven't been cured of their bad habits thoroughly enough. Even now, they don't get the productivity they should considering the wages they pay; it still takes 'em a lot more man-hours to build a car than it does Toyota or Nissan. And, despite all their TV advertising about quality-consciousness, they still turn out too many cars with glove compartments that bounce open when you go over a bump."

The costly protection given Detroit—a course of action which has amounted to an unacknowledged tax on all U.S. consumers—

is only one example of the way in which misperceptions about U.S.–Japanese trade have helped to confuse the American people as to the true nature of our economic problems. The same holds true for the basic cause of Victor Harris's concern: the so-called strength of the American dollar in the first half of the 1980s.

As James Abegglen has pointed out, the 25 percent increase in the value of the dollar vis-à-vis the Japanese yen that occurred between 1980 and early 1985 had a most unhappy consequence: it meant that, even if his basic production costs were identical to those of his American competitors, a Japanese manufacturer could still afford to charge 25 percent less for goods. "Look at it this way," a small Connecticut housewares manufacturer once mournfully urged me. "My Japanese competitors are in fat city. They can sell at prices 20 percent or so below mine, steal all my customers and still make a nice unit profit. Or they can be 'restrained,' sell at prices similar to mine, and earn the same unit profit I do—plus 20 or 25 percent on top of that."

But it was not, of course, just the Japanese who enjoyed this kind of advantage. Since the dollar soared in value against virtually all the world's major currencies during Ronald Reagan's first term, U.S. producers found themselves similarly handicapped in trying to sell against nearly any foreign competitor.

It was this fact more than any other, according to most disinterested students of international trade, that accounted for the rapid increase in U.S. imports and the disappointing performance of U.S. exports between 1980 and 1985. And the majority of experts also agree as to what originally played the major role in sending the dollar through the roof: massive U.S. federal budget deficits and the consequent adoption of tight money policies that kept real interest rates in the United States high—which in turn attracted massive foreign investment in this country and hence produced abnormally strong demand for U.S. dollars.

If logic were the dominant factor in economic policy-making, it might be expected that the undeniable connection between our federal budget deficits and our much-lamented trade deficits would have greatly intensified public pressure upon Congress and the president to embark upon some truly effective budget cutting. But as a practical matter, concern over trade deficits played little role in the adoption of the Gramm-Rudman Act and seems likely to have scant effect on the eventual fate of this congressional experiment in what one cynic has labeled "budget cutting by anonymous consent." The reason for that, moreover, is not hard to find: few people are inclined to harass their congressman about problems of which they are not aware and there is distressing evidence that a great many Americans fail to recognize that when the dollar is overvalued, sales of U.S. products both at home and abroad inevitably are hurt. A New York Times/CBS News poll taken in June 1985, in fact, showed that 60 percent of the people surveyed actually thought that a "strong" dollar was good for U.S. trade.

Admittedly, there are many Americans who fully understand that this is not the case—and such people tend to be found in the more influential positions in U.S. society. Even these relative sophisticates, however, too often preferred to regard the dollar's unnatural strength in the early 1980s as the consequence of malign outside forces rather than of our own national policies. Thus in an article in the *Washington Post* in late 1984 Henry Kissinger charged that Japanese government agencies "manipulate the exchange rate for the yen to favor Japanese exports." Apparently Dr. Kissinger, now a much-sought-after adviser to international businesses, was unaware that several months before he wrote this the U.S. General Accounting Office had specifically investigated this frequently voiced charge and had declared that no evidence could be found to support it.

The fact that it was mistaken, however, was not the only controversial aspect of Dr. Kissinger's statement. From charges such as his it is relatively easy to proceed to the position taken by conservative author and ideologue Kevin Phillips in his book *Staying on Top: The Business Case for a National Industrial Strategy.* In Japanese eyes, Phillips writes, "business has become a continuation of war by other means" and as a result the U.S. faces a threat from Japan that must be taken "almost as seriously" as the threat from the Soviet Union.

How many people in the United States are potentially receptive to Phillips's argument is difficult to appraise. Despite mounting economic tensions, opinion polls taken in 1985 continued to show widespread—if somewhat diminished—respect and even friendship for Japan among ordinary Americans. But a series of appearances I made between 1983 and 1985 on radio call-in shows dealing with Japan left me in little doubt that there is a certain amount of overt hostility toward Japan still extant in this country—and a considerably greater amount of latent suspicion. (During one of these radio conversations an otherwise rational-sounding gentleman from Texas flatly assured me that the design of the Zero fighter plane, generally acknowledged as probably the greatest achievement of Japanese military technology during World War II, was "stolen from Howard Hughes.")

Limited and relatively quiescent as anti-Japanese sentiment in the United States may be, however, implicit exhortations to remember Pearl Harbor can scarcely fail to fan it in some degree. And it is difficult to see what useful purpose that can serve. By presenting the Japanese primarily in the guise of opponents of the United States, arguments such as Phillips's obscure Japan's essential role as a U.S. ally whose continued friendship is necessary to the preservation of American influence and interests in the Pacific. Over time, confusion on that score could conceivably lead Americans to embrace policies damaging to the overall strategic position of the United States. And on a less apocalyptic but far more immediate level, the views of Mr. Phillips and others of like mind in business and politics have a further drawback: they help to perpetuate widespread misunderstanding in the United States about the way the Japanese economy really works.

The most common mistake Americans make when they seek to explain Japan's extraordinary economic growth is to exaggerate the role of the Japanese government in the process. An influential and increasingly sizable minority of U.S. businessmen and academics fall into this error out of a kind of admiration for Japan; they believe that Japanese government agencies, most notably the much-touted Ministry of International Trade and Industry (MITI), orchestrate Japan's industrial life with high skill and efficiency. The conclusion drawn by such people is a plausible one: insofar as is compatible with our very different culture, we Americans should take a leaf from the Japanese book and develop what is variously described as a "national industrial policy" or a "national industrial strategy."

As even the most cursory scanning of the U.S. press reveals, however, the great majority of Americans take a less respectful view of the Japanese bureaucracy's economic role. They are persuaded that the Japanese government not only unfairly restricts imports from the United States by its own actions but also allows and perhaps even encourages private business in Japan to do likewise. And since they regard the existence of "Japan Inc." as undeniable, the members of this most unsilent majority believe Missouri's Senator Danforth was stating an obvious truth when he declared that in its dealings with the Japanese, the United States "should accept nothing less than real market access as measured by additional sales of competitive American products [in Japan]." In other words, the key to increased U.S. exports to Japan lies in better behavior on the part of the Japanese government.

It is, of course, easy to find evidence that seems to justify either—or both—of these two seemingly incompatible views of the Japanese government's economic role. Over the years, efforts on the part of Japanese officialdom to exclude American products have undeniably been legion. What's more, despite Japan's great progress in trade liberalization, such incidents still occur—though nowadays, as a tale recounted by Lee Smith in the May 1985 issue of *Fortune* suggests, they are less likely to reflect avowed government policy than obstruction of it by low-level bureaucrats with deeply ingrained protectionist attitudes. In the case cited by Smith, the villain was a customs officer who received a shipment of forty paddle-tennis paddles which devotees of that sport at Tokyo's American Club had ordered from a New Jersey manufacturer. When he phoned to inquire why the American Club didn't buy such equipment in Japan, the customs man was informed that no paddle-tennis paddles are manufactured in Japan. Unimpressed by this assurance and equally unimpressed by the fact that there is no legal barrier to the importation of paddle-tennis paddles into Japan, he proceeded to sit on the shipment for more than a month before finally surrendering to the increasingly anguished entreaties of the American Club's hapless would-be sportsmen.

If the persistence of some degree of protectionist behavior in Japan cannot be denied, neither can the fact that the Japanese government plays a more active role in guiding and assisting business than the U.S. government does—or, under existing legislation, can hope to do. One of the most striking examples of this that I have ever encountered occurred in the early 1980s when a good friend of mine at MITI informed me that he had changed jobs since we last met. Naturally, I asked what his new assignment was. "Oh," he said with a self-deprecatory chuckle, "I am rationalizing the petrochemical industry."

Somewhat awed by the scope of such an undertaking, I requested further particulars. The problem, my friend explained, was that the cost of imported crude oil, then close to its all-time high, had seriously reduced the competitiveness of Japanese petrochemical producers and as a result MITI had decided that economic logic required substantial shrinkage in the overall size of the industry. But instead of relying essentially on exhortation, as the U.S. government must do in such cases, MITI had quietly organized an informal cartel of petrochemical producers and helped its members work out how much each individual company should reduce its manufacturing capacity in order to achieve an agreed-upon target for the industry as a whole.

To many people in the United States this will surely seem a classic example of national industrial policy in action. Looked at another way, however, it appears less an example of government direction of business than of government encouragement of the consensus-building process to which Japanese are addicted in every aspect of life. It is also significant, I believe, that the role of the Japanese government in the phasing down of "sunset industries" is a lot easier to document than its role in the development of "sunrise" ones. Much as MITI has been lauded for its pronouncement in the late 1970s that "information is the future," it is worth bearing in mind that great segments of American business were acting on that principle well before the late 1970s without benefit of government guidance. And there seems little reason to assume that Japanese businessmen as a group have been any less farsighted in the last twenty years than American businessmen as a group.

What all this suggests is a point put to me, every time we have a drink or a meal together, by Kazuo Nukazawa, a senior—and highly outspoken—member of the staff of Japan's potent Keidanren, or Federation of Economic Organizations. "The heart of our economic miracle," Nukazawa relentlessly insists, "lies on the factory floor, not in central planning."

Amended to make plain the indispensable part played by Japan's able executives as well as by its dedicated workers, Nukazawa's thesis commands the support of some of the closest American students of the Japanese economy and even of some top Japanese bureaucrats. "The people at MITI like to give the impression that our success is all a result of their doing," an economics specialist in the Japanese Foreign Office told me in late

1984. "I suppose that's only human, but the truth is that since the mid-sixties the initiative has been with the private sector." And at about the same time, my closest friend at MITI offered implicit confirmation of this by lamenting the addiction of Japanese businessmen to "selfish interest," i.e., their deplorable habit of acting as their own business judgment dictates rather than as MITI thinks they should.

The point at issue here is one with a direct bearing on America's prospects for achieving a healthier economic relation with Japan. How one appraises the economic role of the Japanese government clearly must affect one's judgment as to what international economic policies the United States should follow. And, in my view, both those Americans who credit Japan's success in great part to brilliant central planning and those who credit it above all to protectionism run riot are lending implicit support to policies that would almost surely prove counterproductive.

By arguing that the United States cannot hold its own against Japan unless it adopts a national industrial policy, the proponents of the central planning explanation unduly downplay the great competitive potential that American business still possesses. And, by so doing, they inadvertently make protectionism seem more attractive. "I can't afford to hang by the neck until this country gets around to adopting an industrial strategy," one New England businessman told me. "That'll take years and my Japanese competitors aren't going to give me that kind of time."

Even stronger and more direct, however, are the negative effects of excessive emphasis on Japanese protectionism, real and alleged. Justified as some of them may be, constant public complaints on that score have convinced too many American businessmen either that there is no point in trying to get into the Japanese market or that all they need do to invade it successfully is to get the Japanese government to give them "a fair shake."

Sadly, some of the voices that are most effective in spreading word of the horrors of the Japanese market belong to people whose function it is to promote U.S. business activity in Japan. This point was driven home to me at a trade fair in Nagoya in March 1985 by Jerie H. Powell, a no-nonsense lady who operated a small trading firm based in Silver Spring, Maryland. "At one time or another," Mrs. Powell said, "I've attended a lot of seminars on how to do business in Japan at which the speakers included Commerce Department officials. Their approach is terrible! They put everything on the basis of 'us,' the Americans, versus 'them,' the Japanese. They think they are trying to encourage Americans to sell in Japan, but they make it sound so hard that they scare people away."

What gave Jerie Powell's comments a particularly ironic twist was that the trade fair at which I met her was sponsored by the Japan External Trade Organization (JETRO) with the sole purpose of bringing small American companies with exportable products into contact with potential Japanese customers for their goods. A quasi-governmental institution, JETRO was originally created to promote the sale of Japanese goods abroad. In recent years, however, it has reversed field and now concentrates primarily on helping American and other foreign firms to do business in Japan.

JETRO's shift of emphasis is a direct reflection of a long-standing Japanese conviction that Americans could do much more business in Japan if they would only try harder. As far back as 1977 the late Nobuhiko Ushiba, then Japan's chief trade negotiator and in an earlier incarnation probably the most popular ambassador his country ever sent to Washington, told me: "You know, after we reduced tariffs on cars, Henry Ford came here and made it plain that he didn't give a damn about the Japanese market. This is the kind of thing I find strange—particularly at a time when Ford cars made in Spain are being marketed here by Honda." And almost a decade later, McDonald's Den Fujita, who spent twenty years in the import-export business, made the same point even more force- fully. "Many American companies don't believe they can sell here when they really could," he said. "Every time I go to the States I see many items I could market successfully here if I weren't so busy with McDonald's—not just high-tech products but ordinary things. For example, a while ago when I was there, I bought my wife a very light General Electric steam iron and everybody who came to our house said 'How fantastic! Where can I get one?' But they aren't sold in Japan—so since then I've had to bring ten more back for friends."

Along with the argument that too many American firms pass up the Japanese market entirely goes an even sharper criticism. As the Japanese see it, many U.S. firms that have tried to sell or produce goods in Japan have been inexcusably inept in their efforts. "They expect to walk in and say to a distributor 'Here's my product,' " sniffs an employee of the Japan Economic Institute. "It just doesn't work that way in Japan." Often, laments economist Saburo Okita, the quality of "ordinary American equipment isn't quite up to standard." And even in a 1985 speech forcefully urging his countrymen to buy more American products, Prime Minister Yosuhiro Nakasone himself couldn't resist citing one particularly sore point. "Japanese traders who do business in America speak English," he said. "I haven't met any American salesmen who are fluent in Japanese." (In fact, there are some, but essentially Nakasone was on solid ground: nearly 90 percent of the U.S. business people in Japan, according to one poll, have never made any attempt to learn Japanese. Even worse, American firms often seem oblivious to the fact that most Japanese cannot cope with product directions or promotional literature written in English; at the 1985 Nagoya trade fair, only a small minority of the U.S. exhibitors came armed with brochures in Japanese.)

Confronted with this litany, it is tempting for an American to reply that the Japanese are simply trying to escape the consequences of their own sins by shifting blame onto American shoulders. But while that is surely sometimes the case, those Americans most knowledgeable about doing business in Japan find a painful degree of accuracy in the Japanese charges. In 1984, Loy Weston, the freewheeling entrepreneur who made Kentucky Fried Chicken a Japanese institution, told an English-language publication in Japan: "I am appalled by the number of American companies who come over here with grandiose ideas of making a fast buck . . . before they learn the rules of the game." In a similar vein, John P. Stern, the head of the Tokyo office of the American Electronics Association, told *Business Week* that many of the representatives of U.S. high-technology companies that came to him for advice were "96 percent ignorant" of the Japanese market. "These companies," he said, "would rather curse the darkness than light a candle."

These are not thoughts that any patriotic Americans can happily entertain. Yet, however reluctantly, a number of thoroughly patriotic Americans familiar with the Japanese business scene have come to share the view of Bill Totten, a onetime market researcher for an American computer software company who successfully launched his own software sales firm in Japan. "In my opinion,"

Totten said back in 1982, "the largest invisible barrier to trade is laziness on the part of Americans."

It would be absurd to suggest that a greater export effort by American business, no matter how massive and intelligently conceived it might be, could by itself wipe out the U.S. trade deficit with Japan. While he was still U.S. trade representative, William Brock confessed to having a "nightmare" in which "the Japanese do all the things we ask them to do—and nothing changes." In essence, that was a confession of the irrelevance of many of the "market-opening" demands the United States has made upon Japan—a confession Brock later reinforced by conceding that in his judgment two-thirds to three-quarters of the U.S. trade deficit with Japan "is our own fault."

What too few Americans recognize is that in order to bring its merchandise trade with Japan into balance, the United States would have to persuade the Japanese to perform something approximating economic hara-kiri. E. S. Browning of the *Wall Street Journal* has calculated how the trade balancing trick might have been accomplished in 1984 when the U.S. deficit was still almost $26 billion below the figure which it ran in 1985. The solution, Browning reported, would have been for the Japanese to import all the beef and oranges they ate from the United States, buy only American telephones, equip their armed forces exclusively with U.S. weapons—and, finally, junk their auto industry, turning over to Detroit not only the entire U.S. car market but the entire Japanese market as well.

Fantastic as that scenario may be, it is a surprising fact that before 1984 when the strength of the dollar induced the United States to go on a worldwide importing spree of unprecedented proportions, Japanese actually spent a bit more per person on goods from the United States than Americans spent on products made in Japan. But since there are only half as many Japanese as there are Americans, each Japanese would have to spend twice as much on imports as each American to bring Japanese-American trade into balance—and since average income in Japan is substantially lower than in the United States, that is scarcely a realistic prospect. For this reason if no other, it seems certain that, barring radical and probably catastrophic economic and political change on the world scene, the United States will continue to run a trade deficit with Japan throughout the foreseeable future.

That fact will clearly impede efforts to establish an economic relationship between Japan and America that is acceptable to both countries and hence does not spark political and diplomatic tensions between them. Yet in the interests of their mutual security—and world peace in general—the United States and Japan *must* achieve such a relationship.

This is a goal which I believe is entirely attainable. I am also persuaded, however, that to achieve it successfully will require certain changes in Japanese behavior and even greater changes in the behavior of both government and business in the United States.

These changes, which will be discussed at length in the final chapter of this book, cannot all come quickly. In particular, the required reshaping of U.S. governmental policies—and of the public attitudes that underlie them—is likely to take years to accomplish. That, however, does not imply that there is any justification or necessity for U.S. business to sit on its hands in the meantime. For in the final analysis, as James Abegglen once reminded me, "governments do not increase trade; private business does."

Even without major changes in U.S. trade and industrial policies, in other words, it is entirely possible for American exporters to increase their sales in Japan significantly—something that would not only help to hold down our trade deficit with Japan but would also spark a welcome growth in export-related employment in this country. And by making additional productive investments in Japan, U.S. companies can ensure a greater flow of interest income back to this country—money that will help to create still more jobs and generally to help maintain the high U.S. standard of living.

Whether or not all this actually happens will ultimately depend on thousands of private sector decisions—decisions by the managers of individual U.S. companies as to whether it is worth their while to invade the Japanese market more aggressively and, if so, what strategy to pursue. These, of course, are questions to which there are no universally applicable answers. Without intimate knowledge of the circumstances of a particular company, no one can sensibly prescribe what course of action it should follow—a point too often overlooked in the growing library of "how to" books about doing business in Japan.

Nonetheless, as I have tried to make plain, the range of U.S. companies that *have* been successful in Japan is so wide and the diversity of their experience so great that almost any corporate manager ought to be able to find in their histories information relevant to his own situation.

So now, as New York's governor Al Smith used to urge his audiences back in the 1920s, "let's look at the record."

4 The Indispensables

A few years ago a reporter for the *Journal of Japanese Trade and Industry* asked Loy Weston, the chairman of Kentucky Fried Chicken Japan, whether he had any advice for foreign companies that wanted to get into the Japanese market. Weston, who by that time had spent more than thirteen years in Japan—so long, he said, that he was thinking of changing his surname to Easton—offered a characteristic reply. "Yeh," he said. "The first piece of advice I'd give them is: 'Don't come.' . . . About four hundred new foreign companies come here each year. In three or four years most of them will be gone. That makes a terrible impression here. So unless they've got a long-term commitment, a product that makes sense to the Japanese market and a tremendous amount of patience, I wish to hell they wouldn't come."

In less colorful and hyperbolic language, many other executives of successful foreign affiliates in Japan express views almost identical to Weston's. It is indeed foolish, the old Japan hands agree, to let lethargy or fear keep your company out of a market as potentially lucrative as Japan. But, they quickly add, it is even more foolish and more damaging to the reputation of U.S. business in general for an American company to burst upon the Japanese scene with a fanfare only to withdraw a few years later in costly frustration. Yet this is a pitfall into which an extraordinary number of American firms, including some highly regarded ones, have fallen in the past—and into which the unwary will surely continue to fall in the years ahead.

By "the unwary" I mean specifically firms that fail to heed the advice given by David Gregg of Control Data Japan in the late 1970s. "A newcomer to the Japanese market should learn everything he can about Japan before he comes," said Gregg. "The key thing is to do your homework first." Obvious as it may sound, this exhortation is all too frequently disregarded—most often for a reason pointed out by George Fields, a bilingual, Japanese-born Australian who heads ASI Market Research (Japan). "Bedazzled by the superficial ease with which Japanese adopt Western ways," writes Fields, many Western businessmen succumb to the illusion that "Japanese are fundamentally no different than Westerners." But the reality, as Fields brilliantly documents in his book *From Bonsai to Levi's*, is that while Japanese obviously do have many things in common with Westerners, doing business in Japan nonetheless differs in a number of highly important respects from doing business in London, Frankfurt, or Saõ Paulo.

Acceptance of that fact, difficult as it may be to swallow, is the beginning of wisdom for any U.S. firm that hopes to prosper in the Japanese market. "To make it in this country," insists Kunihiko Fukuda, the lively, self-assured UCLA graduate who handles public affairs for Ajinomoto General Foods, Inc., "a U.S. company simply has to recognize that there is more than one way to run a business."

Specifically, according to Fukuda and many other veterans of foreign "launches" in Japan, an American company entering the Japanese market must first familiarize itself with certain assumptions and attitudes of mind that are often not highly esteemed in Western business circles but that are indispensable in Japan. Perhaps even more important, the company must consider whether it is genuinely prepared to act upon those assumptions and attitudes in its operations in Japan. It must, in other words, not only identify a set of general principles appropriate to Japanese business culture but must honestly appraise whether it can live within the context of those principles when it comes to making specific strategic and tactical decisions.

This, admittedly, is not an easy task, but it is nonetheless vital to perform. So before considering in detail how particular companies have handled particular business problems in Japan—which is what the next several chapters of this book will do—it seems imperative to present a kind of consensus on underlying principles that emerged from the hundreds of hours of conversation I have held with students and practitioners of business in Japan.

When they are asked to define the basic qualities indispensable to doing business successfully in Japan, the first word that executives of U.S. affiliates there generally come up with is one emphasized by Loy Weston: commitment. What they mean by commitment is a combination of patience, determination and the willingness to pay a high—and sometimes seemingly inordinate—price for admission to the party.

The patience required of anyone who wishes to win a share of the Japanese market takes several forms. Perhaps the most unsettling of these to the typical American corporate manager is the need to postpone gratification in the form of return on investment. Any U.S. executive who feels that he cannot safely present his shareholders and the ubiquitous army of securities analysts with a project that does not promise to make an early contribution to increased profits would probably be unwise to consider a venture in Japan. On this score, I have yet to encounter anyone genuinely familiar with Japanese business who dissents from the judgment expressed by Mark Popiel of Dodwell, a British trading company that has been operating in Japan for more than a century and has helped many American and other foreign companies to launch their products there. "In their initial period here," says Popiel flatly, "foreign companies in Japan simply cannot be concerned with short-term profitability."

One reason for this is that short-term profitability does not dominate the thinking of Japanese corporate managers to the same extent as it does that of most of their American counterparts. In one classic case in point, Japan's giant NEC (Nippon Electric Company) invested heavily in semiconductors for thirteen years before it ever made a single yen's profit from them. And while I do not know of any American subsidiary or affiliate in Japan that has displayed quite that high a degree of patience, those that have been successful have generally waited quite a while before achieving profitability. American Hospital Supply, now the leader in the Japanese health care market, had been operating in Japan for five years before it wrote its first order. Seibu Allstate Life Insurance, which is jointly owned by one of Japan's top merchandising chains and Sears, Roebuck, managed to reach the cumulative break-even point only after it had been in business for nine years. And even Den Fujita of McDonald's, despite his company's stunningly rapid rise to No. 1 rank in the food service business, confesses that "for the first three years I couldn't make money."

There is a significant difference in this respect between U.S. companies that want to market consumer goods in Japan and those that seek to sell parts or equipment to Japanese industry. Generally speaking, it does not take as long to win public acceptance of a consumer item as it does to build a relationship with a Japanese manufacturer and persuade him that your product is not only more cost-effective than competitive Japanese products but also will meet his quality and delivery requirements. In both cases, though, the same broad rule applies: unless a company brings in a product so novel and desirable that is virtually sells itself—and sometimes even when it does have a product of that kind—making a quick buck in Japan can be a danger signal for a foreign firm. As Peter Drucker has pointed out: "Quick results in Japan can mean ultimate failure—you are doing business with the wrong people."

To the uninitiated, Drucker's suggestion that doing business with the wrong people can be a fatal mistake in Japan may seem to border on the self-evident. After all, most entrepreneurs anywhere in the world consider it important to do business with and to cultivate the goodwill of "the right people." But in Japan, this process is not just important, it is crucial—and generally takes far longer to accomplish successfully than it does in a Western society.

One of the most graphic statements of this point I have been exposed to came in a conversation with Haruo Okinobu, the lively, forthright president of Yamatake-Honeywell. A captain of engineers in the Japanese Army in World War II, Okinobu attended Purdue as a Fulbright scholar in the early 1950s and partly for that reason perhaps is more at ease with foreigners than most Japanese of his generation. He is also, however, clearly impatient with foreign businessmen who can't be bothered to learn how the corporate game is played in Japan. "A lot of people say the Japanese market isn't open," he told me in his staccato but highly serviceable English. "That's wrong: it *is* open. But it's like a club; you've got to be a member to enjoy full privileges. Of course, if you want you can apply for membership—but the waiting list is twenty years." Then, obviously pleased with his figure of speech, he chuckled explosively and repeated it: "Oh yes, the club is open all right, but there's a twenty-year waiting list."

Okinobu, I believe, was exaggerating for effect. A foreign company that aspires to membership in the Japanese club can sharply reduce the waiting time required by going into partnership with an established and well-respected Japanese corporation. And even if that proves impossible or undesirable, a new foreign venture can with intelligent management and careful study of Japanese business practices begin to lay the groundwork for a meaningful presence in Japan right from the start. But with the best management in the world it will almost surely take some years to establish an effective network of personal relationships in the Japanese business community and to win the confidence of customers, distributors, bankers, bureaucrats and even potential employees of high caliber.

With inept or mediocre management in its initial stages, of course, a new foreign venture in Japan faces an even tougher time—which is where determination comes in. The maxim "If at first you don't succeed, try, try again" has been the salvation of more than one foreign affiliate now prospering in Japan. According to Japan Tupperware's president, Kazunobu Cho, it took his company three changes in top management and nine years of experimentation to achieve a truly effective distribution system. And Tupperware's early troubles were relatively minor compared to those experienced by General Foods, which first established a wholly owned subsidiary in Japan back in 1954. Initially, thanks to a near-monopoly of the instant coffee market in Japan the company prospered. But then intensified competition combined with short-term business strategies dictated from the States launched it upon what one survivor of those days recalls as "a vicious downhill spiral." Finally, in 1973, General Foods swallowed its pride and turned over a half interest in the subsidiary to the Ajinomoto Company, a highly regarded Japanese food-processing firm with a first-class distribution system. Today, the resulting joint venture, Ajinomoto General Foods, markets a wide array of products ranging from a non-dairy creamer to cat food and has sales of over $300 million a year. (But with characteristic Japanese emphasis on long-term growth rather than short-term payouts, AGF waited until 1983, the tenth anniversary of its founding, to pay its first dividend.)

When they talk about the need for commitment, in short, veterans of the Japanese business scene mean among other things the readiness to make a heavy initial investment—and the investment required isn't always confined to time and money. Some of the best-established American subsidiaries in Japan today are prospering because their managers had the foresight in the past to take risks that other U.S. firms found unacceptable. In the years immediately after World War II when Japan was desperately short of foreign exchange, the Japanese government refused to guarantee any foreign-owned company operating in Japan the right to convert its yen profits into hard currency for repatriation. That killed any interest in Japan on the part of many potential U.S. investors. One exception, however, was Coca-Cola which in 1946 went ahead and established a so-called yen company—and by getting in on the ground floor so to speak laid the foundation for its present dominance of the Japanese soft-drink market.

A variation on this same theme can be found in the experience of Texas Instruments. In the early 1960s, before he underwent his metamorphosis from hard-nosed MITI official to assiduous wooer of foreign investment in Kyushu, Morihiko Hiramatsu decreed that TI would be allowed to manufacture integrated circuits in Japan only if it accepted Sony Corporation as a fifty-fifty partner. This was unwelcome news to the folks back in Dallas who wanted a wholly owned Japanese subsidiary and were thoroughly opposed to taking in a local partner. In the end, though, they decided to gamble on Hiramatsu's promise that after three years of operation in Japan they would be allowed to buy out Sony's share of the joint venture. The upshot, of course, is that TI now owns 100 percent of a company that occupies a strong position in Japan's burgeoning semiconductor industry—while the exact opposite is true of some other technology-based U.S. corporations that did not have TI's foresight. Having declined in the 1960s to go into Japanese ventures in which they could not hold a controlling interest, these firms have since seen their Japanese competition grow so strong that their own prospects of winning any major share of the Japanese market for their products are now much reduced.

The Coca-Cola and Texas Instruments cases are, of course, now history and problems of currency exchange or imposed partnerships no longer exist for foreign companies that decide to enter the Japanese market. But new and different conditions inevitably spawn new and different obstacles and the need for patience and intelligent risk-taking is as great as ever.

If "commitment" is the first word on most lists of the attributes necessary for corporate success in Japan, the second one is apt to be "flexibility." The management styles employed by well-established foreign affiliates in Japan inevitably vary widely and often include distinctively American elements such as private offices for relatively junior executives. Nonetheless, it seems clear that Masahisa Naitoh, a senior MITI official of engaging manner and incisive mind, is on solid ground when he argues that "every foreign company that has been truly successful in this country has in some degree or other 'Japanized' itself." That is to say that the management of such companies has not clung to some Platonic Western model of what a corporation ought to be and how it should be administered but instead has been pragmatic enough to adopt Japanese techniques and behavior patterns where those seem to produce better results than practices favored in the United States.

The first and most important step in this adaptation process according to the majority of people experienced in the matter lies in decentralization—a conscious decision by a parent company in the United States that because the Japanese market differs so significantly from all others the managers of a Japanese subsidiary must be granted more freedom of action than might be accorded the managers of a British or Argentinian subsidiary.

For reasons that no doubt include a substantial admixture of chauvinism and personal ambition, the need for considerable local autonomy is a favorable theme with Japanese executives working for American subsidiaries or joint ventures. But the same proposition has been advanced to me by a fair number of Caucasian executives in Japan—including one who clearly runs a very tight ship himself and who speaks of his U.S. parent company with near-veneration. Yet for all his loyalty to his corporate superiors in the United States, he insists that "absentee management" of a Japanese subsidiary is folly. "If you want proof of that," he told me when I met with him in early 1985, "just look at Procter & Gamble. They've had a very bad time here in the last five years and it's for just one reason: they try to call all the shots from Cincinnati."

According to this man—and many of his peers—delegation and flexibility must be the watchwords from the moment an American company decides to seek a share of the Japanese market, whether by exporting, local manufacture or a combination of the two. The variety of corporate structures U.S. firms have used in establishing a presence in Japan—a subject I shall return to later on—is nothing short of bewildering and not a few of those structures have a jerry-built quality reminiscent of the zany contraptions that Rube Goldberg used to draw. Consider, for example, Teledyne Japan. As Peter Katsuno, that company's deceptively low-key general manager, explained to me, his operation represents some thirty-five of Teledyne's American manufacturing divisions. But there are twenty or so other manufacturing subsidiaries of Teledyne that already had Japanese sales representatives when they were acquired by the conglomerate and in such cases, says Katsuno, "this office doesn't interfere with pre-Teledyne relationships unless it proves absolutely necessary." In other words, a Japanese customer who wants to buy a particular Teledyne product may be able to order it through Teledyne Japan but may equally well have to deal with another entity entirely.

This is a state of affairs that would probably strike most American business school theorists as hopelessly untidy, but in Peter Katsuno's scheme of things the creation of a tidy organizational structure clearly runs a very distant second to the preservation of long-established personal relationships—and quite properly so. For as Holger Wittich, a German-born entrepreneur based in Tokyo, has pointed out: "In Japan, the fact that you like somebody or people like you is very important for business. Even if you offer cheaper or better products, if people don't like you they won't do business with you."

As Wittich's comment indicates, the need for flexibility is by no means confined to such basic strategic problems as finding the best mode of entry into the Japanese market and the most effective organizational structure to employ there. In fact, one of the strongest arguments against "calling the shots from Cincinnati" is that many day-to-day business practices which are commonplace in Japan are either unknown in the United States or run counter to conventional American business wisdom. As a result, only if an American company gives its people on-scene in Japan a relatively free hand is it likely to make intelligent adjustments to Japanese business conditions.

Here again, it is instructive to look at the way Teledyne goes about exporting to Japan an array of American-manufactured products ranging from airborne electronic equipment to special metals such as titanium and niobium. Though the top title at Teledyne Japan is held by an American, he resides in the United States and effective management of the Japanese company is in the hands of Peter Katsuno. And many of the techniques Katsuno employs are ones he learned in the twenty-five years he spent in business in Japan before joining Teledyne in 1972.

"What we really are," Katsuno told me, "is a Japanese trading company. We buy Teledyne products in the U.S. on our own account and then resell them here. We're the only one of Teledyne's overseas operations that does buy and sell on its own account, incidentally. And we do so because, like a Japanese trading company, we help to finance our customers. We will accept 90- or 120-day notes from our customers and then discount them—which, of course, isn't the way things are usually done in the States."

There are also other, less dramatic ways in which Teledyne Japan's operations depart from American practice, according to Katsuno. "For example," he said, "it's very hard to do business on the telephone in Japan. There is a lot more personal selling than in the U.S. In fact, when we have repeat business, we have to go back and meet with the customer a second time. The Japanese customer expects a lot more attention than a U.S. customer would look for."

Onerous—and even outlandish—as a true-blue American executive might find some of Teledyne's accommodations to Japanese business culture, they clearly help to explain the company's success in Japan. And the failure to make such accommodations equally clearly underlies the misadventures that have befallen some other American companies there. It is, for example, not unheard of for a company with a major market share in the United States to be outstripped in the Japanese market by a much smaller American competitor; this is true of Gillette, which sells only one razor blade in Japan for every seven sold by Schick, and it is also the case for Revlon, which, despite a far bigger U.S. base, has never been able to match Max Factor's success in Japan. In both these instances, the firm that was top dog at home faltered in its Japanese venture largely because it did not adapt as thoroughly as its smaller rival to the peculiar intricacies of marketing and distribution in Japan.

Not infrequently flexibility has also proved an effective counter to that most highly publicized of impediments to doing business in Japan: restrictive government regulation. Among the U.S. firms that have demonstrated that is Sears, Roebuck's Allstate insurance subsidiary. In the early 1970s when Sears negotiated a catalog-licensing agreement with Japan's Seibu merchandising chain,

Allstate executives thought they scented an opportunity to pioneer in Japan an insurance sales technique that had served them well in the States. Why not capitalize on the tie-up with Seibu, they asked themselves, by selling life and casualty insurance at booths in Seibu department stores just like the booths Allstate has long had in Sears stores?

There were, as it turned out, a couple of reasons why not. One was that Japanese law does not permit the same company to sell both life and non-life insurance. Another was that there was no assurance whatsoever that the Japanese government would agree to the establishment of any new insurance company, much less one partly owned by foreigners.

In partnership with Seibu, however, Allstate pushed ahead with the necessary legalities. Finally, after a year and a half of bureaucratic contemplation, the Seibu Allstate Life Insurance Company was licensed to do business and set up its sales booths in Seibu department stores. But it took five more years before a change in the regulatory climate made entry into the auto and fire insurance business possible and even then the prohibition on the sale of life and non-life policies by the same company remained.

So today, while the insurance booths in Seibu stores offer essentially the same range of coverage as those in Sears stores in the United States, life insurance is sold from one corner of the Seibu booth by one Seibu Allstate company and non-life is sold from another corner by another Seibu Allstate company. (For simplicity's sake, both companies are sometimes represented by the same sales agent, who shuttles from one corner to the other depending on which hat he is wearing at the moment.)

Though it is really just another form of adaptability, there is one key to successful penetration of the Japanese market so vital that old Japan hands generally treat it as a separate consideration. This is the necessity for employing cultural sensitivity in product design, but people in the business would rarely resort to so highfalutin a description of the matter. Instead, they tend to ring various changes on Loy Weston's down-to-earth statement that a foreign company that wants to establish itself in Japan must first make sure that it can offer a product or service "that makes sense to the Japanese market."

It is sometimes said that to prosper in Japan these days an

American company must possess some form of high technology. A moment's reflection on the triumphs scored in Japan by Schick, McDonald's and Mister Donut is all that is required to demonstrate the fallacy of that proposition. High tech, low tech or no tech, an American company has the first requisite for success in Japan if it is prepared to follow the recipe offered by Kneale Ashworth of Johnson & Johnson—which runs as follows: "Give the Japanese consumer what he wants, not what headquarters back in Boise or wherever decrees he shall have."

Determining what the consumer wants, of course, is always easier said than done and this is no less true in Japan than anywhere else. Indeed, market research in Japan, as I shall discuss later on, has its own peculiar wrinkles. But it is possible to take a long first step toward an accurate reading of the Japanese consumer's mind merely by shedding simplistic cultural predispositions.

This is a point heavily stressed by Yotaro Kobayashi, the enviably handsome and impeccably tailored president of Fuji Xerox. A second-generation captain of industry—his father helped found Fuji Xerox and was for many years president of Fuji Photo Film Company—Kobayashi is a graduate of Philadelphia's Wharton School of Finance and handles English as if it were his native tongue. (The only thing that renders his speech at all "foreign-sounding" to an American ear is an occasional faintly British overtone, perhaps reflecting a year he spent in London working with Rank Xerox.) Partly on the strength of his bicultural background, Kobayashi has identified two mutually exclusive errors that tend to plague American firms starting up in Japan. "One of these," he told me, "is the attitude that whatever sells or prevails in the U.S. should also sell or prevail in the Japanese market. The other mistake is the exact opposite: the assumption that Japan is so different that what works in the United States can't work here."

The second half of Kobayashi's comment was echoed only a few days later by Coca-Cola's Weldon Johnson when I met with him and three of his top subordinates in a conference room at their imposing Tokyo headquarters building. "About a year ago," Johnson said, "some of us were sitting around this same table and we promised ourselves never again to say 'That will never work in Japan.' Instead, we agreed to say 'Let's test that and see if it might work in Japan.' "

A complication that neither Kobayashi nor Johnson specifically mentioned, however, is that sometimes things that work in the United States may turn out to work in Japan as well—but for different reasons. Thus, George Fields of ASI Market Research speculates that while the prime appeal of Tupperware in the United States probably lies in its usefulness in preserving perishables such as food, its primary appeal in the characteristically tiny Japanese home probably stems from its contribution to efficient storage. "Entering the Eastern Culture," writes Fields in *From Bonsai to Levi's*, "a Western product undergoes a transformation and establishes its *raison d'être* [in terms of] Japanese values rather than Western ones. . . ."

To make matters more complex yet, it is not enough for a foreign company operating in Japan to tailor its products to current Japanese values and life-styles; it must also remain constantly alert to the rapid and far-reaching changes which constantly transform Japanese society.

Rapid change is, of course, a characteristic of all modern industrial societies. But the Japanese embrace change more easily and enthusiastically than the inhabitants of any other great nation with which I am familiar. There are, I believe, several interrelated explanations for this: one is that a century and a quarter ago the Japanese recognized that only through acceptance of radical change could they preserve their independence; another is that they operate more on the basis of social consensus than on deeply rooted abstract principles and hence tend to be less rigid in their mind-set than Westerners. Whatever the underlying reasons, however, it is an observable fact that Japanese behavior patterns are perennially in a state of flux—and in ways whose impact on future business conditions and possibilities is extremely tricky to predict.

Not everyone, to be sure, concedes that last point. It is often said by Japanese that if you want to know what life-styles will be like in Japan a decade hence you need only look at what they are like in the United States right now—and it is quite true that many changes in American tastes and behavior patterns are reproduced in Japan after a lag of five to ten years. This, for example, is the case with buying goods from mail-order houses. Though the mail-order business was traditionally regarded with disdain in Japan, it has lately begun to take on the upscale aura there that it acquired some years ago in the United States—so much so, in fact, that both

Young & Rubicam and Doyle Dane Bernbach have now gone into joint ventures with Japanese advertising agencies to design ads for mail-order catalogs.

To assume, however, that developments in the United States will automatically appear later on in the same form in Japan is too easy. In many cases, the new social tides visible in Japan—the rapid aging of the population, the growing role of women in economic life, the emergence of new and different relationships within the family—appear broadly similar to changes that swept the United States somewhat earlier. But they are not, in reality, totally identical to the American developments in either cause or nature—and, as a result, the consequent changes in life-styles and consumption patterns aren't likely to be totally identical either.

Oversimplified cultural generalizations, in short, are just as hazardous in predicting the future tastes of Japanese consumers as in determining those of the present. But difficult as the game is, it is clearly worth the candle. For when it comes to changes in life-styles and buying habits, the behavior of Japan's 120 million prosperous consumers often resembles that of birds on a telephone wire; when one flies, they all fly.

As I have tried to make plain, most of the businessmen I consulted while doing the research for this book felt strongly that any American company entering the Japanese market should come armed with a firm set of general principles carefully chosen for their particular relevance to Japan. But in business as in law, of course, circumstances alter cases, and time and again I discovered that people who espoused the same set of general principles had actually applied those principles to their own specific situations in ways that differed greatly from one another. Both the form these differences took and the reasons why they occurred seemed to me instructive—and best examined by a detailed consideration of each of the major aspects of running a company in Japan.

5 How Firm a Foundation?

Back in the 1930s when even the main thoroughfares of eastern Canada were mostly dirt roads, my father, who had spent part of his childhood there, liked to claim that somewhere in the province of New Brunswick he had once seen a highway sign that read "Choose your rut carefully; you'll be in it for the next 40 miles."

Apocryphal though it may have been, that sign offered advice that any American company with intentions of invading the Japanese market would do well to bear in mind. When it comes to choosing people with whom to do business in Japan, the managers of a new venture there must accept that their company will either be doing business with those same people for a long time to come— or else it will be in trouble.

Sooner or later in any conversation about launching a business in Japan, people familiar with that process are almost certain to emphasize how critical it is for a foreign enterprise to find an appropriate Japanese partner or partners. In so doing, they are not necessarily referring to a partner in the legal sense but rather to a person or firm whose services and cooperation can be relied upon.

In this broad sense, any firm that wishes to manufacture or sell its products in Japan must operate in partnership with local interests. One reason for this is the nature of the Japanese distribution system which is so bloated and complex that Americans exposed to its mysteries almost reflexively describe it as "byzantine." Expounding on "this nightmare" in his crisp British accent, Johnson & Johnson's Kneale Ashworth once explained to me: "In most countries, we sell directly to a supermarket chain which then sells to the consumer. But here you sell to a wholesaler who may well sell to a secondary wholesaler before the product is finally placed in a retail store." And since Japanese retailers, in particular the myriad small ones, tend to buy only from wholesalers with whom they have a long-established relationship, there is little hope of shortcutting this process. The upshot, as Ashworth and most other heads of successful foreign affiliates see it, is that even a 100 percent American-owned firm in Japan is virtually obliged to find de facto partners within the Japanese distribution network.

There is, as Ashworth concedes, one outstanding exception to this rule. From the very beginning of its venture in Japan, Coca-Cola bypassed the traditional Japanese distribution network by setting up its own system modeled on the one it had developed much earlier in the States. Nonetheless, Weldon Johnson pointedly refers to the seventeen bottling companies that handle Coca-Cola's distribution in Japan as his company's "partners" and emphasizes that during Coca-Cola Japan's first year of existence its management devoted its "greatest effort" to the selection of the right bottlers. "It's better," he concludes, "to go with a partner who's a bit smaller than to go with one who can give you a taste of immediate success but who in the long run will put you on a rocky road."

Though it still involves intelligence—or luck—in the choice of a Japanese associate, there is one obvious and common device through which an American company can make money in the Japanese market with minimal risk and little or no direct involvement. This, of course, is for the U.S. firm to license a Japanese enterprise to manufacture its products or, in the service trades, to use the same name and techniques.

One of the most conspicuous recent examples of this approach is provided by the gaudily colored 7-Eleven "convenience stores" that have sprung up all over Japan like mushrooms after a rain and that are operated by the Ito-Yokado Company under license from the Dallas-based Southland Corporation. A $4 billion-a-year retailing giant whose other interests includes 200-odd "Denny's" restaurants which it operates under a licensing agreement with the California firm of that name, Ito-Yokado has worked near-wonders with its 7-Eleven venture. As of early 1985, just a bit more than ten years after it came into existence, Seven-Eleven Japan had more than 2,000 stores and its annual gross had soared to more than $250 million.

Since Southland Corporation is paid a fixed (but undisclosed) percentage of Seven-Eleven Japan's sales, the folks back in Dallas no doubt rub their hands in glee whenever they hear the word "Japan"—and with some justice. Whatever earnings they derive from that country are money for jam, profits that have been achieved with no financial risk and, apparently, with very little investment of time or energy by Southland's management. Indeed, to hear Toshifumi Suzuki, the self-possessed and rather wary president of Seven-Eleven Japan, tell it, it took Ito-Yokado quite a lot of effort to get Southland even to listen to a licensing proposal and the contribution made by Southland personnel to the Japanese company has been negligible.

That, as it happens, is probably just as well since it seems unlikely that an operation with heavy input from Dallas would have come up with the formula that has made Seven-Eleven Japan so successful. Where 7-Eleven stores in the United States are built and owned by Southland and operated by contract managers, Seven-Eleven Japan follows a different pattern based on the Mom & Pop character of much of Japan's traditional retail establishment: its stores are nearly all franchise operations and the typical franchise is held by a married couple who before converting their shop to a 7-Eleven were running it as a liquor store or small grocery. Similarly, instead of relying on company-owned distribution centers as Southland does, Seven-Eleven Japan uses Japan's regular wholesale network as much as possible and many of the fast foods sold in its stores, such as snacks to be eaten with rice, are distinctively Japanese. In short, as President Suzuki rather insistently notes, "there are very few common factors between American 7-Elevens and ours in Japan."

Happy as its results have been, however, the 7-Eleven case nonetheless is a reminder of one of the potential hazards an American firm can face in making a licensing deal in Japan. For a firm which does business in many nations or which draws its customers from many nations, it can often be vital to present essentially the same face to the public everywhere. And while that is not a significant consideration for the Southland Corporation, it is one of supreme importance for Walt Disney Productions. Accordingly, even though it, too, decided to resort to licensing in Japan, Disney followed a very different course from Southland.

When I met with him in a sterile cement office building conspicuously devoid of the architectural fantasies that characterize the rest of Tokyo Disneyland, Disney vice-president Jim Cora recalled that caution and patience were the company's watchwords in Japan right from the start. So much so, in fact, that Disney executives spent five long years negotiating with their prospective Japanese partners. "Back then," said Cora, a crew-cut-haired veteran of twenty-six years with the Disney organization, "we didn't understand that with Japanese you don't have to put it in writing."

Finally, in 1979, a license-and-royalty contract was signed with the Oriental Land Company, a specially formed partnership between the Mitsui Real Estate Development Corporation and the Keisei Electric Railroad Company. The agreement called for Oriental Land to build, own and operate Tokyo Disneyland—but under the close supervision of Walt Disney Productions Japan. At first, in fact, every Japanese in an executive position at Tokyo Disneyland had an American counterpart on-scene, and while the initial number of Americans has subsequently been reduced by having some of them serve as counterparts to two or more Japanese, a substantial American cadre will remain, according to Cora, for the forty-five-year life of the license agreement.

The reason for this is that, although the need for American training and technological assistance at Tokyo Disneyland diminishes as time goes by, Disney's concern that there be no distortion of its corporate image remains as keen as ever. "We accommodate to the Japanese market where that doesn't conflict with the Disney way of doing business," says Cora succinctly. That, he implies, constitutes no great problem since "Disney culture is a lot like Japanese culture." But where the two do conflict, it is Disney culture that prevails. Thus, although most Japanese amusement parks sell sake, Tokyo Disneyland does not, for to do so would be plainly incompatible with the clean-cut style that has become Disney's worldwide hallmark.

All in all, then, the licensing agreement with Oriental Land appears to have been a sound move for Disney. To be sure, while its annual royalties from Tokyo Disneyland are substantial—in its first year of operations the venture grossed $300 million, of which Disney's share was more than $20 million—they are by no means as great as the profits that would be realized from actual ownership of the venture. On the other hand, by opting for the licensing agreement rather than full ownership, Disney avoided tying up well over half a billion dollars in construction and start-up costs in

Japan. And in addition to royalty fees, the company has also derived some indirect but highly tangible benefits from Tokyo Disneyland: in the two years immediately following Disneyland's grand-opening ceremonies, sales of Disney-licensed consumer products in Japan surged by 25 percent, attendance at Disney films increased substantially and the travel agency that Disney operates in Japan performed much more strongly than most of its competitors.

Despite the fact that it has worked so well, Disney's hands-on approach to licensing is relatively unusual. But licensing of a more permissive kind akin to that practiced by Southland is very widespread indeed and has, of course, been a major vehicle for the acquisition of U.S. technology by Japanese industry. All told, U.S. companies currently collect between $800 million and $900 million a year in payments from Japanese licensees and the figures continue to grow.

While it undeniably offers an easy way to tap the Japanese till, however, licensing is regarded with a certain disdain by some experts on Japanese-American business relations. In a lecture he gave at the Japan Society in New York in 1983, Kenichi Ohmae, who heads the Japanese arm of McKinsey & Company, characterized licensing as a strategy often adopted by "risk-averters" who were prepared to settle for a very small piece of the action as long as it was a guaranteed piece. And, subsequently, in a book that Ohmae's staff prepared for the United States–Japan Trade Study Group, the same point was made even more dramatically: since licensing fees typically run between 1 percent and 5 percent of the licensee's sales, so the argument ran, American firms had sold, for $800 million a year, technology that may have accounted for as much as $60 billion a year in sales of goods in Japan. The inference was obvious: if there were fewer American risk-averters, Japanese-American trade balance figures might be rather different.

Here, as in so many cases, however, generalization seems perilous: sometimes the alternative to half a loaf really is no bread at all. But one thing does appear reasonably clear: for a manufacturing company there are substantially more potential hazards involved in licensing than there are for most service companies. For one thing, a U.S. manufacturer who licenses his technology to a Japanese firm may find that he has created a new competitor for himself in third markets. As far back as the 1960s, in fact, I recall hearing an executive of Combustion Engineering complain that his firm had just been underbid on a sizable Canadian contract by its Japanese licensee.

That particular risk, of course, can be averted by careful drafting of the licensing agreement, but there are other risks that are difficult—or even impossible—to guard against contractually. Luciano Cohen, a former Olivetti executive who became a business consultant in Tokyo, once pointed out that a foreign company that licenses manufacture of its product by a Japanese firm surrenders two important things: it loses control of how the product is manufactured in Japan and it loses control of the Japanese market as well. And, as Cohen stressed, if the foreign company is a multinational, to surrender the latter can prove a serious strategic error.

For precisely the reasons advanced by Kenichi Ohmae and Luciano Cohen, many a U.S. company decides that licensing is too unenterprising—or too risky—and that some form of direct participation in the Japanese market is far preferable. But that decision promptly raises a paradoxical problem. "Brand loyalty in Japan, once you have won it, is like no place else in the world," says Max Factor's Victor Harris. "The trouble is you can't force your way onto the retailer's shelves."

Harris's point here is that no introductory advertising and promotional effort, however extensive and expensive, will by itself persuade Japanese retailers that they had better stock your product. Once again, the *gaijin*—or "outside person" in the implicitly disdainful phrase that Japanese apply to all foreigners—is confronted with the near-necessity of acquiring a mentor who already occupies an established position inside the Japanese distribution system.

For a U.S. company that recognizes this imperative yet is unprepared to go into a joint venture or establish a Japanese subsidiary, the commonest solution is to sign up a Japanese sales agent to market its products. Traditionally, many foreign firms have entrusted this function to one of Japan's major *sogo sosha*, the giant trading companies that deal in innumerable different products and perform an extraordinary range of business functions including the financing of distributors (who lack easy access to bank credit) and distribution service. Today, however, the most famous of the *sogo sosha*—firms such as Mitsui, Mitsubishi, C. Itoh and Sumitomo—often turn out to be already handling products competitive with those of a would-be newcomer to the Japanese market. Increasingly, therefore, U.S. firms that seek to penetrate the Japanese market are turning to other channels: straight sales agents, smaller Japanese trading companies, foreign trading companies long established in Japan such as Britain's Dodwell, aggressive retailing chains such as the Seibu Group and even industrial companies such as Sony, which has served as an agent for imported products ranging from furniture to sporting goods.

Lining up a sales agent, no matter how prestigious, does not, of course, guarantee success in the Japanese market—a fact dismayingly demonstrated by the experience of Apple Computer, Inc. In 1977, when Apple's then boss Steven Jobs negotiated an exclusive-distributorship arrangement with Tokyo's ESD Laboratories Company, Apple became the first company of any nationality to offer a personal computer for sale in Japan. "If they had done things right back then," says one Japanese computer marketer, "they'd be No. 1 in Japan."

Unhappily, Apple proceeded to do things all wrong. Its machines were not designed to process the Chinese characters used in written Japanese—which tended to limit its market to those who speak English. The company failed to provide Japanese instruction manuals for its equipment. And, perhaps worst of all, despite its exclusive agreement with ESD Laboratories, Apple sold computers to a number of other Japanese importers, who then undersold ESD.

All this inevitably damaged Apple's reputation. "Nobody trusts them anymore," asserts ESD's chairman Toshio Mizushima. And even though the company now has its own Japanese marketing subsidiary, Apple Computer Japan, it is starting from behind its own goal line: in 1984, its estimated sales amounted to substantially less than 1 percent of the 1.2 million personal computers purchased by Japanese consumers.

Even with less of a death wish than Apple manifested, moreover, reliance on a Japanese sales agent can pose difficulties. Secure in his exclusive distribution rights, the sales agent may not push the product aggressively enough—or he may set retail prices so high as to restrict sales. And in a country where long-term business ties are so highly valued, it can be difficult and damaging to break off relations even with a demonstrably incompetent or unsatisfactory agent.

All that being said, however, it must also be noted that some of the outstanding successes scored by foreign products in Japan have been the result of happy marriages between foreign manufacturers and Japanese sales agents. Here the classic instance is that of Schick razor blades—which have become so much a part of the Japanese scene that a highly cosmopolitan Japanese official of my acquaintance was startled when I told them they were manufactured in Connecticut. "I've used Schick razor blades for years," he said with some bemusement, "and I always thought they were Japanese."

In reality, up until about twenty-five years ago, very few Japanese had ever laid eyes on a Schick razor. In the late 1950s, roughly 80 percent of the razor blade market in Japan was held by Japanese manufacturers, primarily a company called Feather whose success rested in part on the fact that it was based in Seki, a town famous in feudal Japan for the high quality of the samurai swords its craftsmen produced. Virtually the only foreign competition that Feather and its smaller Japanese rivals faced was from Gillette, which had managed to carve out close to 20 percent of the market. Such few Schick blades as were sold at all in Japan were brought in on its own hook by K. Hattori & Company, a Japanese trading company which has since blossomed into Hattori-Seiko, one of the world's leading watchmakers.

All this began to change in 1960 when Schick, then the Eversharp Schick Company, decided to sign a sole agency agreement with Hattori. Trying to find out what happened next is a bit like watching *Rashomon*, the classic Japanese movie in which a single crime is perceived in very different fashion by each of the people who were involved in it or witnessed it. But even if it is impossible at this remove in time to determine precisely who deserves primary credit for each particular judgment along the way, the overall picture is clear. "What you have here," says Sam Maugeri, president of Warner-Lambert Japan and as such the current overseer of Schick's Japanese operations, "is a classic example of doing everything right."

One of the places that Schick and its advisers at Hattori were conspicuously right was in their judgments on product introductions. Though double-edged blades were then dominant in the Japanese market, Schick decided that the first product it would bring to Japan was its injector razor—and this gamble on the gadget-mindedness of the Japanese promptly proved successful. Three years later Schick struck again by introducing the first stainless steel blades sold in Japan and although its competitors swiftly followed suit it was by then too late to freeze the feisty new boy out: as of 1965 Schick had acquired 5 percent of the market. Then, in 1971, learning that Gillette was planning to put the twin-blade cartridges on sale in the Tokyo area for the first time, Schick executives in Japan took preemptive action and put in an urgent appeal to the company's Milford, Connecticut, plant which had already begun production of its own version of the twin-blade cartridge. In response, Milford not only air-shipped a supply of the cartridges to Japan in time to meet Gillette's launch day but sent a sufficient quantity so that Schick was able to introduce the new product on a nationwide basis rather than on a purely regional one.

Shrewd as these product judgments were, however, their impact was vastly enhanced by Hattori's skill at promotion and distribution. In the mid-sixties, for example, when Schick finally decided to sell double-edged blades, gift packages of blades were sent to 3.5 million Japanese homes, a promotional strategy never before employed in Japan on such a scale. Currently, Schick promotional devices range from the sponsorship of football matches to the presentation of sample shaving kits to scores of thousands of college freshmen. And because of its high reputation in the remotest reaches of the Japanese distribution system, Hattori has been able to establish a stable and classically Japanese system for getting Schick products into the hands of the ultimate consumer: from one super sales company, Schick's wares go to five distributors. These distributors in turn deal with 800 wholesalers who between them cover some 200,000 to 300,000 retailers.

Cumbersome as that may seem to anyone familiar with the American distribution pattern, it nonetheless works in Japan—whereas the system used by Gillette, whose Boston headquarters rides closer herd on its Japanese operations than Warner-Lambert's does, is much less effective. In keeping with corporate policy at the time, Gillette established a wholly owned subsidiary in Japan in 1968 and began dealing directly with some 150 distributors. Subsequently, this figure was reduced to 33, but even that, according to Hattori sources, is so large a number that no single distributor does enough business with Gillette to have a really strong interest in pushing its products.

The result of all this is that Gillette today holds only 10 percent or less of the Japanese razor blade market. A roughly equivalent share is still held by Feather—which made the twin mistakes of clinging too long to the double-edged blade as its primary product and spending too little on advertising. As for Schick, it faces the rather pleasant problem that it cannot realistically hope to increase significantly its current 70 percent share of the blade market. Accordingly, it is aggressively pushing such ancillary products as shaving lotion (where it already has the biggest-selling brand in Japan) and shaving foam.

Not surprisingly, it is sometimes suggested that Schick's triumph in Japan has primarily been the work of Hattori-Seiko and that Warner-Lambert's chief contribution to the process was to preserve the Schick-Hattori relationship after it acquired control of Schick in 1971. That, however, seems to me to underestimate Warner-Lambert's admirable flexibility and very real managerial input, and in a conversation I had with Sam Maugeri in 1985 it became quite clear that he felt the same way. "We [at Warner-Lambert] develop the marketing plans and strategies," he said. "And we develop all of the advertising and promotion materials ourselves. . . . Obviously, Hattori-Seiko are the ones who are out there pushing the product and they have to agree with the strategy or they won't do a good job. So we try to coordinate with them on promotion strategy and oftentimes on some features of products and the packaging aspects. But at the same time it's our business and we want to have the final decision on it."

In still another example of the *Rashomon* phenomenon, executives of Hattori-Seiko tend to stress the joint character of some of these decisions more than Maugeri does. But at bottom these differences seem more matters of nuance than of basic substance. "We think of ourselves almost as part of Warner-Lambert," says Masao Sasaki, the planning manager for the Hattori-Seiko department that handles Schick. And Maugeri himself is quick to admit: "I think the single most important factor in Schick's success here has been consistency of distribution."

Clearly, in short, no one at either Warner-Lambert or Hattori-

Seiko has any intention of jeopardizing what has proved to be an extraordinary happy and fruitful marriage. "Brand strength is very important in Japan," says Sam Maugeri in a direct echo of Victor Harris. "It took us twenty years to get it, but now we've got it and I don't think we're going to lose it."

It is, obviously, exceptional for a U.S. company to find a Japanese sales agent that will serve it as brilliantly as Hattori-Seiko has served Schick. For that reason, many American firms with aspirations of capturing a solid share of the Japanese market for their products have chosen another mode of entry: the establishment of a joint venture with an existing Japanese company.

Like everything else to do with Japanese-American business relations, the advisability of joint ventures is a subject of debate. At one end of the spectrum is the view advanced by Herbert F. Hayde, the chairman of Burroughs & Company's Japanese subsidiary and the president of the American Chamber of Commerce in Japan for 1985. A stocky, bustling man who, among other things, stands out in my memory as the first person ever to telephone me from an automobile, Hayde is a quintessentially American figure who makes no bones about his low regard for certain aspects of Japanese business culture. And while the company which he heads was at one time a joint venture between Burroughs and a Japanese firm, Burroughs bought out its Japanese partner as soon as it was legally able to do so. Nonetheless, Hayde insists, "It's important for a company coming into this market for the first time to look for a partner. . . . I hate to think what it would have been like for Burroughs to try to develop in this marketplace without that original joint venture."

Hayde, moreover, is far from alone in that view. A few months earlier when an interviewer asked him whether a U.S. company entering Japan should try to go it alone or enter into a joint venture, Kentucky Fried Chicken's Loy Weston replied: "Depends entirely on the situation. . . . But all things being equal, I'll come down on the side of the joint venture. . . . If you need to go through the Japanese distribution system, you'd better have yourself a joint venture because of all the entangling alliances."

In recent years, however, the desirability of joint ventures has increasingly come under challenge. According to Robert Talbott, until recently the chairman of Caterpillar Mitsubishi, by no means are all Japanese as enthusiastic about the concept as they once were. "These days," argues Talbott, "Japanese are more inclined to say 'We don't need your technology any longer. Or at least we don't need to pay so high a price for it. We can develop it ourselves if we have to, so why should we give you half of the venture?' "

On the American side, too, doubts about joint ventures seem to have grown stronger. By general agreement, a joint venture has little chance of working well unless there is mutual trust between the two parent companies—and that, of course, isn't always present. When Texas Instruments was obliged by MITI to accept Sony as a partner in its semiconductor venture in Japan, part of the arrangement was that TI must make its patents available to its Japanese partners. But while it lived up to the letter of the agreement, TI reportedly took great pains not to disclose any of its proprietary know-how to Sony. "It's up to them to figure out how to use the information we provide," one TI executive allegedly declared.

Since the deal between Sony and Texas Instruments was only slated to last for three years, that attitude was perhaps understandable, but such behavior clearly doesn't offer the basis for a fruitful permanent relationship and in any case is apt to prove no more than a delaying action. "After a while, the Japanese learn the technology," Tokyo-based business consultant Lyle B. Stuart told Susan Chira of the *New York Times*. And when that happens in a situation where the Japanese and American sides question each other's motives, an erstwhile joint-venture partner can suddenly emerge as a bitter competitor.

Another frequent criticism of joint-venture arrangements is one emphasized by McKinsey & Company's Kenichi Ohmae in an article he wrote for the *Wall Street Journal* in March 1985. "Joint ventures," Ohmae asserted, "tend to get outmoded in today's increasingly volatile business environment since they are based on contracts that specify not only what companies can do but what they cannot. There is little room for initiative or for accommodating changes. As markets and competition shift, disputes over investment and resource allocation become frequent and frustrating. . . . If partners have to dash back to the original contracts rather than to a round-table discussion, you know they are in trouble."

That Ohmae has a point cannot be denied; too many Japanese-

American joint ventures have either failed or performed disappointingly for precisely the reasons he suggests. At the same time, it's important to remember that mutual mistrust and legalistic constraints are insuperable problems in a joint venture only if the parent companies involved let them become so. They are not, in other words, an inherent concomitant of the joint-venture approach and anyone who doubts that assertion has only to study the history of Fuji Xerox, whose corporate structure strongly recalls the case of the bumblebee, a creature which, according to the laws of aerodynamics, ought to be totally incapable of flight.

Though many people are unaware of the fact, the Xerox Corporation of the United States has no direct stake in Fuji Xerox at all. Back in 1956 when Xerox first decided to go international, it formed a joint venture with Britain's Rank Organisation and vested in the resulting company, Rank Xerox Ltd., all rights to manufacture and market Xerox products everywhere in the world outside the United States and Canada. Accordingly, when Japan's Fuji Photo Film Company decided that it wanted to get into the copier business using Xerox technology, it was legally barred from striking a deal with the mother church in Rochester, New York. Instead it had to go into fifty-fifty partnership with Rank Xerox and legally that situation has never changed; even today Xerox chairman C. Peter McColough and the other executives of the American company who sit on the board of Fuji Xerox technically do so in their capacity as directors of Rank Xerox Ltd.

In 1962, when Fuji Xerox came into existence, this state of affairs posed some obvious problems. At that time, the only major font of Xerox technology was in Rochester. Yet initially, Fuji Xerox president Yotaro Kobayashi recalls, "Xerox went to almost extreme lengths in honoring its commitments to Rank Xerox. They were very shy about developing any direct ties with Fuji Xerox and, in fact, for the first couple of years all the technological information that Fuji Xerox received came through Rank Xerox."

Before long, however, it became clear to everyone, including the people in charge of Rank Xerox, that Fuji Xerox would make faster progress if it was able to deal directly with Rochester. And without any rewriting of contractual provisions that was the course adopted. Since 1970 most of the Fuji Xerox people sent abroad for training or information exchange have gone to Rochester, not London. And on technological questions, according to Kobayashi,

Fuji Xerox now deals directly with Xerox in the United States "about 99 percent of the time."

This triumph of realism over legalism was paralleled by an equally remarkable flexibility in the delegation of power. Understandably, both Rank Xerox and Xerox wanted from the beginning to place some of their own people in the Japanese operation. But the management of Fuji Xerox had seen too many expatriate executives misperform in Japan either because they tried to operate on a purely Western basis or because they alienated their home offices by becoming "too Japanese." As a result, says Kobayashi, "we told our friends at Xerox and Rank Xerox, 'Please wait until we here think the time is ripe.' " And with what Kobayashi terms "a unique degree of self-restraint," Rochester and London did, in fact, wait until Tokyo gave them the come-ahead signal—which was not until 1972 by which time Fuji Xerox was ten years old.

Given this history, it is hard to quarrel with Kobayashi when he describes the relationship between the partners in Fuji Xerox as "probably the best of any of the joint ventures." Certainly, it is a relationship that has paid off handsomely for the Western partners. On the most obvious level, they hold a half interest in a business which now boasts sales of well over a billion dollars a year and which in the first half of the 1980s increased its earnings by an average of nearly 13 percent a year. Perhaps equally important, however, is the increasingly strong contribution that Fuji Xerox is making to the international competitiveness of the other members of the Xerox group. According to Kobayashi, the 1045 Xerox copier sold in the United States and Britain incorporates features originally developed by Fuji Xerox for its model 3500, and two other Fuji Xerox copiers have actually been adopted intact into the newest model series offered by Xerox and Rank Xerox.

More and more, in fact, the members of the Xerox group are moving toward what Kobayashi calls "a joint approach to our product portfolios." But along with a broad division of labor in research and development goes a certain amount of deliberate duplication of effort. Says Yotaro Kobayashi: "In the most important segments of the market, we want to have two different horses running—two candidates, each of which has the possibility of becoming the market standard. Precisely because we have been able to maintain a strong sense of trust and confidence in each other, we can also maintain a healthy sense of competition within the group."

Fuji Xerox in short constitutes something done close to a textbook illustration of the potential benefits of the joint-venture approach to the Japanese market. Acquiring a partner of the stature of Fuji Photo Film gives an American company an instant credibility in the Japanese business world that no amount of prestige and success at home in the United States can confer. One of the most candid admissions of this came from Loy Weston whose Kentucky Fried Chicken Japan is 50 percent owned by Mitsubishi Corporation. Said Weston: "Even though Mitsubishi didn't do a lot for us in the beginning in terms of involvement they gave us their name. . . . If Mitsubishi's got their thumbprint on it, the real estate people, the supermarkets or whoever you're dealing with tend to believe you're going to hang around."

Where the Japanese partner *is* prepared to play a highly active role in the joint venture as Fuji Photo Film was, still further advantages accrue to the Western partner. For one thing, the Japanese parent firm constitutes a built-in source of Japanese executives of a higher caliber than those American firms can readily recruit on their own. (At Caterpillar Mitsubishi, for example, the presidency is traditionally occupied by a former top executive of Mitsubishi Heavy Industries.)

By the same token, the Japanese partner in a joint venture can supply indispensable know-how in coping with the various pervasive and frequently mutually hostile branches of the Japanese bureaucracy. In dealing with their government, Japanese companies often use a go-between—generally a retired senior bureaucrat himself. The advantage of this is that the go-between is familiar with all the twists and byways of the corridors of power. Such a person, as Peter Drucker has pointed out, "has been to the same university as the men now in authority and can therefore talk to them over drinks rather than in their offices. He can, in turn, be told what the score is and how his client, the business, should behave to get what it wants."

Theoretically, of course, there is no reason why an entirely American-owned firm should not acquire the services of such a figure and some well-established companies actually have, a case in point being Texas Instruments Japan, whose chief executive, Hideo Yoshizaki, was at one time a very senior official of MITI.

But for a firm just coming into Japan this is not as a rule a realistic option. For as Drucker has also noted, "Unless a foreign investor has a Japanese joint-venture partner, it is not always easy to identify the right go-between."

Along with these considerations, others that can make the joint-venture approach attractive are demonstrated by the experience of Nike, the West Coast wonder child that parlayed the jogging and running fad into something approaching a billion-dollar-a-year shoe and apparel business. Nike's founder, former University of Oregon miler Phil Knight, was at one time a U.S. distributor for Asics Tiger, Japan's major purveyor of running shoes, and perhaps for that reason he prides himself, according to one subordinate, on "copying Japanese philosophy." (One Japanese business principle which Knight has not only adopted but pushed to its logical extreme is avoiding swollen payrolls and excessive investment in plant by letting others do much of your manufacturing. Nike, in fact, does no manufacturing at all. Though it designs the products that it markets, its shoes are all made by contract manufacturers, many of them in Korea, and the same holds true for its apparel.)

In 1981, after having sold its wares in Japan on a license basis for a number of years Nike decided that the potential there was so great that it wanted to be directly involved in the marketing process. But that presented some significant challenges. Asics Tiger had a solid grip on the lion's share, so to speak, of the running-shoe market in Japan and in addition to Nike a number of other well-known companies such as Adidas were trying to carve out a niche for themselves.

The route Knight finally decided upon was to establish a joint venture in which 51 percent of the shares were held by Nike and the great majority of the remainder by Nissho Iwai, Japan's sixth biggest trading company. This at one stroke assured Nike Japan of excellent commercial intelligence—all of Japan's major trading companies have communications networks superior to those of most governments—and, even more important, guaranteed it an effective distribution system. At the same time, it kept to an absolute minimum the capital investment required of Nike. "Nissho Iwai has played a critical role in our financing," says Gary Kurtz, Nike Japan's boyish-looking chairman and chief executive officer. "Even though they don't guarantee our debt, they largely support our bank borrowing. And like many joint-venture companies, we're all debt, all leveraged with just a nominal equity position by either parent. By American standards, I suppose we're all bankrupt, but that's the accepted style of doing business here."

As Gary Kurtz is the first to admit, the verdict on Nike Japan is still out. In its first three years of existence, the company's revenues surged to $60 million a year. "But we're still in the middle of a fight for that solid No. 2 position in the market—a position well below Asics Tiger," says Kurtz. "We haven't won that fight yet by any means." All the same, Kurtz adds, "we're comfortable with where we're going." And he is clearly comfortable, too, with Nike's decision to team up with Nissho Iwai.

"Outstanding" as he declares relations between Nike and Nissho Iwai to be, even Gary Kurtz concedes that it is harder to satisfy two or more masters than it is to satisfy one. Neither that undeniable reality nor the dangers of legalistic rigidity posed by Kenichi Ohmae, however, seem to constitute as fundamental an objection to the joint-venture concept as the one voiced to me by an American executive who himself plays a leading role in a major fifty-fifty venture. After emphasizing just how well the American and Japanese partners in his company worked together, this gentleman in a sudden access of candor rhetorically demanded of me: "But who wants to share if he doesn't have to?"

At least in the unsaintly world of commerce, the answer to that question clearly is "hardly anybody" and in keeping with that spirit some of the most successful U.S. corporate invaders of Japan have managed to retain or ultimately acquire total control of their operations there. Besides such well-known examples as IBM, Coca-Cola and Texas Instruments, the list of wholly owned American enterprises includes some which, at least in their Japanese context, are less often heard about. Among the latter are DuPont Japan, whose chemical sales run well over $300 million a year, and the Weyerhaeuser Company, which disposes of some half a billion dollars' worth of newsprint, paper and other forest products in Japan each year. (Weyerhaeuser's performance is apt to come as a surprise to those who remember the uproar that U.S. trade negotiators have repeatedly raised over Japan's unabashed restrictions on imports of a number of forest products. It may, however, be relevant that Weyehaeuser has gone to great pains to familiarize its U.S. millworkers with Japanese quality requirements and that

David B. Baskerville, who heads the company's operations in Japan, not only speaks Japanese but is given to staging the kind of fancy corporate social bash so dear to the hearts of Japanese businessmen.)

In a few cases, wholly owned American enterprises in Japan are entirely the product of historical accident. One of the most ironic of these accidents involved the American Family Life Assurance Company of Columbus, Georgia, whose enormously successful Japanese venture is not even a subsidiary but merely a branch of the U.S. company. On a visit to Japan in the mid-sixties, American Family's chairman and chief executive officer, a patriarchal figure named John B. Amos, noticed the gauze masks that many Japanese wear in winter in the hope of warding off respiratory infections and concluded that people with that kind of concern for their health might be good customers for one of his company's chief products—a policy insuring the holder against the astronomical medical costs faced by anyone who contracts cancer. But when American Family approached Japanese insurance companies in search of a joint-venture partner the answer was unanimous: "It will never sell in Japan." On the strength of that presumably informed judgment, the Japanese Ministry of Finance concluded that cancer insurance was a non-starter and when Amos insisted that he wanted to go ahead anyway the Ministry offhandedly decided that there was nothing to be lost by letting American Family open a branch in Japan.

In this instance, as it turned out, the conventional wisdom could not have been more wrong. By 1985, just over ten years after John Amos got his Japanese branch, there were fifteen or sixteen companies peddling cancer insurance in Japan, but 70 percent of the policies sold were being written by American Family—and the only Japanese to share in the company's handsome and rapidly burgeoning earnings were the tax authorities.

For obvious reasons, American Family's experience must be considered something of a fluke. Far more typical of the out-and-out U.S. subsidiaries in Japan are those owned by companies that have been doing business there in one form or another for a very long time. IBM punch cards first hit the Japanese market in 1925 and Burroughs began exporting adding and billing machines to Japan in the 1930s. Even these pioneers, however, were Johnny-come-latelies compared to Kodak, which began selling its products in Japan nearly a century ago and which, if it had played its cards differently, might be a far more formidable force there today.*

In their dealings in Japan, a number of these corporate veterans have followed a common pattern of evolution: they started off purely as exporters, marketing their wares in Japan through sales agents. Subsequently, as sales or sales potential seemed to warrant it, they moved toward the establishment of Japanese subsidiaries, frequently with their own manufacturing capability.

In some instances, this was a relatively simple and straightforward process: Victor Harris, whose father before him was involved in the company's Japanese operations, recalls that Max Factor moved directly from a distributorship to a "yen company" in 1954—gambling, along with Coca-Cola, that it would in time become possible to convert yen profits into dollars.

In other cases, however, such as that of Johnson & Johnson, the evolution was a complex and multistage affair. Because it had successfully sold such things as baby powder and Band-Aids in Japan through importers before World War II, J&J was relatively quick to return to the market after the war, this time using as its sole agent the Japanese arm of a British-owned trading company called Cornes. In 1961, this relationship blossomed into a joint venture in which Cornes had a 60 percent interest and J&J 40 percent—an arrangement that observed the letter but not the spirit of a MITI regulation which then required that at least 50 percent of any company established in Japan must be owned by a local partner. (Unable to deny that Cornes & Company was a local firm, MITI swallowed its deal with J&J but promptly rewrote the regulation in question to specify that in future the local partners in a joint venture must be Japanese.)

Though the joint venture prospered, what J&J really wanted was its own enterprise and in 1975, after the local partner requirement was finally dropped, it proceeded to buy out Cornes. But even then the company's regulatory problems were not ended. With Cornes out of the picture, J&J converted its Japanese oper-

---

* Back in the 1930s, as Kodak Japan's president Albert Sieg tells it, a Japanese chemical company asked George Eastman to build a film-manufacturing plant in Japan in a kind of joint venture. On the advice of his engineers, who argued that Japan's high humidity would make it hard to dry the film base, Eastman rejected the proposal—whereupon the Japanese, undeterred, established what has since become Fuji Photo Film, one of Kodak's strongest worldwide competitors.

ations into a branch of the U.S. company and only after some time had elapsed did someone in the Japanese government suddenly remember that it was illegal for the Japanese branch of a foreign company to own land or possess manufacturing facilities—both of which the J&J branch did.

The solution to this awkward situation, according to Kneale Ashworth, the boss of J&J Japan, was "a typically Japanese compromise." No financial or legal penalty was imposed on J&J; instead, the company was requested to make formal apology to the authorities and to establish a *kabushiki kaisha*, or Japanese joint-stock company, to take ownership of its manufacturing facilities. "By then," adds Ashworth, "the bureaucrats who had made the original mistake had all retired, so no face was lost."

Today, of course, a U.S. company entering Japan no longer finds itself virtually required to perform the kind of fancy footwork that Johnson & Johnson was obliged to indulge in. With a more receptive attitude toward foreign investment on the part of the Japanese government and far fewer encumbering regulations in force, a newcomer can base its choice of the best mode of entry into the market more heavily on straightforward business considerations. As a result, in very recent years a number of American firms have decided to skip the joint-venture stage. Instead, companies as diverse as G. D. Searle & Company and Monsanto Electronics Materials Company have opted to buy or lease plant sites in Japan and go into business there on their own from scratch. And while it is still too soon to be sure how enduring all of these recent entrants will prove to be, some, such as Sheldon Weinig's Nihon MRC, appear promising.

Meantime, yet another way of getting into the Japanese market with both feet has also begun to look more feasible than it used to. Partly because Japanese companies tend to see themselves more as social organisms and less as pure profit-making entities than their American counterparts, large corporate mergers and acquisitions are far less common in Japan than in the United States. And for many years this tradition, sometimes reinforced by government policy, effectively prevented any foreign firm from buying control of a major Japanese corporation and thereby acquiring readymade facilities and staff in Japan. Today, however, this principle is sacrosanct no more.

The breakthrough on this front was made by Merck & Company, America's fifth largest pharmaceutical house, which in the mid-1950s began marketing its products in Japan through a joint venture with Tokyo's Banyu Pharmaceutical Company. By the early 1980s, Merck's sales in Japan were running some $140 million a year, a substantial sum but by no means the kind of share of the $16 billion-a-year Japanese drug market that the New Jersey company aspired to. Accordingly, in October 1983 Merck plunked down $314 million for a 50.5 percent interest in Banyu itself—and to almost universal surprise met with no demur from the Japanese government.

Behind the surprise lay the fact that Banyu, with annual sales of close to $300 million, is among Japan's fifteen biggest pharmaceutical firms and is listed on the first section of the Tokyo Stock Exchange, a kind of honor roll of solidly established companies. Never before had foreigners acquired control of a Japanese corporation of such stature and the implications seemed plain. Between Banyu's earnings, its own Japanese sales and those of Torii & Company, a smaller, Japanese drug house in which it also acquired a controlling interest at about the same time, Merck had put together a group with annual revenues of better than half a billion dollars—and, not so incidentally, a whopping 1,200-man sales force. All this, it appeared, could well lay the groundwork for realization of Merck's unconcealed dream of establishing itself as No. 1 in the Japanese pharmaceutical industry.

Before long, however, some of Merck's competitors began to jeer that in acquiring Banyu the company had bought a pig in a poke. Merck, they said, had not been fully aware of Banyu's weaknesses: heavy overstaffing, a lamentably poor record in research and development and excessive dependence on sales of older products such as generic antibiotics whose prices the Japanese government has been relentlessly beating down in an effort to contain health care costs. In short, the critics argued, the only reason Merck had been able to buy control of Banyu was that the company had been badly mismanaged.

All that being said, though, it could well prove to be Merck that has the last laugh. To realize its hopes for Banyu, Merck will doubtless have to display an abundance of patience and commitment—those twin imperatives for all foreign investors in Japan. At least one U.S. pharmaceutical executive in Japan, in fact, believes that the only way Merck can hope to make a success of its bold venture will be through the highly tricky process of consolidating Banyu into the Merck organization. But assuming that Merck has the stamina and skill to make the Banyu acquisition work in the end, it will have pulled off a coup that will change the face of the pharmaceutical industry in Japan.

As for the proposition that any Japanese company available for acquisition by foreigners is more than likely to prove a troubled one, that does not strike all U.S. businessmen as an automatic turnoff. Nearly a year after Merck's purchase of Banyu, Richard T. Lindgren, the chief executive of Michigan's Cross & Trecker Corporation, told a *Wall Street Journal* reporter that because Japan's machine tool industry had acquired far too much productive capacity, it was bound, in his opinion, to go through a serious shakeout sooner or later. When that happened, Lindgren suggested, it might be a good time for an American machine tool maker to pick up a Japanese company cheap.

To the orderly minded, it might well appear that the various corporate arrangements I have been discussing are pretty much mutually exclusive, that it is necessary to choose between licensing and a joint venture, say, or a joint venture and a wholly owned subsidiary. But that, of course, is emphatically not the case. Teledyne's Japanese operations, in which outside sales agents coexist with a wholly owned subsidiary, is far from unique. Many of the most flourishing U.S. enterprises in Japan have developed hybrid structures which at first blush appear classic examples of a horse designed by a committee.

The diversity of forms assumed by these hybrids is nothing short of bewildering. Among the more notable variants are these:

- Max Factor's manufacturing arm in Japan is a wholly owned subsidiary, its marketing arm is a branch of the U.S. parent and its distribution is handled by five separate regional companies, some of which are independently owned but some of which are owned by Max Factor itself. (All of the distribution companies were originally independently owned but, according to Victor Harris, Max Factor eventually bought two of them as a favor to aging owners who wanted out.)
- In addition to Schick with its symbiotic relationship to

Hattori-Seiko, Warner-Lambert's Japanese subsidiary operates a thriving confectionary business and a small pharmaceutical business. But the health technology and hospital products operations that Warner-Lambert also has in Japan are not under the control of its Japanese subsidiary. Instead, they are part of businesses centrally run on a worldwide basis from the United States.

• Johnson & Johnson now has no fewer than five wholly owned Japanese subsidiaries—plus a joint venture in the pharmaceutical field. Organized for the most part around a particular product line, the individual J&J companies are essentially marketing and sales organizations. For such things as financing, administration and personnel, they all have to rely on centralized services in keeping with Kneale Ashworth's belief that "in Japan, the larger the group the greater the synergy."

Sometimes, as we have seen, these hybrid structures are primarily a result of historical accident. But more often they have been adopted out of sound business considerations and in recent years the trend toward hybridization seems if anything to have grown stronger.

One striking evidence of this is supplied by the recent history of IBM Japan. A wholly owned subsidiary since 1937, IBM Japan for many years followed certain business practices religiously: it marketed all its products itself and, while it procured many of its components from subcontractors, it eschewed any formal partnership with outside firms.

Under the leadership of Takeo Shiina, who became its president in 1975, however, IBM Japan has moved in some radically new directions. It has had not just components but entire machines produced by outside contractors. To expand its marketing capabilities, it now allows carefully chosen independent dealers to sell some of its computers. It has gone into joint ventures in computer leasing, the marketing of office equipment and advanced information network systems with firms ranging from Japanese trading companies to Morgan Guaranty International Financing. And in perhaps the biggest departure of all it decided in 1983 to try to secure a stronger foothold in the small-computer market by buying a 35 percent interest in the Japan Business Computer Corporation, better known as JBCC. (The manner in which this last deal was consummated affords a revealing insight into Japanese business mores. "When IBM Japan first showed interest in JBCC," confessed JBCC president Kazuzo Taniguchi, "we were perplexed and doubtful—until Shiina-san came to me saying 'Do lend us a hand.' We then had a heart-to-heart talk.")

Though in all—or nearly all—these things, IBM Japan's behavior has been paralleled by that of its U.S. parent, the hybridization pursued by Shiina has clearly been in response to Japanese conditions. "Our experience," he wrote in early 1984, "has clearly shown that so-called 'traditional' marketing and business operations practices may not be enough in the rapidly moving Japanese market. However, unique approaches are possible and solutions exist for those who will look."

6 The People Problem

Of all the conversations I have held in Japan over a period of forty years, few have aroused my sympathy more than one that I had in early 1985 with the chief executive officer of a U.S. subsidiary there. A man of obvious intelligence and ability, he had arrived in Japan a year or so earlier with no prior knowledge of the country and was the solitary American in the organization that he headed. And when the talk turned to the differences between doing business in the United States and in Japan, his usual quiet decisiveness gave way to an oddly tentative tone. "Communication takes a lot of time here," he mused. "It takes a long time for you to understand what they're saying—not just their words but their concepts. And you've got to make sure they understand you. Normally, in the States if a problem comes up, you have a meeting about it and it takes maybe fifteen minutes. Over here the same type of meeting would probably take two hours."

He hesitated a minute and then went on: "I don't know what the reason is. Maybe it's the basic language problem. And then, of course, you have to be more diplomatic. I'm reluctant to really chew ass here, because I'm not sure how they'll react. Some people tell me that's silly, that you can treat 'em just like Americans, but I don't know."

This man's plight and the incredibly bad advice he was getting from other Americans who presumably fancied themselves knowledgeable about Japan serve to underscore a crucial point: even more important than the mode of operation that a U.S. company chooses to employ in Japan is its choice of managers for the venture. In 1983 when the Study Group on Direct Foreign Investment in Japan asked some 285 foreign affiliates to identify their biggest problem more of them listed personnel and labor concerns than anything else. And so far as personnel problems go, one of the most delicate ones is clearly working out the relative roles of Americans and Japanese in the top management of a subsidiary or joint venture.

The tensions at work here are obvious enough. Quite rationally, any U.S. company involved in a Japanese venture is primarily concerned with the advancement of its own interests and corporate strategies and is likely to conclude that this requires giving trusted Americans control of the levers of power in the Japanese operation. With equal logic, however, the Japanese involved in the venture, whether they are partners or merely employees, will be bent on protecting *their* interests and in seeing operations conducted in a manner compatible with Japanese values.

This, once again, is a problem for which there is no textbook solution. Indeed, successful American ventures in Japan have dealt with it in a variety of different ways. Coca-Cola Japan, which is wholly American-owned, has an American president and nine or ten other Western executives (out of a total staff of 800). Japan Tupperware, which is also wholly American-owned, has a Japanese president and no American employees. As for IBM Japan, which for many years made a great point of the fact that there were no Americans among its top managers, it can still make that boast, but just barely: in 1985 an executive dispatched from IBM Canada took charge of its marketing operations.

Among joint ventures, there is perhaps an even greater variety of answers than there is among out-and-out subsidiaries to the question of how much authority the U.S. parent should exercise and by what means. One common pattern, employed by companies as diverse as Yamatake-Honeywell, Yamazaki-Nabisco and Seibu Allstate, is for a joint venture to have a Japanese chief executive officer but an American executive vice-president. Some joint ventures such as Ajinomoto General Foods, however, have no American executives permanently assigned to them at all. And at the other extreme is Caterpillar Mitsubishi which, in a sense, maintains a dual hierarchy.

"We do not bring Americans over to be in the line organization at Caterpillar Mitsubishi," I was told in early 1985 by Robert Talbott, then the chairman of the company. "We're scrupulous about that. We bring them over to make input into a good, effective operating company staffed by Japanese." Nonetheless, Talbott, who ended a twelve-year tour in Japan shortly after we talked, appeared to look upon Caterpillar's Peoria, Illinois, headquarters much the way a Mormon missionary abroad might look upon Salt Lake City. "Expert as our Japanese executives are," he went on, "they don't know Caterpillar the way we Americans do—and what we're building are Caterpillar products. So what we do is bring in senior people from Caterpillar who are experts at the job they're being assigned to here—which can be manufacturing, quality control, purchasing, data processing or anything else in which they may have a little bit of advanced state of the art as it applies to Caterpillar. That certainly doesn't mean there isn't excellent data processing here, but the important question for us is how do we use it in building Caterpillar products. And in that respect we're always finding that we have experts who can come over here and help us both by answering questions on the job or by knowing where to go in Caterpillar to get some of the answers."

What Caterpillar has devised, in other words, is what Talbott called a "counterpart" system. "I'm the chairman," he said. "My counterpart, so to speak, would be the president, who is Japanese. He is really the operating officer, but we're both held accountable for the smooth operation of the company: I'm held accountable by Caterpillar and he would be held accountable in their way by Mitsubishi."

The same kind of relationship, Talbott added, exists between Caterpillar Mitsubishi's managing director for production who is Japanese and his American counterpart. "The Japanese has the line authority and the American doesn't interfere with that. But if he feels something needs to be changed in terms of strategies or objectives—not in terms of how to put a bolt on—he'll work it out with his Japanese counterpart."

One advantage of the counterpart system, according to Talbott, is its flexibility. "When a particular area is running really smoothly, we can phase the American there out and replace him with somebody else in a different area that can use attention," he said. And, increasingly, there is the possibility that the American who goes home will not be replaced at all. Between 1963 when Caterpillar Mitsubishi was founded and the early 1980s there were always better than twenty Americans working there at any given time, but lately the number has diminished somewhat. "There's no point to having a costly American if you don't need him," Talbott noted.

Though Robert Talbott insisted that Caterpillar Mitsubishi's twin-track system is "one of the key reasons we have been successful," it is not one that arouses enthusiasm among many of the Japanese I have met who are executives of companies with American affiliations. For although Talbott could not be expected to admit it publicly, the Americans at Caterpillar Mitsubishi obviously are not there purely as helpful advisers; they also perform a watchdog function which can scarely fail to dilute in some degree the authority of the Japanese executives. And the prospect of being second-guessed by American colleagues is one that most Japanese managers understandably dislike.

Today Japanese holding senior positions with American-owned firms or joint ventures constitute a unique and increasingly significant factor in the economic life of their country. Necessarily different in outlook both from expatriate American executives in Japan and from the managers of purely Japanese companies, some thirty of them have obeyed the powerful Japanese inclination to band together in affinity groups by forming something called the Study Group on Foreign Affiliates. At a small dinner party which some of the members of this rather special fraternity held in the plush precincts of Tokyo's Seabornia Men's Club in January 1985, I was particularly impressed by two things: the uncommonly high energy and intelligence level of those present and the evident depth of their conviction that any company operating in Japan had best be managed by Japanese.

Neither at the Seabornia Club nor in any of the other conversations I held on the subject with Japanese did anyone come up with a handy-dandy formula as to what percentage of American executives a U.S. affiliate in Japan ought to have. It was clear, however, that, if forced to pick a round number, quite a few of my informants would have opted for zero. "You should depend 100 percent on Japanese to manage a joint venture," Yamatake-Honeywell's president Haruo Okinobu told me. "Too often Americans like to stick their nose in. This is the biggest mistake U.S. companies make in Japan." And McDonald's Den Fujita was equally adamant: "It's just like I told Mr. Ray Kroc years ago. You can send engineers and food technologists; that's fine. But to control Japanese people you must have a Japanese president. I saw many joint ventures—Kraft Cheese, Heinz—start up in Japan and do badly because they had American managers."

In most such pronouncements by Japanese, there is surely a certain amount of chauvinism and an even larger admixture of self-interest. As Fuji Xerox's Yotaro Kobayashi notes: "Japanese with capability want as good a chance as anyone else to make it to the top—even in a foreign affiliate." But the fact that it may in part rest on personal ambition does not, of course, automatically invalidate the argument the Japanese make. Other things being equal, a Japanese executive is, in fact, likely to possess a surer hand in dealing with other Japanese than an American. And in a kind of reverse English, so to speak, Japanese chauvinism can sometimes work to the advantage of a company's American owners. In 1974, the year that Kazunobu Cho was formally made the first Japanese chief executive of Japan Tuperware, the company's sales in Japan doubled. "Our dealers wanted to show that a Japanese president could be successful," Cho explained to me. "Their feeling was 'Now we have a Japanese president—so let's do it.' "

Significantly, too, the doubts that so many Japanese voice concerning the effectiveness of foreign executives in Japan are occasionally echoed by foreign executives themselves—though in more qualified fashion. Kneale Ashworth of Johnson & Johnson, for example, argues that there is a legitimate place for Western executives in Japanese operation—and not just in the kind of exalted slot that he himself occupies. "There are certain areas such as marketing in which it is difficult to fill jobs effectively in this country," Ashworth told me. "The kind of product brand management espoused by companies such as Procter & Gamble, Unilever and ourselves cuts right across the Japanese way of doing things: in the broad sense, Japanese managers are generalists not specialists. And there's an age-generated problem as well: sales directors tend to be considerably older than product managers and since no thirty-five-year-old Japanese is going to tell a fifty-five-year-old where to get off, this means that in meetings and so forth the marketing people get drowned out by the sales people. So we try to put in one or two senior foreign marketing people who've been around the company a while and earned their stripes. Because he's a foreigner, a person like that is allowed to get away with a little more and he's less likely to be shy about coming to the president and saying 'Hey, those sales people are really screwing up'—which a Japanese, of course, would never do."

That said, however, Ashworth was quick to add: "I strongly

believe that all general managers should be Japanese. . . . My thoughts about how to be successful in Japan do not include having foreigners try to run the business day by day." And as a man who first came to Japan in 1969, is married to a Japanese and speaks the language fluently, he is scathing about the basic ignorance of Japan that characterizes too many of the U.S. executives stationed there. "One of the most important elements in managing a business in this country is continuity," he remarked to me. "Yet it is difficult to find an American who is prepared to commit himself to work here for any length of time. According to the American Chamber of Commerce here, most foreign executives who come to Japan come for only three and a half to four years and in my view most of them just skate along the surface. They live in *gaijin* ghettoes, hang out in the American Club* or the Press Club and don't speak the language—which prevents them from truly learning the marketplace. In many cases really their company almost operates despite them."

Obviously, executives who possess some or all of the characteristics Ashworth describes are unlikely to share his views. Indeed, one veteran member of the American business community in Japan took almost the opposite tack. While he conceded that the top man in any U.S. subsidiary or joint venture "should be here a while to demonstrate continuity," he felt it was wrong in career terms for less senior people to spend more than six years in Japan and told me that, as a result, he did not encourage his American subordinates to learn Japanese. "In the time period they're here for," he said, "there are more important things for them to learn." And yet another senior U.S. executive bluntly informed me that in his view his company should have more Americans "in key jobs such as financing, engineering, marketing, etc." Upon further questioning, however, it turned out that what he had in mind was increasing the number of Americans among his company's nearly three thousand

---

* A huge, hotel-like structure which boasts excellent recreational facilities and serves good Western food including such nostalgic items as sourdough bread, Tokyo's American Club is a thoroughly pleasant place and has a number of Japanese members. But is is undeniably a bit of home away from home and in the eyes of some critics has a distinctly colonialist image. The fact that it is located right next to the Soviet Embassy in Tokyo can be regarded as highly ironic or totally suitable depending on one's point of view.

employees from two to five or six—and that he wanted all of those five or six to speak Japanese fluently.

In short, although the word is a highly elastic one, the people involved in the most successful U.S. ventures in Japan generally agree that the permanent American staff assigned to such a company should be kept "small." That, however, by no means has to imply an arm's-length relationship between the Japanese company and its American parent. Increasingly, U.S. companies have found that an effective way to maintain close contact with their Japanese offspring is to send U.S. executives in for short or relatively short stints and with specific missions—to impart a particular kind of expertise not available in Japan, to acquire expertise in areas where the Japanese have shown themselves innovative or to coordinate strategies of one kind or another. "I don't believe there is ever a day when we don't have at least one visitor here from the U.S.," says Fuji Xerox's Yotaro Kobayashi.

This executive flow, moreover, is by no means a one-way affair. Among wholly owned U.S. subsidiaries, in particular, a popular means of ensuring the maximum feasible adherence to the corporate culture of the U.S. parent company and the special business practices it employs is to send Japanese managers to the United States, often to perform real jobs in the American company for a year or more. This is a device favored, for instance, by Johnson & Johnson where, so Kneale Ashworth proudly allows, "we send Japanese to the States who do so well that the domestic companies sometimes try to steal them." The same approach has been used for even longer by IBM—with conspicuous success but sometimes also with unexpected side effects, as was confessed to me some years ago by a very senior executive of IBM Japan who at one point managed an IBM facility in the American South. "Not long after I returned to Japan," this man recalled, "I was being driven somewhere late at night and fell asleep in the car. Eventually, we had to stop for some highway construction, which woke me up. As I came to, I noticed that the flagman on the construction project had a Japanese face and found myself wondering in a sleepy way 'Hey! What's a good Nisei boy doing holding down a nothing-ball job in the boondocks of North Carolina?' "

Broadly speaking, the advantages of relying heavily or even primarily upon Japanese managers seem to loom larger the longer a foreign affiliate is in business in Japan. In the survey conducted by the Study Group on Direct Foreign Investment in Japan to which I alluded earlier, only 82 out of 285 companies cited "management by Japanese staff" as having been one of their strong points immediately after they first went into business in Japan. But when the companies surveyed were asked how they felt after having been in business for some time, the number that cited Japanese management as a strong point jumped to 131.

In part, that increase may have reflected heightened recognition of the desirability of relying on Japanese managers by some of these companies as they gained experience. To a greater extent, however, it probably reflected the fact that it is much more difficult for a fledgling company—and particularly one with foreign ties— to attract capable executives in Japan than it is in the United States. As a rule of thumb, a new foreign affiliate in Japan must assume that it will take several years and a seemingly inordinate amount of effort to assemble a truly topflight Japanese management team.

There are several reasons for this, perhaps the least often considered being a limitation which most American companies impose on themselves and which was drawn to my attention in almost identical language by Hideo Yoshizaki of Texas Instruments Japan and Kazunobu Cho of Japan Tupperware. Cho, like Yoshizaki, speaks English fluently, but there was nonetheless a faint hint of derision in his voice when he said: "Most Americans think a guy who speaks English is smart and tend to rely on his judgment."

Clearly, easy communications between an American company and those who manage its Japanese operations is a necessity and it is far easier to find an English-speaking Japanese executive than a Japanese-speaking American one. But the fact remains that linguistic skill is not synonymous with good business judgment and that those American companies that will not hire a senior employee who does not already speak English automatically reduce by a considerable amount the pool of capable Japanese executives available to them.

In all fairness, however, most of the difficulties encountered by foreign affiliates in their efforts to acquire topflight Japanese executives are the product of Japanese cultural attitudes rather than American ones. And to overcome these difficulties successfully, it is necessary not only to accommodate to Japanese psychology to some degree but also where possible to manipulate it.

As anyone even faintly familiar with Japan is aware, the large modern firms that constitute about a third of the Japanese industrial establishment practice what is generally but somewhat misleadingly called "lifetime employment." (In reality, what is involved is guaranteed employment up to a fixed and often rather early retirement age.) In return for this, such corporations feel entitled to demand extraordinary loyalty from their employees. Partly for this reason and partly because of the strong group orientation generally characteristic of Japanese, executive job-hopping has traditionally been looked upon with great distaste in Japan and the few people who indulged in it were apt to pay a high price for their "flightiness." A Japanese friend of mine who switched from one company to another in his late thirties bitterly recalls that after he had been with his "new" company for twenty years, other executives there still made it plain from time to time that they regarded him as a Johnny-come-lately and not truly one of them.

As we shall see shortly, the tabu against job-hopping is no longer as sacrosanct as it used to be. It is, however, still strong—strong enough to constitute a real constraint upon executive recruitment by firms with foreign ties. "In a country where you own people for their entire working lives," says Kneale Ashworth, "you have to think very carefully before hiring anyone." True enough, but in many cases before a firm with foreign ownership, particularly a relatively new one, can even think of hiring a Japanese executive it must first persuade him that he really can reasonably expect to spend the rest of his working life there.

On that score, suspicion sometimes runs very deep. To a degree, the repeated executive shake-ups at places such as Apple have tarnished the image of U.S. businesses in general. "Japanese still tend to see U.S. companies as quick to hire and quick to fire," says Hideo Yoshizaki of Texas Instruments. And the number of U.S. companies that have withdrawn from Japan because they lacked the commitment to pay the price of success there has served to keep alive another fear. "There is real concern among many Japanese," notes Fuji Xerox's Yotaro Kobayashi, "about the permanence and survival of foreign affiliates. They see a much greater sense of continuity in Japanese businesses."

Even where these concerns are not operative or can be allayed, the quarry is not necessarily in the bag. A Japanese executive himself may well be persuaded that he will find both security and greater satisfaction by joining up with a foreign affiliate and then may still be talked out of making the move by his family. Despite the fact that their society is remarkably egalitarian in material ways, Japanese remain intensely status-conscious and, with relatively few exceptions, association with a foreign firm does not confer the same kind of status that association with an established Japanese firm does. "Japanese wives," I was told by Seiro Takehara, one of Tokyo's top executive recruiters, "like to be able to say 'My husband works for Mitsubishi or Sumitomo.' " And that attitude is often shared by Japanese fathers, mothers, uncles, cousins and aunts. Early in 1985 a Japanese friend of mine who had been working in the United States for one of Japan's biggest trading companies accepted a job offer from a leading American corporation that has been established in Japan since long before World War II. By American standards, the move was an eminently sensible one: the new job offered a substantial pay increase, the prospect of swifter advancement and, somewhat ironically, an opportunity to return to Japan at a time when, for family reasons, that seemed peculiarly desirable. Nonetheless, my friend confided, his elderly father in Tokyo was horrified by the switch, refusing even to take consolation in the prospect of seeing far more of his grandchildren.

In the face of this kind of family pressure, it's scarcely surprising that Japanese executives sometimes agonize for months over a job offer from a foreign affiliate. "We've been dickering for a long time with one guy," Albert Sieg of Kodak told me. "He wants to come work for this company in the worst way, but his wife doesn't like the idea, his parents don't like it and I'm not all sure that in the end he's going to make it."

One reason that mid-career job changes by executives remain much less common in Japan than in the United States is that, traditionally, major Japanese companies have chosen their top managers from an in-house elite whose members have never worked anywhere else. To assure themselves of a constant supply of potential senior executives, most such companies recruit a fresh crop of new university graduates each spring. In theory, these officer candidates, so to speak, are chosen on the basis of a corporate entrance examination which is held each winter about five months before college graduation time. In reality, however, the examinations are more or less a formality: anyone whom a corporation invites to take its exam has already been given the nod by company officials who attended the same university and have been alerted to the young man's desirability by their own former professors. ("The professor," notes Kenichi Ohmae, "is a kind of godfather—a trusted counselor both to the students and to the company men who are his former students.") And once they actually go to work, the members of this handpicked elite are typically rotated through a variety of different jobs rather rapidly to make sure that those who ultimately rise to the highest level in the company will have as broad a background as possible.

Comparative status, of course, plays a major role in this process, too. As a rule, the topflight students from Tokyo University, which in Japan has the cachet of Harvard, Yale and MIT all rolled into one, will only consider signing on with Tokio Marine and Fire Insurance, the Mitsubishi or Sumitomo trading companies, Hitachi, Fujitsu or another of a dozen or so such blue-ribbon companies. Less prestigious Japanese companies must settle for Tokyo University graduates with less impressive credentials or for graduates of less prestigious institutions. (In Japan, the educational pecking order is broadly the reverse of what it is in the United States: the most respected universities by and large are government-supported public schools.)

Today, most well-established foreign affiliates in Japan try to emulate Japanese companies in their college recruitment efforts—and they do so with greater success each year. As of 1985, IBM Japan had risen to ninth on the list of companies for which science and engineering graduates of top Japanese universities wanted to work. But the process of developing an "old boy network" at Tokyo University and its leading rivals such as Kyoto University takes years of effort reinforced by the acquisition of great public prestige. As a result, most foreign affiliates—and in particular those which are entirely American-owned—must resort to private universities such as Aoyama Gakuin, which in 1984 sent graduates to such companies as American Hospital Supply, Nippon Univac, Bank of America, First Chicago Corporation and Japan Motorola. But while it is a thoroughly respectable institution, Aoyama Gakuin is a distinct cut below Tokyo or Kyoto universities in general esteem and in that of the Japanese bureaucracy—which means, among other things, that its graduates are less likely to have powerful and widespread contacts inside the government in decades to come.

With the passage of time, the ability of foreign affiliates to recruit successfully among the most sought-after college graduates will surely increase. "Change, while subtle, is clearly going on in that respect," says Fuji Xerox's Yotaro Kobayashi—who adds that his firm can already recruit top college graduates because it is regarded as "an independent Japanese company." And in any case not all executives of U.S. subsidiaries are totally sold on the traditional Japanese recruitment system.

"Most Japanese companies think Tokyo University graduates are automatically good people," Tupperware's Kazunobu Cho told me. "But in my view some are and some aren't. We have key executives from [private universities such as] Waseda, Keio and Jochi. . . . There aren't tailor-made good people or bad people and you don't need geniuses to run everything. Good people are people who can do well what you want done and in that sense even a mediocre person properly developed can be a good person." In a slightly different vein, a senior American executive in Tokyo complains: "In the U.S. people with recently earned degrees in computer sciences are full of ideas; they can come directly from university to industry and start being productive early in the game. But it's my observation that with a recent Tokyo University graduate, you have to tell him what to think about."

Whatever the merits or demerits of conventional Japanese-style college recruitment, however, it is a tool that is rarely available to a newly established foreign venture or a small and relatively unknown one. And it is of no use either to a company that must fill as soon as possible a senior management position for which no in-house candidate is available. For these and other reasons, a considerable number of foreign affiliates in Japan resort on a fairly regular basis to hiring experienced executives away from other companies, either by direct raiding or by employing the services of a headhunter.

Executive head-hunting, at least in its contemporary form, is a relatively new profession in Japan and is still regarded by many Japanese as a somewhat dishonorable one because its practitioners encourage people to flout obligations which they have incurred under traditional Japanese mores. Nonetheless, there are now dozens of executive search firms officially registered with Japan's Ministry of Labor and many more that operate quietly without government sanction. Generally regarded as the largest of the officially approved head-hunting operations is IMCA (for International Management Consultant Associates), which is run by Seiro Takehara, a plump, moon-faced man whose staccato English consists essentially of nouns and verbs devoid of connective tissue and whose office wall is adorned with a motto that translates roughly as "Make something out of nothing." When he started IMCA in 1967, Takehara focused primarily on recruiting Japanese executives for foreign firms and he claims to have received a letter of appreciation from "the chairman of Coca-Cola in Atlanta" for his help in recruiting nearly sixty middle managers for Coca-Cola Japan.

Not surprisingly, Takehara has very definite ideas on what foreign ventures must do to attract the services of established Japanese managers. "Nowadays," he told me, "good U.S. companies [in Japan] offer lifetime employment." And just as in the States, financial incentives are a significant consideration: most of his clients, Takehara said, got salary increases of 10 percent or more when they moved and in some cases substantial lump-sum payments as well. "But Japanese," he quickly added, "are very position-oriented people; that's more important than money. Good Japanese can be attracted by power." And conversely, he warned, they could be turned off by the awareness that the top slot in a foreign venture would always be reserved for an American or by the prospect of having to cope with a clutch of "young American MBA technocrats"—a phrase he pronounced with all the disdain of a U.S. conservative inveighing against "knee-jerk liberals."

To a large degree, Takehara's analysis is borne out by some of the senior American executives in Japan with whom I have discussed mid-career hiring. "Basically," Kodak's Albert Sieg said, "what a U.S. firm can offer a guy that it wants to hire away from a Japanese company is more rapid advancement, the opportunity to operate on a more individualistic basis and the chance of exposure to opportunities outside Japan."

Those are undeniably potent attractions but the U.S. raider may also be laying up for the job-hopper—and for itself—a considerable amount of grief. To acquire a general manager for his new plant in Kyushu, Materials Research Corporation's Sheldon Weinig lured a man away from a nearby facility of Texas Instruments Japan—whereupon the new recruit proceeded to persuade several other TI personnel to come with him. Understandably, this did not please Texas Instruments' management and, by unhappy coincidence, TI happened to be Materials Research Corporation's best customer in Japan. "That was something of an embarrassment," says Dr. Weinig dryly. "We put a stop to it."

Raiding can also be expensive as well as embarrassing. Some Japanese companies actually have regulations forbidding employees to resign without the permission of their boss. Such provisions are apparently of dubious legality, but it is by no means unheard of for a company that has been raided to bring suit against the headhunter and/or the corporation he is assisting for "stealing" the services of an employee. And in some cases either the new employer or the job-hopper himself feels it prudent to negotiate a cash settlement with the old employer.

Employee-snatching, in short, can still be a source of considerable *angst* in Japan. In an interview with Susan Chira of the *New York Times* in November 1984, one Mitsuo Ogishima, who left a Japanese trading company to join Nihon Digital Equipment as a marketing specialist, somewhat plaintively remarked: "Changing a job is just like a divorce." But just like divorce, it is also becoming a much more commonplace feature of life in contemporary Japan. A 1984 survey conducted by the prime minister's office found that nearly half of all Japanese between twenty and twenty-nine expressed a preference for an "employment changing" job environment to the assurance of lifetime employment. And in another survey conducted by a large job-placement firm, a quarter of the college graduates interviewed actually had changed jobs at least once.

The gradual but very perceptible weakening of the Japanese addiction to lifetime employment has already considerably expanded the pool of executives and potential executives in which foreign affiliates in Japan can fruitfully fish. As late as the 1960s, when such a firm wanted to acquire Japanese managers it often had to fall back upon former employees of the Occupation forces or U.S. government agencies in Japan. And while some of these people, such as Tupperware's Cho, Johnson Wax's Koyama and

McDonald's Den Fujita, proved to be outstandingly capable, there were others who had little to offer beyond the fact that they spoke English.

Today, however, an American subsidiary or joint venture can reasonably insist upon relevant business experience when it goes hiring in Japan. With each passing year, for example, there is a larger supply of high-caliber Japanese managers who have worked in the U.S. branch of a Japanese firm and have thereby acquired both a familiarity with the American business environment and a taste for its relatively free and easy character.

This group, in the eyes of some headhunters and corporate personnel offices, constitutes probably the single most fertile source of managerial recruits for foreign affiliates in Japan. "Our success has often come through hiring Japanese in the U.S.," says Albert Sieg of Kodak. "Many of the people we have acquired have spent time in the U.S. but wanted to come back to Japan for their children's sake or whatever." In a variation on this theme, others prefer to focus on Japanese who have already returned from an overseas assignment. But in such cases, according to executive recruiter Michael Stockford of PA International Consulting in Tokyo, timing is of the essence. "After a man has been back for a year," Stockford told Bernard Wysocki, Jr., of the *Wall Street Journal*, "he has forgotten that he has ever been overseas. So you have about six months in which to strike and get him."

The steady expansion of the pool of available executives with demonstrated track records, however, is only part of the story: where what is sought is potential rather than experience some promising new personnel possibilities have been opening up for U.S. ventures in Japan. A number of companies have begun to pay closer attention to Japanese women, who are becoming notably more career-minded but still find it difficult to get executive-track jobs with top Japanese corporations. (Among the 110 university graduates hired by Tokio Marine and Fire Insurance in 1984, for instance, there was not a single female.)

By exploiting this long-neglected resource, some foreign affiliates have significantly increased the effectiveness of their college recruitment programs: in 1984, Salomon Brothers' Asia Ltd. landed its first Tokyo University graduate by accepting a woman. And American Family Life Assurance has capitalized very heavily on womanpower. "We can't recruit the cream of the masculine crop from Tokyo University or other universities comparable to your Ivy League schools," I was told by Yoshiki Otake, senior vice-president of the company's Japan branch. "But we can get women—outstanding women who are graduates of good colleges and universities. And we recently put a woman who worked for some years for the IMF in the U.S. in a management position."

Along with women, other sources of potential executive talent that were once overlooked or were extremely limited in scope have begun to assume greater importance. Partly because of the burgeoning of the Japanese business community abroad, there is a growing number of Japanese who have received some of their education overseas. Such people have in the past often been regarded by Japanese companies as too cosmopolitan and individualistic, but they can also possess an independence of mind that equips them to deal effectively with Westerners. So IMCA's Seiro Takehara keeps on the lookout for young Japanese who have studied in the United States, including—for all his horror of "technocrats"—those who have earned MBAs at American universities.

At the opposite pole, Takehara also seeks out what he calls "the new *gaijin*." By this he means young Americans who speak Japanese and have an understanding of Japanese culture—people such as William Pfeiffer, son of IBM World Trade's Ralph Pfeiffer, who spent one of his college years at Tokyo's Sophia University and who at twenty-six became director of marketing for a U.S. pharmaceutical company in Japan.

The new *gaijin* are still in relatively short supply, but they are considerably easier to find today then they were even as recently as the 1970s. While the number of Japanese-language students at U.S. colleges is still minuscule compared to students of Spanish, French or German, it totaled more than 16,000 in 1983—which was a whopping 40 percent increase over the figure just three years earlier. And from my own contacts with young people at Columbia University and elsewhere, it has become clear to me that considerably fewer of those who study Japanese nowadays are preparing for an academic career than used to be the case; more and more often their avowed motive for learning Japanese is that it will give them an edge in pursuing a career in business, journalism or government.

This opens avenues which Herbert Hayde of Burroughs strongly believes U.S. companies with Japanese interests should actively pursue. Noting that he had recently made a place on his staff for a young American who studied Japanese at the University of South Carolina, Hayde told me in early 1985: "I've said to my corporation that we ought to make the investment in language-capable international managment personnel." Hayde's point was not just that this would be useful in Japan itself, moreover. "We need to make that investment," he said, "so that we can get some people on the U.S. end who are, let's say, Japan experts."

In this view, he is by no means alone. Yoshi Tsurumi, who is professor of international business at Baruch College of the City University of New York, argues forcibly that one reason U.S. companies often find themselves outcompeted by Japanese companies is that, unlike many of their Japanese counterparts, "very few chief executive officers [of American corporations] have had any direct experience in the international business end of their firms." And judging from what Herbert Hayde has observed, the premium which the Japanese place on international experience is, if anything, increasing. "Japanese firms," he told me, "are taking managers they trained in their American companies and bringing them back here—and you can see the resulting Western influence within some of these companies."

In so saying, Hayde underlined one aspect of a phenomenon that will bear close attention from U.S. ventures in Japan. When he first went into the head-hunting business in the late 1960s, Seiro Takehara recalls, 70 percent of the companies that employed his services were foreign and only 30 percent Japanese; by 1985, however, those percentages were almost reversed. "Nowadays," Takehara reported, "big Japanese companies are scouting out good Japanese managers in American companies." What's more, he went on, some of them were also making passes at the new *gaijin*. "Oh, yes," he said with a large grin. "I recruited three bilingual Harvard graduates for Japanese companies. Former students of Ezra (*Japan as Number One*) Vogel."

In the same week that I met with Seiro Takehara, I asked Kneale Ashworth just how tough it really was for a foreign affiliate to put together an outstanding management team in Japan. "It's difficult," he shot back, "but not at all impossible." Clearly, if they wish to keep conditions that favorable, U.S. business with interests in Japan are going to have to keep a sharp eye on their Japanese competitors and remain untiring, aggressive and innovative in the search for high-caliber personnel.

7 Something Old, Something New

"There are times," a well-read Japanese bureaucrat of my acquaintance told me a few years ago, "when the behavior of some American companies here reminds me of the charge of the Light Brigade. Perhaps you remember what a French officer who was present as an observer said about that: 'It's magnificent, but it isn't war.' Well, when an American company tries to function in Japan strictly according to American principles of management, it may reflect great corporate discipline, but it isn't good business. The truth is that when it comes to management practices, every U.S. company that has been successful in this country for any period of time has 'Japanized' its operations at least to some extent."

That observation, in my view, is accurate enough as far as it goes, but it still leaves some crucial questions unanswered. How far can a U.S. company carry localization of management in Japan and still retain ultimate control of its investment? No less important, who is in the best position to judge what degree of Japanization of management style will be both productive in the Japanese market and compatible with the best long-term interests of the American parent?

The answer to the latter question, according to the managers of some highly prosperous U.S. ventures in Japan, is: the men on the spot. One proponent of that argument is Japan Tupperware's Kazunobo Cho, a man who can scarcely be accused of blind rejection of U.S. business practices. He is, for one thing, the only Japanese executive I have ever met who is sufficiently comfortable with American informality to receive a visitor to his office in shirt sleeves. More important, he freely admits that he has "benefited much from the experience of Tupperware people in the U.S. and elsewhere" and feels deeply indebted to a now-retired American executive who launched him on his managerial career at Tupperware and counseled him for many years ("He is like a father to me"). For all that, however, Cho is adamant on one point: "If you ask me what made Japan Tupperware successful, this was the key: we had clear understanding from headquarters: 'Leave Japan alone and they will do it.' "

Inevitably, many U.S. companies find this degree of decentralization impossible to swallow even when the top man on the scene in Japan is an American who has proven himself in the parent company. Drawing, presumably, upon his observation of other companies, Kodak's Albert Sieg told me: "If an American executive in Japan starts talking too much in the long term, the home office guys are apt to say: 'You've gone native; you've lost your American business perspective.' " And when that happens the result can easily be the kind of second guessing in the States which, as Kazunobu Cho noted, creates a destructive situation in which "the manager in Japan is sandwiched between his Japanese employees and the head office in the U.S."

Not surprisingly, a number of the American affiliates in Japan that have successfully avoided this problem are ones whose U.S. parent is accustomed to giving its managers a good deal of independent authority. This, for example, is true of Johnson & Johnson and is cited by Kneale Ashworth as one of the primary strengths of J&J Japan. "Having put together a competent management team here," he says, "New Brunswick trusts us to run the business. Of course, we agree on strategic plans and on an operating plan for each year. But I've worked for the company for nine years now and I've yet to receive a direct order from New Brunswick."

Along with local autonomy, Ashworth is also a strong proponent of Japanese management style—up to a point. But fitting into the Japanese scene, he argues, has required less adjustment on the part of Johnson & Johnson than is the case with most American companies. "Back in 1942 or so," he told me, "General Johnson wrote a basic credo for J&J by whch, although it's been somewhat revised over the years, we are still required to run our businesses. That credo spends a lot of time talking about quality, about responsibility to the end user of our products, about responsibility to one's staff, responsibility to the environment and, last of all, responsibility to shareholders. . . . We took these basic principles in which we happen to believe and found that they dovetailed very much with the way Japanese think. So we have maximized them. When we recruit at universities we center heavily on that credo . . . and I think that J&J has rightfully picked up a reputation for concern for its people."

In stressing the value of the Johnson & Johnson credo, Ashworth is undoubtedly right. At my encounter with Japanese executives of U.S.–owned firms at the Seabornia Men's Club, much of the conversation turned around the fact that Japanese tend to attach more importance to the existence of a strong corporate philosophy than Americans do. But as one of the senior Japanese present pointed out, the mere fact that a U.S. company has a well-defined corporate philosophy—even one that Japanese find acceptable in the abstract—doesn't by any means ensure that there will be a meeting of the minds as to how its Japanese operations should be managed. "In my experience," this man said, "Americans and Japanese working for the same multinational can sincerely subscribe to the same set of corporate principles and still differ significantly as to what those principles require in the way of concrete action in a specific situation."

The validity of that observation becomes clear when one looks at the management styles actually employed by U.S. subsidiaries and joint ventures in Japan. In my conversations with the heads of such companies, somewhat more than half assured me that they relied upon a blend of Japanese and American management practices—and many of them phrased that assertion in virtually identical language. Yet, as it turned out, they were far from identical in their recruitment, salary and promotion policies. And to complicate the picture further there were sometimes strong similarities in practice between companies which professed to combine Japanese and Western styles and those which claimed to follow "a generally Japanese system."

When Americans try to analyze Japanese management practices, they almost invariably focus entirely on the large modern companies that have spearheaded Japan's international economic triumphs. Such corporations, as it happens, account for only 50 percent of Japan's industrial production and about a third of its industrial employment. The rest of the Japanese industrial establishment, which the great corporations use as a source of low-cost labor and parts, consists of small companies that in general pay poorly, offer little if any job security and go bankrupt in startlingly large numbers.

Nonetheless, it is the modern companies with which U.S. ventures in Japan chiefly compete both in the marketplace and in the recruitment of managerial and white-collar personnel. And by now certain stereotypes concerning the way such companies are managed have been widely disseminated in American business circles.

Anyone who has sampled the studies of Japanese business techniques produced in ever-increasing quantities by American academics, management consultants and others has learned that the employees of top Japanese companies are not only blessed with extraordinary job security but also, except at the higher levels of management, with automatic promotions and salary raises based on seniority alone. And a diligent reader will surely have encountered the concept of *marugakae*, or "total embrace"—the management philosophy that impels major Japanese corporations to provide their workers with everything from company commissaries and athletic facilities to company vacation homes.

The explanation commonly offered for the practice of *marugakae* is that it is a way of maximizing the traditional tendency of Japanese to turn any group to which they belong into a kind of extended family. (Foreigners with limited knowledge of Japanese are sometimes confused by the fact that the word *uchi*, which basically means "home," is also frequently used by workers to refer to their company.) To some Americans, this conscious attempt to induce workers to regard their company as far more than just an employer seems a manipulative and basically cynical means of securing a docile labor force. Other, more receptive American observers argue that it reflects an intelligent concern for people and worker motivation too often lacking in contemporary U.S. industry. But both cynics and admirers agree that *marugakae* does, in fact, help to account for one of the great strengths of the modern sector of Japanese business—workers deeply dedicated to the survival and prosperity of the company that employs them and confident that if they serve it well their own interests will also be well served.

By general agreement, too, it is not just material inducements that lead Japanese to identify so strongly with the company that employs them; it is also the fact that, however humble their position, all those who work for a major Japanese corporation are, according to the stereotype, given some sense of participation in its management. At the blue-collar level, this manifests itself in the warm encouragement accorded suggestions on how to cut costs or increase efficiency. (In 1981, Toyota received 1.3 million such suggestions from its 48,000 employees—and implemented 90 percent of them.) But what has fascinated American students of the sociology of Japanese business even more than this has been a phenomenon which occurs above the blue-collar level—something called *ringi seido*.

In his book *How to Do Business with the Japanese* the late Mark Zimmerman, who for some years ran Sterling Drug's operations in Japan, defined *ringi seido* as decision-making that goes "middle-up as opposed to the American decision-making process of top-down." It is, in other words, a concept which rests on the proposition that in Japanese companies important policy proposals often originate not with top executives but in the middle or even lower echelons of management. When such a proposal emerges, it will first be subjected to a process called *nemawashi*— a word that refers to the careful handling that must be given the roots of a tree before it can be transplanted. In the corporate context, this means that everyone who is likely to be affected by the proposal will be consulted about it on an informal basis and only if a consensus in its favor can be achieved will it be officially bucked up through channels for the approval of top management. And by that time, so the more extreme interpretations of *ringi seido* have it, the approval of top management is essentially a formality since there is already company-wide support for the policy.

For reasons I shall explain later in this chapter, I have reservations about the usefulness of the *ringi seido* stereotype—and, indeed, about all other stereotypical analyses of Japanese business practices, including my own. Stereotypes, of course, are almost by definition misleading and in Japan, where form and substance are even more frequently at odds than in most places, they can be particularly deceptive. What foreign students of Japanese business too seldom emphasize, in my opinion, is that successful Japanese companies differ from one another in their management styles just as often and just as greatly as successful American businesses do.

That being said, however, there obviously are certain management techniques and practices that can legitimately be held to be particularly characteristic of Japanese business. And a look at which of these have been adopted by various existing American ventures in Japan offers at least some clues as to which can contribute significantly to success in the Japanese market—and under what circumstances.

For obvious reasons, those foreign affiliates in Japan which are or claim to be entirely assimilated in terms of management practices are mostly joint ventures—firms such as Fuji Xerox, Ajinomoto General Foods and Yamatake-Honeywell in which there is at least a 50 percent Japanese interest and whose executives are exclusively or almost exclusively Japanese nationals. But even among wholly owned American subsidiaries—and especially among those which have been operating in Japan for a long time—there are some that have gone very far toward adopting the "total embrace" approach. One such is Johnson Wax Japan, whose chairman, former University of Illinois Fulbright scholar Hachiro Koyama, proudly proclaims that, because the Japanese management practices he employs are reinforced by the socially conscious policies of the U.S. parent company, "Our firm is actually 120 percent Japanese." Much the same holds true for Max Factor where President Victor Harris told me: "We completely follow Japanese management practices—particularly as they apply to personnel. We have company unions, company vacation homes, promotion by seniority, lifetime employment—the works." And there is no doubt in Harris's mind that this has paid off. "Look at Revlon," he said succinctly. "In most of the world they've been highly, highly successful. But they got themselves in a terrible jam here and the reason was that they wouldn't follow Japanese practices of any kind."

By the same token, it would seem no accident that IBM Japan is not only the biggest of U.S. subsidiaries there but also among the most thoroughly Japanized. Like Kneale Ashworth at Johnson & Johnson, IBM Japan's president Takeo Shiina argues that, rather than requiring special adjustment to the Japanese environment, much of his company's management style simply reflects the character of its American parent. "Many elements of IBM's corporate culture and business style," he wrote in the *Journal of Japanese Trade and Industry,* "closely parallel those of Japanese business . . . Japan has proved fertile ground for the IBM tradition of corporate social responsibility." Those are surely valid observations. But in the same article, Shiina emphasized that "executives of our parent corporation have always been good listeners, alert to local requirements." Just how alert they have been is suggested by his comment that "Japanese companies provide family allowances, health insurance, health care programs, recreational facilities, educational programs, house ownership promotion programs and . . . job security. IBM Japan is consistent with Japanese practices in all these key areas."

Even those American subsidiaries which stop far short of "total embrace," moreover, are careful for the most part to try to mitigate their reputation for "foreignness." Sometimes this effort can take seemingly trivial forms such as IBM Japan's decision in 1981 to abandon its traditional Christmas holiday. (Though many Japanese regard it as something of a special occasion—much as some New Yorkers without Irish roots look upon Saint Patrick's Day—Christmas is not a legal holiday in predominantly non-Christian Japan.) More often, however, the attempt to avoid "foreignness" involves matters which, while essentially mundane, will be instantly recognizable to anyone who has ever managed any enterprise at all as fraught with explosive potential—problems such as who gets what kind of office space.

Traditionally, Japanese have regarded the possession of private offices by anyone except the two or three top executives of a firm as inappropriate and inefficient—inappropriate because an office is a place where one goes to work, not to display pictures, grow plants or engage in meditation, and inefficient because things get accomplished faster if the boss is right out there in the bullpen with the rest of the folks, keeping a constant eye on everything that's going on and available at all times to answer questions and field unexpected problems. My own belief is that these avowed arguments for the open office, all sternly practical, are reinforced by some unavowed and perhaps even unrecognized emotional ones: the fact that most Japanese find it psychologically uncomfortable to be physically separated from other people very much of the time and that many of them tend to be rendered jealous by conspicuous displays of privileged status.

That, however, is speculation and there are signs that, whatever its origins, the tabu against private offices and individual cubicles in Japanese business is now fading somewhat. On person who is convinced that such a change is occurring is President Yotaro

Kobayashi of Fuji Xerox who in early 1985 reminded me that some first-line Japanese corporations had lately built themselves new headquarters with offices so plush "that it is hard to see how they justify it." And even in his own firm, which he asserted was generally regarded as "an independent Japanese company," Kobayashi conceded that "executive board members and directors can if they wish have private rooms as well as a desk in the common areas."

But where a purely Japanese firm or one that is perceived as Japanese may feel free to break ground, companies with strongly American identities occasionally feel it safer to adhere to traditional Japanese practices. At Nike's Tokyo headquarters, even Chairman Gary Kurtz occupies a desk in a large communal work space. And two out-and-out U.S. subsidiaries that originally gave all of their supervisory personnel at least a private cubbyhole have had second thoughts in recent years.

One of these is Texas Instruments which in its Tokyo headquarters had created a veritable maze of small offices on the floor where President Hideo Yoshizaki is ensconced. When I commented on this while visiting the company in January 1985, Yoshizaki, whose square, handsome features customarily bear a somewhat saturnine expression, looked even more saturnine than normal and confided with what seemed a certain degree of triumph that he intended to have all the partitions knocked out shortly. (As TI's president, Yoshizaki presumably planned to retain his own private office but since it was of a size and simplicity that some Ivy League university professors would regard as beneath their dignity, this would scarcely constitute a flaunting of privilege.)

A similar development, I also discovered, had occurred at Warner-Lambert Japan—but with something of a twist. There, sometime in 1983, management sounded out the employees on the issue of private offices and discovered that in most of the company's operations there was a consensus in favor of a more open system. "So we actually tore out some offices and where the staff wanted it our managers are now in open positions among their people," President Sam Maugeri told me. "Anyone who reports to me directly still has a private office, but other than that there's just a handful that does."

An even touchier aspect of "foreignness" than office layout, however, is the question of what the dominant language shall be in the headquarters of a foreign affiliate. To many Americans, the answer to that seems so obvious as to require no consideration: clearly, the *lingua franca* of an American-based multinational enterprise must be English. After all, the reasoning goes, even though it may be called Nihon Consolidated Widget in Japan, it's basically an American company, isn't it? And, indeed, as a practical matter, English is not just the only feasible means of corporate communication between a U.S. venture in Japan and its American parent, it is also—with relatively few exceptions—the only feasible means of communication between the Americans the parent company sends to Japan and the Japanese staff whom they are supposed to oversee or advise.

There are, however, certain practical disadvantages to widespread use of English in an enterprise located in Japan. Not surprisingly, when a Japanese walks into an office in his own country and finds its senior people communicating with each other in English, his reaction is apt to be very similar to that of an American who finds all the bigwigs in a Manhattan office talking German or French to each other; even if he isn't resentful, he is unlikely to accept the firm in question as an integral part of the local business community. Beyond that, even if it were desirable it would be virtually impossible to staff any sizable office in Japan entirely or even primarily with people who both possessed the requisite business skills and were comfortable in English. Though untold millions of Japanese have earnestly studied English, most of them for a variety of reasons never become truly proficient in it. And among those who do there are, as I suggested earlier, a certain number who have little else to offer—enough of them, in fact, to have inspired coinage of the phrase *eigoyasan* (English-speaking incompetent).

In the face of all these conflicting considerations, U.S. firms with ventures in Japan have, predictably enough, adopted a variety of approaches. "Internal communication in some U.S. affiliates," according to headhunter Seiro Takehara, "is now 70 percent in Japanese and only 30 percent in English." And in some basically Japanese-managed joint ventures, there is probably even less use of English than that. At Ajinomoto General Foods, public relations director Kunihiko Fukuda says that senior executives don't have to speak English at all. In fact, says Fukuda—who professes to be "a sort of mixed breed" because he spent his youth in the United

States and went to UCLA—he himself is "just about the only bilingual one" among the company's senior managers. And even at Yamatake-Honeywell, where English is apparently more widely used, President Haruo Okinobu roundly declares: "I select the people who get promoted here—and I don't worry about whether they speak English."

Inevitably, however, a very different pattern prevails at most wholly owned U.S. subsidiaries—and especially those with Western chief executive officers. In such companies, broadly speaking, communication at the blue-collar, white-collar and even lower-management levels is generally entirely in Japanese but at the higher levels of management things change. "We don't require anyone in this company to speak English unless he wants to go up the ladder," says Kneale Ashworth of Johnson & Johnson bluntly. "This is Japan and the Japanese have a proverb which basically means 'when in Rome, do as the Romans do.' I believe in that. However, a Japanese who wishes to go to executive board level in a multinational must accept the fact that one of the things he's got to do is to learn to speak English."

Ashworth makes it plain that, in his view, there is more involved here than the deplorable American tendency to monolingualism. "After six o'clock when I go out for drinks with my guys, it's Japanese only," he says. "They feel happier that way. In fact, the most effective use a foreigner gets out of the ability to speak the language is in the evenings when the lobbying and the interfunctional communication get done—which, in this society, as you know, happens out of the office. If a foreign manager wants to be part of the *nemawashi* process, it's much better that he be able to speak the language. But while it's nice to be able to exhange courtesies in Japanese with our wholesalers when they come visiting—and 99 percent of them don't speak English—I don't do serious business in Japanese. I don't believe in doing business or trying to negotiate in Japanese and I don't think that's what a foreigner is here for."

In fact, though Ashworth himself didn't explicitly make the point, there are knowledgeable academics as well as businessmen who are convinced that it is highly risky for an American to try to conduct truly important business in Japanese. Without a knowledge of the nuances of Japanese far more extensive than one can reasonably expect to acquire in two or three years of study, it is

painfully easy to misinterpret just what the person one is negotiating with is really saying. And even a thorough mastery of the
nuances of the language won't necessarily save a *gaijin* from another hidden bear trap. In his years in Japan with Sterling Drug,
Mark Zimmerman wrote, he came to recognize that Japanese
"don't like to see Americans become so Japanese in their outlook
and approach that they . . . always try to react as the Japanese
themselves do in business situations." Because of the high value
they place on group solidarity, Zimmerman concluded, Japanese
don't like Japanized Americans any more than they like Ameri-
canized Japanese.

In feudal times, the Japanese had a saying that "the castle is people." The contemporary equivalent of that—"the company is
people"—is the cornerstone of modern Japanese business management and is reflected in the preoccupation many Japanese executives display with the material and physical well-being of their
workers.

It is not, however, merely a generalized sense of social responsibility that underlies such behavior on the part of Japanese managers. It is also the fact that the inherent docility and workaholism
of the Japanese labor force is by no means as great as Westerners
often assume it to be.

One striking evidence of this is provided by a survey that social
researcher Daniel Yankelovich conducted for the Aspen Institute
and the Public Agenda Foundation early in the 1980s. In his poll,
Yankelovich discovered that the percentage of Japanese workers
who assented to the statement "I have an inner need to do the best
I can regardless of pay" was actually slightly smaller than the
percentage of American workers who did so. Judging from the
Yankelovich survey, in fact, it is not so much devotion to the work
ethic that prompts Japanese to labor so hard as the conviction that
it is in their personal interest to do so: some 93 percent of the
Japanese workers polled by Yankelovich believed that they would
be the primary beneficiaries of any increase in their own productivity; by contrast, only 9 percent of the American workers polled
thought that.

In apparent confirmation of Yankelovich's findings, most American executives in Japan have discovered that to keep a Japanese
staff functioning smoothly involves constant attention to motiva-

tion, psychic as well as material. Indeed, to manage a Japanese staff successfully demands even more diplomacy—and a different kind of diplomacy—than is generally practiced in U.S. business.

One of the prime skills required of any executive in Japan is the ability to cope calmly and effectively with factionalism. The existence of factions or cliques is, of course, common enough in American corporations, as are power struggles between such groups. But where factional power grabs in the United States are usually masked by at least pro forma concern for efficiency, in Japanese offices they are often open and unabashed. Typically, a large Japanese business abounds in small cliques, each built around an *oyabun*, or father figure, who strives to carry his *kobun*, or children, along with him as he rises in the corporate hierarchy.

In his book *Japan: The Fragile Superpower*, my old friend Frank Gibney, who presided over the Encyclopaedia Britannica's Japanese operation in its glory days, vividly describes how this process works. "Distinguished Japanese businessmen," writes Gibney, "will walk into the president's office and argue passionately for the promotion of a grossly inefficient subordinate on very simple grounds: Mr. Ikeda has worked a long time directly under Mr. Sakai. If Mr. Ikeda is not promoted, it is a reflection on Mr. Sakai. Another division head in the same firm contends with equal passion that a department must be put under his jurisdiction primarily because this arrangement will gain him peace of mind [and] he could then go on to handle the problems piling up on his desk with renewed vigor."

In both the situations Gibney outlines what is basically at stake is *kao* or "face"—and, foreign as the concept may be to them, face is something that perceptive U.S. executives in Japan have learned to take very seriously indeed. When he was managing Sterling Drug's ventures in Japan, Mark Zimmerman recalled, "I tried very hard not to make or even imply any criticism of one of my subordinates or Japanese associates in front of others and when I did have some corrective suggestions to make, I used to spend at least ten minutes privately with the individual emphasizing the positive side of his work and character . . . before delivering one or two suggestions for improvement in vague, indirect and diplomatic terms. Once or twice my irritation got the better of me and I was more direct in my criticism; the result was that the employee was shocked and angry—though he wouldn't show it—and the situation only deteriorated."

While most American managers in Japan sooner or later come to recognize that public criticism of their subordinates is tabu, there is a corollary principle which some find harder to accept: in a Japanese company, even public praise has to be ladled out very judiciously. As Allen Zecha of Medtronics Japan once noted: "Something that might work in an American company but not in a Japanese company would be giving out an award for the most outstanding worker. In Japan, everybody else would get jealous and the guy chosen for the award would feel very uneasy, too. The person you are trying to give the incentive to may be ostracized by his own group."

While they don't like being singled out for public attention, however, Japanese workers do expect what they consider proper regard to be paid to their dignity as a group and they are quite capable of bringing pressure to bear on the boss himself to extract this. Back in the 1970s, for example, George Fields of ASI Market Research arrived at a decision that he wanted to have executed quickly and unilaterally issued a memo to that effect to his staff. Before long criticism of this move became so intense that Fields felt obliged to call a meeting with his employee association—a meeting at which he carefully explained the reasons for the decision and asked why the staff was so hostile to it. "Ah," replied a spoksman for the employees, "it is not the decision we object to, Fields-san, but the way you made it."

All of the phenomena I have been describing—promotions to save face, the muffling of thoroughly justified criticism and the toleration of employee nitpicking about questions of managerial style—will surely strike most American businessmen as irrational and unjustifiable. And quite properly so—unless, as Frank Gibney has pointed out, "you happen to be an American in business in Japan, in which case you ignore this kind of reasoning at your peril."

The peril to which Gibney refers can take a number of forms. Contrary to the assumption of some Westerners, Japanese workers are capable of turning very militant if they feel ill-used. And even short of an actual work stoppage or a working strike—where employees contine to do their jobs but wear armbands to show that they are doing so under protest—a Japanese staff can find many ways to crimp an American manager's style. After confessing that he had reluctantly decided not to replace a burnt-out senior executive with a highly competent younger man, the president of one major U.S. subsidiary in Tokyo told me: "Of course, I could say 'Just do it my way and don't give me any argument. Make it happen!' But you know what would actually happen if I did that? They'd make the change in titles, but they'd go right on running things just as before. My guy would get ignored—and maybe I'd get ignored, too."

Rather than court the perils inherent in a purely American management style, most U.S. affiliates in Japan—or at least most of those that have prospered for any considerable period—make significant adjustments to the Japanese environment. One of these, to which I have already alluded, is to restrict sharply the number of American executives that they import.

One reason for this is that offered by Warner-Lambert's Sam Maugeri, who is the only American on permanent assignment in Japan for his company. "Bringing in expatriates," he explains, "is demoralizing to the Japanese staff because it closes off the top jobs to them." But there are also powerful financial deterrents to doing so. "The tax situation in Japan," notes Fuji Xerox's Yotaro Kobayashi, "makes remuneration of American executives difficult." And reinforcing the stiff Japanese income tax—which runs to 80 percent of any salary over $150,000—is the extremely high cost of maintaining anything like an American standard of living in Japan. In one case with which I am personally familiar a U.S. company found itself paying a middle-ranking American executive in Tokyo salary and benefits amounting to almost twice what he would have received in a comparable job in this country. Though he lived in what would have been considered a painfully small home in any American suburb and had only two children, his housing, educational and cost-of-living allowances alone very nearly equaled what his entire salary would have been in the States.

This was admittedly an exceptional situation, stemming largely from the fact that the man's basic salary was relatively modest. Still, as of 1984, according to a Conference Board survey, a $60,000-a-year U.S. executive stationed in Tokyo typically received an additional $21,759 annually in living allowances. And on top of that he and his family would normally expect a paid home leave every two or three years.

This sort of thing is not only inordinately expensive but can arouse jealousy among Japanese employees who hold jobs comparable or nearly comparable to that performed by an expatriate executive but are far less handsomely rewarded. And that resentment can be greatly compounded if an American is given a status in his company's Japanese venture equal or superior to that of older Japanese; in Japan, where as a matter of principle rank and age are expected to go hand in hand, it can be fatal to office morale to require a group of fifty-year-old division chiefs to report to a thirty-seven-year-old "MBA technocrat."

Perhaps to avoid this situation, some established U.S. ventures in Japan, such as Texas Instruments which once had a fair number of expatriates in permanent assignment, now bring Americans in only for specific missions and for relatively short periods. Since these people are only "advisers"—or "tourists," as TI's boss Hideo Yoshizaki calls them—and do not appear on the Japanese company's permanent organization chart, the question of comparative age and status does not become a problem in the eyes of the Japanese staff.

Among those U.S. ventures that do have expatriates on permanent assignment in Tokyo, however, the conventional wisdom increasingly seems to be that it is desirable to leave them in place for several years. "I tell people we are thinking of bringing over here that they shouldn't come if they can't contemplate with comfort a five-year assignment," says Kodak Japan's Albert Sieg. For one thing, Sieg argues, excessively rapid turnover of its American executives tends to raise doubts about the depth of a company's commitment to Japan both in the eyes of its own staff and in those of the Japanese firms with which it hopes to do business. Beyond that, he believes, it can create what might be called a lame-duck problem. "If your Japanese staff know you're only going to be here for two or three years," he says, "there's a possibility that they may not take overly seriously any changes you try to effect, figuring that they will still be here when you're long gone."

As Sieg's comment indicates, expatriate executives in Japan often display a special concern for their relationships with Japanese subordinates. Yet in at least one respect most of the foreign affiliates I have investigated proved to be remarkably consistent in their handling of Japanese personnel. When it came to the question of salary raises and promotions, nearly all of them, joint ventures and wholly owned subsidiaries alike, admitted that in the early stages of a Japanese employee's career seniority counted for considerably more than it normally does in American business life. But all of the chief executives with whom I talked also insisted that even at lower levels their companies factored individual competence and merit into promotion decisions in some degree—and many were quick to point out that an increasing number of purely Japanese corporations were also moving away from completely automatic raises and promotions in the lower ranks.*

But while they seem to have little trouble swallowing heavier emphasis on seniority than is usual in the United States, American executives in Japan tend to be somewhat less comfortable with the concepts of "middle-up" management and the elaborate consensus-building of *nemawashi*. And their reservations in this regard cannot simply be dismissed as manifestations of cultural chauvinism. Sociological theorizing to the contrary, consensus management has never been by any means universal in Japanese business. Such men as Isao Nakauchi, the dynamic, self-assured founder of the huge Daiei supermarket chain, and Keizo Saji, the restless, highly cosmopolitan head of Suntory Ltd., exercise a degree of personal authority in their companies every bit as great as Lee Iaccoca does at Chrysler. (It is revealing that Saji is both president and chairman of the board of Suntory.)

Even in Japanese corporations which are less dominated by a single personality, moreover, authority is often considerably more centralized than it may appear to be to foreigners. "Consensus management is frequently misunderstood abroad," Isamu Yamashita, one of the elder statesmen of Japanese industry, told me some years ago. "Daily business is conducted from the bottom up, but long-term plannning is top-down. Basic policy does not originate at lower levels."

---

* It is some measure of the speed with which change occurs in Japanese business that in 1980 Taiji Ubukata, then the president of Ishikawajima-Harima Heavy Industries, predicted to me that the wage system for non-executive employees of Japanese companies—which at the time was 80 percent to 90 percent based on seniority—would "gradually" be modified until it was perhaps 30 percent to 40 percent based on merit and productivity. Within five years, his prediction was close to being the reality.

Even more succinctly, the late Yoshiya Ariyoshi, an outspoken maverick who eventually rose to the top of NYK, Japan's biggest shipping line, indignantly declared on one occasion: "The top men in Japanese companies aren't just figureheads, you know—idiots who sign off on ideas presented to them by their subordinates. The leader of a company is also a teacher." In practice, what Ariyoshi meant by this was that, while he took the need for consensus-building very seriously and saw great virtues to it, the *nemawashi* process could and should be to some extent manipulated. He himself, he admitted, would frequently plant policy ideas that he favored in tentative form with people three or four levels below him on the executive ladder and then greet these ideas with feigned judiciousness when they subsequently came up to him as formal proposals from the staff.

By dint of trial and error, more than one American chief executive in Japan has learned to follow essentially the same practices that Ariyoshi did. "Consensus *is* important here," Warner-Lambert's president Sam Maugeri conceded as we chatted in his office one sunny Saturday. (Belying the stereotypes of the workaholic Japanese and the sybaritic American, Maugeri was the only Warner-Lambert executive in the office that weekend morning.) "But there are ways of leveraging all that from the top," he went on. "I'm sure that in Japanese companies they often make things sound as though they originate at the bottom when it's really a combination. . . . All the boss has to do is subtly spread awareness of what his desire is in a particular situation and all of a sudden it becomes a proposal from below."

Like Maugeri, most American executives of established U.S. ventures in Japan pay at least formal obeisance to *nemawashi*. And some, particularly those who have spent several years in Japan, have discovered that one of the most effective ways of conducting *nemawashi* is to go out with their Japanese colleagues to one of the "hostess bars" or other drinking establishments where the members of Japan's managerial class regularly congregate after office hours. In between the often risqué badinage that characterizes such sessions a great deal of informal and apparently casual consultation on company affairs can be accomplished. And the evening drinks ritual serves another, somewhat related purpose as well. As Mark Zimmerman of Sterling Drug wrote: "Japanese businessmen do not hang out in bars after work in order 'to get away from it all'; in fact, their reasons are just the opposite. They feel obliged to engage in these activities to maintain *ningen kankei* (personal ties) among themselves, for good *ningen kankei* among the people in a company is what makes the company successful."

To this statement, however, Zimmerman added one important cautionary note: Japanese, he observed, "are likely only to resent it if a foreign boss is willing to go out with them for a drink after work but is unwilling to become truly interested in their personal affairs. Most Japanese prefer a boss who demands a lot but is understanding and supportive of their personal problems to one who is not so tough but is aloof."

Though nearly all of them recognize the need for some adaptation to Japanese business culture, the expatriate executives associated with U.S. ventures in Japan generally stop well short of blanket acceptance of local management practices. In particular, few would quarrel with Johnson & Johnson's Kneale Ashworth when he says: "There are some things one has to be very Western about. For example, one has to insist on a certain amount of responsibility at a senior level. In a typically amorphous Japanese organization responsibility tends to be diffused among the group as a whole. I accept that up to a point, but if a guy wants to be the president of one of our companies, he's got to damn well take responsibility for that company and he's got to deliver."

Predictably, another source of cultural clash is *nemawashi*, the mere mention of which tends to elicit wry smiles and ill-concealed impatience even from U.S. executives who profess to have found ways to manipulate that process. "*Nemawashi* is used here," says Herbert Hayde of Burroughs. "We have a consensus system and it fits in well with the culture." But as Hayde quickly makes plain, what Burroughs really has is a modified consensus system. "One of the things I *dislike* about the *nemawashi* system," he says, "is that you don't have as much creativity coming forth; it takes too long to get an idea to the surface. . . . In the information-processing industry, you can't take forever to make a decision; if you do, you're going to be looking at the back end of your competition. So even when you are trying to work within the *nemawashi* system, there are times when somebody has to make a decision—and I reserve the right to make those decisions when I consider it's appropriate."

Such departures from Japanese practice have to be carefully calculated, however, if they are not to prove destructive. One American who heads a company that is otherwise entirely staffed by Japanese confessed that when he first arrived in Tokyo he tried to strike up relationships with promising younger executives two or three rungs below him on the corporate ladder. "In no time at all," he recalled, "I had people coming into my office very upset because I was talking directly to their subordinates. At the end of my first six months if the key managment people here could have thrown me out they absolutely would have." That hostility, he insisted as much to himself as to me, had eventually dissipated. "I think I've slowly become their partner," he said. "But I still don't feel . . . oh, I don't know what to say. Sometimes you feel it's real, sometimes it's token."

Along with *nemawashi* and strict observance of the chain of command, some expatriate executives also have mixed feelings about Japan's vaunted lifetime employment system—which, while helping to promote labor peace, inevitably protects mediocrity. "The Western president," George Fields of ASI Market Research has perceptively observed, "strives to retain the ablest [employees]; the Japanese president contrives and maneuvers to get the most out of the average."

Worse yet, in the eyes of some American bosses, lifetime employment deprives them of the ultimate sanction against demonstrable incompetence. In virtually all Japanese corporations that have lifetime employment there is a group of workers known as the *madogiwa-zoku* or "the tribe that sits by the window." These are salaried employees who because they have performed inadequately have been assigned to a desk by a window and are given little or no work to do. To the individual involved, this is extremely humiliating punishment, but that can be cold comfort to a Western manager who finds himself carrying expensive deadwood on his payroll. (One result of this, as President Haruo Okinobu of Yamatake-Honeywell happily notes, is that like their Japanese competitors, many American executives in Japan operate on the principle that "it's smarter to invest in automation than to hire more people.")

As I have suggested, it is primarily in wholly owned American subsidiaries rather than in joint ventures that concern about "excessive Japanization" of management practices occurs. This again, however, is not necessarily a manifestation of simple chauvinism; it can also reflect a legitimate worry that Japanese employees totally steeped in their own business culture will simply fail to comprehend some of the realities with which a corporation headquartered in the United States has to cope. "For example," says President Weldon Johnson of Coca-Cola Japan, "Japanese find it difficult to understand our system of corporate reporting to Wall Street. That's totally anathema to them." And it is to bridge such gaps quite as much as to train people in specific skills that Coca-Cola like so many other U.S. companies in Japan regularly dispatches Japanese staff members to work in the United States for a year or two. Says Johnson: "We try to give them exposure to the Western way of doing business because it helps them to understand some corporate decisions better."

Coca-Cola, in fact, has been one of the most selective of U.S. companies in Japan in its adoption of Japanese ways. "We have done our best to be good corporate citizens of Japan without losing sight of our heritage," says Weldon Johnson in his soft Georgia drawl. The manifestations of Coca-Cola's American heritage range from the totally unJapanese practice of demanding cash on the barrelhead from retailers to installing the majority of its employees in private offices. And, contrary to much of the conventional wisdom, Weldon Johnson is convinced that all this is an advantage in recruiting able Japanese employees. "With all due respect," he said, "I think the people we attract are looking for a more Western company. We've been very fortunate in being able to get people from some of the better universities here who want the best of both worlds, so to speak."

There are, in fact, others besides Johnson who believe that changing attitudes among younger business people in Japan make certain aspects of American management style increasingly congenial to them. There is considerable evidence that a salary system based right from the beginning primarily upon ability has become appealing to those young Japanese who are—or think they are—extraordinarily talented. "If you are really capable, you're better off working for an American company," says Yasuo Takahashi, a 1966 graduate of elite Kyoto University. And Mr. Takahashi's own history illustrates yet another advantage American companies can offer—the willingness to let an executive specialize rather than rotate Japanese-style through a wide variety of jobs designed to give him the broadest possible experience. When he left the university, Takahashi joined C. Itoh, one of Japan's major trading companies, and at a relatively early age was made head of the company's foreign-exchange trading operation in New York. In due course, because of his outstanding performance in that position, he was brought back to Tokyo and promoted to chief of C. Itoh's country-risk analysis department. But, though that clearly put him on the high road to C. Itoh's highest echelons, what Takahashi really enjoyed was dealing in foreign exchange—and so in the summer of 1984 he joined the Chemical Bank in Tokyo as vice-president in charge of its foreign-exchange trading room.

What all this would seem to suggest is that before he sets about adapting his management style to the local environment, anyone responsible for launching a new U.S. venture in Japan should first be sure that he knows what contemporary Japanese business practices really are. Perhaps the pithiest comment on this score I have heard came from Eiji Irino, a soft-spoken man whose unlined, almost boyish features seem incompatible with his rank as executive director of Yamazaki-Nabisco. "Japan is still Japan in its way of thinking and for that reason so-called localization of management is necessary to get successful results here," Irino told me. "But, of course, management style itself is changing in Japan every day and becoming more and more a mixture of Japanese and Western elements."

Then, as if to offer living proof of his statement, Irino confessed that he himself was a financial man with no production experience at all. This is a background which was traditionally considered too narrow to qualify someone for a top executive position in Japan— a fact which has sometimes been cited as a peculiar strength of Japanese industry. But today, so Irino informed me, more men with exclusively financial backgrounds are moving into Japan's executive suites—just as has long been the case in the United States.

8 Coming Up with the Goods

Toward the end of 1984 a New York executive of my acquaintance invited me to an inspirational meeting at which an ostensibly omnicompetent management consultant offered guidance to businessmen whose companies were eager to win a foothold in the Japanese market. To achieve that goal, the consultant sternly declared, any American enterprise had to meet one of two conditions: it must come up with a product that was either demonstrably superior to equivalent Japanese products—or, alternatively, one that offered a clear cost advantage over competitive Japanese goods.

Somewhat dryly, one of the businessmen present observed that this was a formula that would work pretty well in any market. What I found most troubling, however, was not that the speaker was belaboring the obvious but that he was indulging in grievously misleading oversimplification.

The reality, as I see it, is that any serious study of successful American business ventures in Japan leads inexorably to what at first may seem a thoroughly frustrating conclusion—namely that it is impossible to find a single rule of thumb that serves to explain why some U.S. products and services are embraced by the Japanese while others are rejected. To be more precise, perhaps, there *is* a valid universal formula but it is the unserviceably vague one that the key to success in the Japanese marketplace lies in selling something peculiarly suited to the perceived needs and/or tastes of Japanese buyers.

That, of course, is essentially circular reasoning, but any attempt to generalize a bit less broadly almost immediately runs afoul of an inordinate number of exceptions. Thus, to return for a moment to the New York consultant's advice, it is undeniably true that many

U.S. products or products produced by U.S. affiliates in Japan have sold well because they are in some respect demonstrably superior to competitive products offered by Japanese manufacturers; an obvious case in point—though the U.S. edge here is now diminishing—is American-designed computer software. But how about Schick razor blades, McDonald's hamburgers, Coca-Cola's soft drinks or Kentucky Fried Chicken? Though I intend no aspersion on the quality of these products and am myself at least an occasional consumer of all of them, I find it hard to believe that it is any quantifiable superiority over all comparable Japanese products that primarily accounts for their dominant market positions in Japan.

Similarly, the suggestion that offering a cost advantage is an infallible recipe for the success of a U.S. product or service in Japan does not stand up to close scrutiny. To be sure, it has been a major competitive tool for certain U.S. ventures: even though it isn't permitted to use price comparisons in its advertising, Seibu Allstate Life Insurance clearly owes a substantial portion of its sales to the fact that it charges lower premiums than its rivals. Particularly where manufactured items are concerned, however, many American affiliates in Japan simply cannot match the prices of their Japanese competitors and at best find themselves in the same situation as Teledyne, where General Manager Peter Katsuno concedes: "We are not consistently lower in price in the Japanese market." Yet remarkably often this does not prove an insuperable handicap: as I shall discuss in a later chapter, price, while important, seems to be a less decisive consideration for Japanese buyers, whether individual or corporate, than it is for Americans—and sometimes pricing one's products below those of the competition can actually be a strategic mistake in Japan.

Besides those aired at the séance I attended in New York, there are, of course, a number of other generalizations about what will and won't sell in Japan that have gained currency in the United States in recent years. Increasingly, American politicians and businessmen have taken up the theme that the Japanese as a people prefer domestic products to foreign ones. The only response to that assertion that is both concise and accurate is that sometimes they do and sometimes they don't.

Most of the managers of U.S. affiliates in Japan with whom I have discussed the matter agree that there has in fact been a change over the years in the prevailing attitude toward foreign products in

Japan. "Japanese used to regard Western products as generally superior to their own," Chairman Kenzo Sasaoka of Yokogawa-Hewlett-Packard told me in 1985. "That didn't change essentially until recent years." But that it has changed, largely because of the vastly improved quality of Japanese products, is now generally agreed. "Having a foreign image used to make products more attractive," said Eiji Irino of Yamazaki-Nabisco. "However, that's not so true any longer." And in some cases this has actually led to a change in advertising tactics by U.S. affiliates. "Up until the 1970s," said Masao Sasaki, who manages the division of Hattori-Seiko that markets Schick blades, "we used to emphasize that Schick was American—and that helped. Now we don't stress it anymore."

For all that, however, there are product areas where having an American image is still a distinct asset. This is particularly true of what might be loosely lumped together as "life-style" products—such things as Levi's, Ralph Lauren shirts and Arnold Palmer golf accessories. But it is also the case for certain beverages and comestibles. "I guess that because coffee is seen as non-Japanese, having a bit of a non-Japanese image is a plus for our instant coffee," Kunihiko Fukuda of Ajinomoto General Foods reflected. And the same rationale presumably helps to explain the brisk business done by Mister Donut, Baskin-Robbins and Häagen-Dazs—the last of which is now marketed in Japan by Suntory Ltd. and as of 1985 was the "in" ice cream in the more chic districts of Tokyo. So helpful is the international aura in such cases, in fact, that it has led to some rather schizophrenic behavior on the part of Warner-Lambert Japan: while the company doesn't emphasize the American provenance of Schick blades, it doesn't emphasize either the fact that although they carry American names such as Dentyne and Chiclets, most of the chewing gums and candies that it sells in Japan are manufactured locally. "We try in the main to label these products in English to establish a foreign-brand image," I was told by Warner-Lambert president Sam Maugeri.

Closely akin to the question of foreign image is that of adaptation of products to the Japanese market and on that score a common generalization—though admittedly one more frequently cited by Japanese than by Americans—is that U.S. companies too often try to pass off upon the Japanese goods that are specifically designed for American tastes and conditions. There is, sadly, no denying that this approach has indeed been the undoing of many a U.S. venture in Japan. As I noted earlier, Apple Computer missed a golden opportunity in Japan by failing to produce computers capable of dealing with *kanji* (Japanese ideographs) and there are even some who argue that IBM's fall from No. 1 to No. 3 in the Japanese computer market resulted at least in part from the fact that it was slower than its Japanese competitors in coming to grips with the problem of processing information in *kanji*.

Predictably, however, the classic example of self-destructive American behavior in this respect has been provided by the U.S. auto industry. If you ask an American auto company executive why so few U.S. cars are sold in Japan nowadays he will almost certainly tell you—with complete accuracy—that for many years American cars were effectively frozen out of the Japanese market by various protectionist devices. Very possibly, he will add—still with considerable accuracy—that in a country with as many narrow streets and as relatively few first-class inner-city highways as Japan there isn't a mass market for cars of the size Detroit prefers to build.

What the man from Detroit almost certainly won't tell you, however, is that between the late 1970s and 1984 sales of American cars in Japan plummeted from 20,000 a year to about 2,000 a year and the lion's share of the prestige foreign car market in Japan was taken over by European automakers. (Between 1980 and 1984 BMW alone increased its sales in Japan from just under 3,200 cars a year to nearly 9,000.) Though it is hard to put a monetary value on all this, I would calculate that the U.S. auto industry has lost a minimum of somewhere between $300 million and $500 million a year in potential Japanese sales and the reason why is quite clear: while European automakers created good service organizations in Japan and supplied their Japanese dealers with the right-hand-drive vehicles appropriate to a country where people drive on the left, America's Big Three resolutely declined to be bothered with such irksome concessions to customer requirements.

Yet to conclude from such cautionary tales that no U.S. products or services can be marketed in Japan without major alterations would be a great mistake. Indeed, some of the most flourishing U.S. affiliates in Japan rely on products that are either identical to products sold in the United States or whose chief appeal is their similarity to a U.S. product. The rapid growth of Seibu Allstate Life Insurance has stemmed in considerable part from the fact that it introduced to Japan the American concept of life insurance policies that are primarily designed to provide protection rather than a combination of savings and protection. The razor blades and empty gelatin capsules for pills that Warner-Lambert sells so profitably in Japan are indistinguishable from those it sells in the United States. The formula used in Japan to make what I have reluctantly learned to call Classic Coca-Cola is identical to that used in the United States. And Den Fujita of McDonald's Japan makes a positive fetish of duplicating exactly the culinary delights that are available at the Golden Arches in Old Saybrook, Connecticut, or Orlando, Florida. "The only thing different is that Japanese like orange juice a lot," Fujita says. Then, with a shrug, he adds: "So I'm selling orange juice."

Den Fujita's departure from his U.S. model in the matter of orange juice reflects awareness of an awkward fact: when it comes to determining whether an American product or service will prove acceptable in Japan a kind of Catch-22 comes into play. Mistaken as it is to assume that nothing American will sell in Japan in its original form, it is even more mistaken to go to the opposite extreme and assume that success can automatically be achieved in the Japanese market by making available in unaltered form something which has proved popular in the United States. Particularly among items designed for personal consumption, some of the greatest success stories have been achieved by products that at first blush seem identical to those offered under the same brand name in the United States but that have in fact been modified to increase their appeal to Japanese.

One of the commonest reasons for such tampering with a tried-and-true U.S. product lies in the many differences between Japanese and American taste—in the most literal sense of that word. "We've modified some U.S. products because the Japanese consumer prefers milder, less strong flavors," Yamazaki-Nabisco's Eiji Irino told me. "We had to reduce the sweetness of Chips Ahoy cookies, for example, and also the salt level of Ritz crackers." On the same principle, the frozen french fries that Ore-Ida sells in Japan are substantially less salty than those generally marketed in the United States, while the salads served in Kentucky Fried

Chicken shops in Japan have only half the sugar content of those made in the U.S. shops. And horrifyingly—at least to my own small children, who consider mashed potatoes smothered in gravy one the world's supreme joys—anyone who wants potatoes with his Kentucky Fried Chicken in Japan has to settle for french fries. "We tried a taste test," said Kentucky Fried Chicken's Loy Weston, "and it turned out that Japanese didn't like mashed potatoes and gravy." As partial compensation, however, the Kentucky Fried Chicken menu in Japan includes milk shakes, yogurt, and fish and chips—none of which is available in the company's American outlets.

If they are startled by what they encounter in a Kentucky Fried Chicken shop, first-time U.S. visitors to Japan can also be in for a surprise when they buy some familiar "American" beverages. "The Maxim's instant coffee that we sell is different in formula from that sold in the States," Kunihiko Fukuda of Ajinomoto General Foods told me. "Japanese consumers in general insist on higher-quality instant coffee than Americans do." And while Coca-Cola, as I noted earlier, is identical in Japan and the United States, it is quite literally the only Coca-Cola product sold in both countries of which that can be said. "Japanese don't really care for the flavor of limes so we've taken much of the lime out of Sprite," Weldon Johnson of Coca-Cola Japan informed me. "And Fanta here is very different from what it is in the U.S. Because Japanese are probably the most ingredient-conscious people in the world, we've taken all the artificial coloring out of Fanta; it's all natural color here."

Somewhat paradoxically, I thought, Johnson then proceeded to point out that Coca-Cola Japan does not bother to make any caffeine-free colas. "With the consumption of green tea as high as it is in this country," he explained, "caffeine isn't really an issue here." But this, obviously, is less a reflection of differing tastes than of differing cultural attitudes—and cultural attitudes inevitably are another major force impelling many U.S. affiliates in Japan to modify their products and product lines.

One way in which this process sometimes works can be found in the experience of Max Factor Japan. "Though most people don't know it," Victor Harris remarked when I met with him in 1985, "Max Factor himself invented makeup. In fact, he coined the word 'makeup' and our single biggest-selling product in Japan today is still pancake makeup—which is nearly fifty years old. Yet, despite that, probably 75 percent of what we are selling in Japan today consists of products developed here specifically for this market."

The explanation for this state of affairs, Harris went on, was that in certain respects Japanese and American women approach self-beautification quite differently. "In the U.S.," he said, "the business is basically lipstick, eye makeup, nail polish and fragrance. There's very little attention paid in the U.S. to skin care; in fact, American women tend not to worry much about skin care until it's too late. In Japan, on the other hand, a girl doesn't start wearing lipstick until she's eighteen and most women don't use fragrance. But a Japanese girl *does* start creaming her skin at twelve. So a much bigger percentage of the business here is in creams and lotions."

Somewhat surprisingly, at least to a layman like myself, cultural attitudes toward skin are also an important consideration for Kodak Japan—so much so that the company uses a different color balance in the film it sells in Japan than the one it uses in film destined for the U.S. market. "The Japanese consumer," Kodak's Albert Sieg explained to me, "is not interested in having his subject's flesh tone look too yellow. He like to have it look a little more pink. That's a characteristic that in Caucasian markets is called 'beefy flesh tone' and isn't considered desirable. But here it is. So we've moved our product toward the Japanese preference and to the extent you can measure it's had a positive effect on sales."

Besides gratifying the Japanese shutterbug's taste for "beefy flesh tone," Kodak has also made significant modifications in the products it sells to Japan's graphic arts industry, a market in which the company holds a very strong position. In this case, however, the reason for the adaptation was quite different from that which prevailed in the amateur film field. "The graphic arts industry in Japan is probably one of the most advanced in the world," Sieg told me. "But it's unusual in one important respect. In the rest of the world graphic arts people prefer to work in darkrooms. Here they prefer to work in subdued yellow lighting—what we call room light. I think that's a result of the limited space available here; I don't think a Japanese print shop has the luxury of being able to wall off a whole big area for a darkroom. In any case, we have to make products for this market that can be used in room light."

The need for this kind of adjustment to the peculiar realities of life and work in Japan helps to explain why so many U.S. affiliates there end up localizing product design in at least some degree. As I noted earlier, the space restrictions mentioned by Albert Sieg have also been cited as one reason why Tupperware with its potential for efficient storage appeals to Japanese housewives. But another reason for its popularity is clearly the shrewdness with which President Kazunobu Cho and his staff have tailored their product line to the Japanese environment. Sometimes they have done this through the development of products which would not be functional in the United States, such as a "kimono keeper." On other occasions, they have simply altered American products to suit Japanese needs: by taking what is sold in the United States as a "cracker keeper" and putting a grill in it to drain off blood, Cho & Company came up with a "fish keeper"—an especially useful item in Japan where fish still constitutes a far more important part of the national diet than it does in the United States. And while such changes can scarcely be hailed as epochal advances in technology, the contribution they have made to the prosperity of Japan Tupperware is significant—and easily quantifiable. "Only about 25 percent of the items in our product line were developed here in Japan," Cho told me in 1985. "But those items now account for 50 percent of our sales."

It is not just products developed in the States and transplanted to Japan that can require modification, moreover. For reasons ranging from cultural preferences to differences in the social and political environments the same is often true of services as well.

Sometimes the necessity for such changes is obvious, as it was in the case of American Family Life Asssurance's cancer policies. "In the United States, where there is no national health insurance, the benefits we pay differ according to the site of the cancer and the special procedures needed," I was told by American Family's Shinichiro Adachi. "But here there *is* national health insurance which covers the actual surgical procedures and so forth. So our Japanese policies don't specify a particular amount for a particular type of cancer but rather a fixed benefit regardless of type."

Sometimes, however, the implications of Japanese conditions and attitudes are far from as self-evident as they were in American

Family's case. "When we were planning Tokyo Disneyland, the Japanese kept telling us 'keep it Western,' " Disney vice-president Jim Cora recalled. Presumably Disney's Japanese partners were using "Western" in the sense of "Occidental," but as things turned out, they could well have used the word in its common American sense as well. "The riverboat and the Westernland attractions have proved to be much more popular here than they are back home," Cora told me. (In at least one respect, however, Tokyo Disneyland is distinctly non-Western in any sense of that term. "We need much less security here," Cora reported. "We don't have to have the kind of rigid crowd control that we need in the States to keep people from jumping lines. Here, once people are queued, they stay queued.")

From the examples I have offered so far, it should be apparent that it is possible to prosper in Japan by (a) selling U.S. products in unmodified form, (b) selling U.S. products that have been adapted to Japanese conditions, (c) selling products specifically designed for the Japanese market, or (d) doing all three of the above simultaneously. The trick obviously lies in determining which of these approaches or combinations thereof is most fruitful in one's own particular business. And since bringing wares to the marketplace untested can be a very costly way of learning that they are not quite what the consumer wants, U.S. affiliates that have established a solid long-term position for themselves in Japan often rely heavily on market research and market testing.

Such is the case, for example, at Johnson & Johnson Japan where, according to Kneale Ashworth, "We do all the normal things—focus groups, the usual marketing stuff. If we find we've got a product that's of interest to Japanese consumers but needs amendment in packaging or a slight change in formulation, we make those changes. Then normally we go into test marketing—or perhaps a full-scale launch."

As Ashworth's final clause hints, however, many Western executives with extensive business experience in Japan are more ambivalent about market testing than their counterparts in the United States. "It may seem suicidal to launch a full-scale marketing effort without any testing," wrote Mark Zimmerman of Sterling Drug. "But if the testing takes longer than three months, it may turn out to be . . . a bad move." Zimmerman's reasoning: if it is at all prolonged, "any form of testing tips off Japanese competitors and gives them enough time to copy the product. . . . By the time the Western company completes successful testing, numerous local competitors will have already prepared excellent imitations and introduced them in forms that are particularly suitable for their market."

As for market research in Japan, it presents if anything even more complications than market testing. In trying to decide whether a particular U.S. product or service will go in Japan, both Japanese and Americans too often accept as market research what are essentially no more than seat-of-the-pants judgments based on generalized observation of Japanese habits and attitudes. Glancing around his spacious, handsomely appointed office in the upper reaches of one of Tokyo's fanciest new skyscrapers, Den Fujita told me with a triumphant chuckle that when he announced the launching of McDonald's Japan the conventional wisdom in local business circles was that "Japanese will never eat standing up"— and that, as a result, he had great difficulty in finding a bank prepared to lend him the start-up money that he needed.

The same order of prescience was displayed by a marketing consultant that Tupperware engaged in the early 1960s to appraise its chances of success in Japan. Tupperware's prospects, the consulting firm decreed, were dim because both its sales method and the material it employed were inappropriate: it was not the custom in Japan for women to give parties for their friends, and for food storage Japanese housewives wanted containers made of ceramics, metal or wood—almost anything in fact except plastics. In its own foolhardy way, however, Tupperware decided to plow ahead and soon discovered that what on the surface seemed insuperable barriers in fact were not. Today, the Japanese housewife like her American sister has surrendered to the convenience of plastic. Meantime, the Tupperware sales party has proved so compatible with Japanese social mores that it has been copied by purveyors of other goods as diverse as underwear and health foods.

When it comes to determining the viability of a product in the Japanese marketplace, in short, broad cultural attitudes are a very chancy guide—and that is just as true of those that seem favorable as those that seem negative. Some years ago Ajinomoto General Foods introduced—without serious preliminary testing—a powdered fruit beverage. This was a product which because of its compactness might theoretically have been expected to benefit as Tupperware has from the perennial shortage of storage space in Japanese homes—and in Japanese refrigerators as well. But in sad reality, sales figures—or, more precisely, a dismaying lack thereof—soon made it plain that the Japanese consumer, as AGF's Kunihiko Fukuda candidly put it, "thinks powdered fruit beverages are for the birds."

Conceivably, the powdered drink's chief positive aspect—its ease of storage—was outweighed in Japanese minds by the strong distaste for artificial ingredients that prompted Coca-Cola Japan to change the formula for Fanta. But to determine whether that was actually the case would not be easy. A company that hopes to find out with some certainty what cultural attitudes are evoked in Japanese consumers by a particular product and just how those attitudes interact does not have a lot of options. Unless, like Tupperware, it has 42,000 built-in market researchers in the form of sales agents recruited from the ranks of its natural customers, it must as a rule invest in detailed professional probing into the reactions of potential buyers to the product in question.

Often resting on the use of the "focus group," which is market research jargon for assembling a clutch of consumers around a table to discuss a specific product in depth, this probing process can on occasion be extremely effective. In *From Bonsai to Levi's*, George Fields of Tokyo's ASI Market Research recalls the instructive tale of a cake mix marketed in Japan in the mid-1960s by a company jointly owned by General Mills and a big Japanese confectionary concern called Morinaga. At the time, ovens were not yet a standard feature of Japanese kitchens but automatic rice cookers were; accordingly, General Mills had gone to considerable pains to develop a cake mix that could be baked in an automatic rice cooker. Despite the apparent shrewdness of this move, however, Japanese women showed little interest in the mix and Fields and his colleagues were asked to find out why. The most important reason, which ultimately emerged indirectly from some seemingly tangential conversation at a focus group, was one no Japanese marketer had foreseen: though rice consumption in Japan has fallen notably in recent decades, rice continues to possess a mythic or semisacred quality for Japanese, and housewives were irrationally fearful that the flavoring in a cake mix might somehow "psychologically" contaminate rice subsequently prepared in the same cooker.

Inherent in Fields's story is a lesson that many U.S. businessmen in Japan have learned the hard way: the pervasive Japanese distaste for confrontation and the obliqueness in social intercourse that it fosters make market research an even more delicate art in Japan than it is in the United States. "Too often," remarked Victor Harris of Max Factor Japan, "American companies coming in here translate a questionnaire that worked beautifully in Ohio and hire a team of people from Chicago to run the survey. What they don't know is that the little Japanese woman who answers the door isn't going to insult them by telling them she doesn't like their product and isn't going to make any suggestions about how it could be better."

Getting over that hurdle is, in fact, a continuing challenge even for U.S. enterprises in Japan that are fully aware of its existence. "It's easy enough to present people with a lot of photographs and get them to tell you which ones they prefer," said Kodak Japan's Albert Sieg. "But finding out why they prefer the ones they do is a different matter. It was difficult to find why they liked pictures with beefy flesh tone, for example, because some Japanese found it difficult to express the reason. They knew why all right, but they couldn't verbalize it. So you had to figure it out by indirection."

In a similar vein, Disney's Jim Cora reported that in certain situations the visible reactions of audiences at Tokyo Disneyland can be actively misleading. "When they watch a show, their emotions are sometimes so much in check that you wonder if it's bombing," he said. "They'll sit there and when it's over they'll smile politely and walk out and you'll think 'Well, that didn't make it'—when, in fact, they may have loved it. So when we want to know how successful a show is, we have professional surveyors ask people certain tested key questions as they're leaving it."

For all its complexities and potential pitfalls, however, market research is an indispensable tool not only in arriving at the most salable possible product but in determining how best to advertise it as well. A great many intelligent people have devoted a great deal of thought to the differences in the way Japanese and Americans respond to various kinds of advertising, but so far at least no one has succeeded in distilling any universally accepted set of scientific principles out of all this theorizing. Perhaps for that reason,

Johnson & Johnson Japan among others declines to rely exclusively on the judgment of professional advertising people in deciding what ads to run. "Our practice," Kneale Ashworth told me, "is to expose Japanese consumers to Japanese versions of American, British and/or German ads for a particular product and also to two or three locally produced versions. And we let the consumers choose which they find most effective."

As with product selection, though, the history of U.S. enterprises in Japan demonstrates that there is a place for intuition in advertising, too. In the late 1960s Coca-Cola Japan was presented with a proposed TV commercial that showed a young man drinking Coke directly from the bottle. Because this was considered unmannerly in Japan at the time, many people earnestly advised against airing the commercial, but the company did so anyway and promptly created a new national fad. "Drinking bugle-style," as the Japanese call it, was, it transpired, a break with tradition that suited the mood of Japanese youngsters at that particular moment.

The success of Coca-Cola's convention-defying commercial was a minor manifestation of a major reality that U.S. ventures in Japan must reckon with day in and day out. We Americans quite rightly regard rapid and continual change as one of the hallmarks of our society. But it is an even more notable characteristic of Japanese society. Since the end of World War II in particular the pace of social, economic and technological change in Japan has been nothing short of breathtaking; in fundamental as well as superficial respects today's Japan bears far less resemblance to the country I entered with the Occupation forces in September 1945 than today's United States does to the United States of my boyhood. And there seems no reason to think that this process of constant transformation will not continue for the foreseeable future.

For the businessman, of course, this means that both the hazards and the potential rewards of the Japanese marketplace are uncommonly great. Rapid changes in consumer tastes as well as in industrial needs and technologies obviously inspire equally rapid changes in the salability of particular services or products. A product such as cancer insurance which didn't exist in Japan a decade ago or ones like health foods in which the Japanese then showed little interest can almost overnight become hot items. By the same token, a product that was a money-spinner for years can unexpectedly lose favor, as now seems to be happening with instant cameras in Japan. (The reason for this development, some marketing experts speculate, may be the advent of quick film development services, which reduce the appeal of instant cameras for the amateur photographer.)

For U.S. affiliates in Japan that are involved in high-technology industries such as information processing, identifying new needs and scrambling to develop products that will meet them is a self-evident condition of survival. But while the fact is sometimes overlooked, the same often holds true in less glamorous and seemingly more stable industries where a technological imperative is less readily apparent.

To attempt to offer an exhaustive appraisal of how current trends in Japan are likely to affect the future business decisions of U.S. affiliates there is beyond the scope of this book. Inevitably, however, some of the executives with whom I spoke did comment on the social and economic trends that they saw going on around them and on the impact which those changes had already had on their industries or threatened to have in years to come. And among the most instructive of those comments were ones reflecting the often oblique consequences of alterations in Japanese living patterns.

Almost to a man, my informants agreed with Tupperware's Kazunobu Cho on the most important single trend in Japanese life: "Growing prosperity." With each passing year, Japanese consumers have more money to spend: between 1970 and 1983, to cite just one piece of evidence, the average hourly wage of a manufacturing worker in Japan almost quadrupled. (In the United States the average increase in manufacturing wages for the same period was only 250 percent—and since inflation made greater inroads in the United States the relative gain made by Japanese workers was even greater than the wage figures alone would suggest.) At the same time, the Japanese have been showing greater willingness to spend their money: the personal savings rate, which ran as high as 22 percent of income in the postwar years, had dropped to 17 percent by 1985 and among younger Japanese, who are more inclined than their parents to demand instant gratification, the use of personal credit is growing.

All this has obvious implications for durable luxury goods and even for chic comestibles such as Häagen-Dazs ice cream. But it also, as Kunihiko Fukuda of Ajinomoto General Foods pointed out, created a market for something which few Americans think of as a luxury item. A generation ago, he reminded me, few Japanese felt they could afford pets and those who did mostly had animals of uncertain and undistinguished ancestry whom they fed scraps. "But lately," he went on, "people have begun to acquire better breeds of dogs and want to treat them nicely. So we introduced our Gaines dog food and have kept adding to the line with things like special food for puppies, special food for big dogs and, most recently, cat food." In the new, more affluent Japan, Fukuda concluded, pet food looked like a growth area and in that opinion he was clearly not alone: as of early 1985 Kal Kan, a subsidiary of the privately owned Mars Company of Chicago, decided to try its luck in Japan, too.

Still another reason for the greater open-handedness of Japanese is a large increase in the number of two-income families in Japan. Much as it did in the United States, at a somewhat earlier period, a growing appetite for consumer goods and other attributes of the good life such as expensive vacations has helped to inspire a major influx of married women into the Japanese work force in recent years. Besides a number of predictable social consequences such as a surge in attendance at day-care centers, this has had some unanticipated commercial fallout. "The door-to-door cosmetics business has gone to hell," Victor Harris of Max Factor told me. "For one thing there aren't as many women at home when the sales ladies call anymore. For another, it's getting harder and harder to find people who are willing to work part-time as sales ladies since nowadays women are more apt to want to work full-time."

The latter problem is one of considerable concern to Tupperware's Kazunobu Cho, whose products are sold exclusively by housewives who work only part-time. But Cho finds a silver lining to that cloud in the fact that married women with full-time jobs have less opportunity and/or willingness to go to the trouble of preparing time-consuming traditional meals for their families. This leads him to cherish high hopes for a material patented by Tupperware with which it is possible to produce frozen-food containers that can be moved directly from a freezer into an oven or microwave and then used at the table. "With products like that, we can grow," Cho says confidently.

Still another major social trend in which various U.S. ventures in

Japan scent opportunity is the steady increase in the number of elderly Japanese. Between a relatively low birthrate (the average Japanese couple now has only 1.7 children) and greatly increased life expectancy (eighty for today's Japanese woman as opposed to fifty in 1945), the average age of Japanese is inexorably increasing and estimates are that by the year 2020 nearly 25 percent of the population will be over sixty-five. With this in mind, American Family Life Assurance Company in 1984 supplemented its cancer insurance business with the introduction of "senility insurance"— policies designed to alleviate the financial burdens attendant upon Alzheimer's disease or other forms of senile dementia. In rather cheerier vein, Yamazaki-Nabisco's Eiji Irino noted that his company had a special interest in "the development of products appealing to older people, who tend to prefer cereals and generally healthier foods." And at Ajinomoto General Foods Kunihiko Fukuda suggested that delayed emulation of U.S. life-styles might combine with the "graying of Japan" to make calorie counting and weight control the wave of the future in the Japanese marketplace so far as packaged foods were concerned.

In a basic sense, of course, there is nothing uniquely Japanese about any of this: responsiveness to changing social and economic patterns is the hallmark of intelligent business management anywhere. The difference is that in Japan—or so some U.S. executives with long experience there believe—the wave of the future tends to arrive sooner and to sweep away seemingly well-entrenched habits and preferences more easily than is the case in most other countries. "There's an enormous premium on innovation here," President Weldon Johnson of Coca-Cola Japan told me in the opening days of 1985. "Right now 25 percent of our sales in this company come from products and packages which were not even on the market three years ago."

9 Tough Customers

"Nature is neutral," Adlai Stevenson once remarked, and, so far as U.S. enterprise is concerned, essentially the same can be said of the business environment in Japan. Any American company which seeks to operate there will almost certainly encounter some conditions that seem inherently adverse, some that appear inherently favorable and many that can be either harmful or beneficial depending on how they are handled.

That same statement, of course, can equally well be made of the business environment in the United States. But just as spin casting for bass in the St. Lawrence does not adequately equip a fisherman for fly casting for trout in Nova Scotia, so experience gained under American business conditions is far from an infallible guide to the precise nature and intensity of the forces at play in Japan's business world. And while we have already explored some of the ways in which American models can prove misleading in a Japanese context, the list is far from exhausted. For that reason, this chapter and the three immediately following it will deal with what managers of U.S. subsidiaries and affiliates see as special constraints and opportunities that they have encountered in the Japanese marketplace.

Some years ago, while on a business trip to Japan, I wandered for the first time into one of the coffee bars that were then just beginning to become a fixture of the Tokyo scene. Sitting down at a counter, I found myself somewhat to my confusion confronted with a blackboard listing my options. Depending on how much I was prepared to spend, I could get a cup of coffee freshly brewed from beans grown exclusively in any one of several exotic locations ranging from Colombia to Jamaica's Blue Mountains. Or, if

I preferred, there were carefully specified blends of beans from two or three different places. What I could not do, however, was what I was accustomed to doing at New York coffee shops; that is, in response to the mumbled request "Cuppa coffee, please" get a mug of anonymous brown liquid whose provenance was known only to the purchasing department of some unidentified corporation.

In their own way, the coffee bars in Tokyo reflect a fact that no one who wishes to do business in Japan can safely ignore: whether they are buying fish for dinner or robots to run their company's new assembly line, Japanese are among the most finicky and quality-conscious customers in the world. "The standards in our industry in Japan start with perfection," Max Factor's Victor Harris told me. "You can't sell lipstick here if it has the slightest blemish on it. In the States people don't think twice about such things, but here even if it costs you another fifteen cents to put a lipstick through a flame again to get a little mark off it, you've got to do it. Otherwise, you won't sell it."

When they first encounter it, some American manufacturers dismiss the extreme quality-consciousness of Japanese buyers as simply perverse. This is a reaction painfully familiar to Mark Popiel, who is a senior executive in the Tokyo branch of Dodwell, a British-owned trading company which acts as sales representative or marketing adviser in Japan for a number of American and European firms. "There's no question but what Japanese standards are extremely high," Popiel told me. "We get instances where we have quality problems with a foreign-made product and when we refer them back to the supplier, he gets indignant and says 'We don't get these complaints from the rest of the world.' "

In these circumstances, there is a natural temptation for an American manufacturer to conclude that Japanese customers are unrealistic in their demands and that they must learn to settle for what in the United States is sometimes rather ambiguously termed AQ—or "acceptable quality." One such instance was recounted in a letter to a Japanese newspaper written by Kenichi Ito, a professor of electronics engineering at Tokyo Agricultural and Industrial University who claimed to have investigated problems with American-made equipment experienced by a number of Japanese corporations. According to Ito, one of the companies he looked into imported chemical-analysis equipment from a U.S. manufacturer.

"So many of the ICs (integrated circuits) broke down," wrote Ito, "that they had to send the equipment back and ask for proper treatment. What they got was a near threat by the U.S. company that if they were so concerned about breakdown, they should use ICs designed for the military, which would cost several times more." The upshot, Ito reported, was that the Japanese corporation redesigned the equipment and replaced the American-made ICs with Japanese ICs—whereupon the breakdowns ended.

How often such incidents occur is difficult to say since most Japanese corporations are reluctant to admit publicly to having problems of this kind for fear of exacerbating further the already troubled economic relations between Japan and the United States. Even Professor Ito, for all his whistle-blowing, declined to identify for a *New York Times* reporter the firms involved in his story. And I myself encountered similar reticence when I tried to find why some Japanese importers of agricultural products had begun to buy their corn from China rather than from the United States. (Between the end of 1984 and mid-1985, the U.S. share of the Japanese corn market slipped from 97 percent to less than 86 percent and virtually all the business the Americans lost was picked up by the Chinese.) Privately, several knowledgeable Japanese assured me that part of the reason for the switch was that the Chinese corn arrived in Japan in better condition: it had fewer broken kernals and less water content. None of my informants, however, was willing to be quoted by name and none would identify specific U.S. suppliers who, they said, had been ignoring Japanese complaints on this score for twenty years.

Touchy as the subject is, though, there clearly have been enough such incidents as well as enough cases in which individual Japanese have been disappointed in the quality of American consumer goods to have had a generally adverse effect on the reputation of U.S.–made products in Japan. "There is a widespread feeling here," Herbert Hayde of Burroughs told me in early 1985, "that the quality of U.S. products is not as good as that of Japanese products."

This is a generalization which clearly disturbs Hayde, who insists—quite accurately as far as I can determine—that "the products Burroughs is selling today are as reliable as any Japanese product." And there is undeniably both a measure of chauvinism and a considerable degree of exaggeration in the blanket assertions of superior quality which some Japanese make for their country's manufactured goods. The fact that Kodak, for example, continues to hold 85 percent or more of the Japanese market for professional film clearly attests to the excellence of its products—none of which as of 1985 were manufactured in Japan. And Kodak is by no means an isolated case: in a wide array of products ranging from tennis rackets to medical and dental equipment the label "Made in U.S.A." still bespeaks exceptionally high quality even in Japan.

Nonetheless, Japanese charges that American goods are often less well made and less reliable than their Japanese counterparts can't simply be brushed aside. If they could, American consumers would surely have stopped buying Japanese automobiles in large numbers as soon as there was no longer any great initial cost advantage to doing so—and the same essentially holds true for a variety of Japanese electronic devices.

The perception that Japanese manufacturers often build more quality into their products does not, moreover, rest on purely anecdotal or subjective evidence. The American semiconductor manufacturers who filed charges of unfair competition against a number of Japanese producers in late 1985 may have had certain grounds for complaint. But to attribute the success of Japanese chip makers primarily to predatory pricing or marketing techniques is to ignore an important piece of industrial history: In 1980 when California's Hewlett-Packard Company ran tests on 16K RAM (random-access memory) chips purchased from three American and three Japanese suppliers, the results were devastating for the home team; the highest-quality American chips proved to have six times as many defects on average as the lowest-quality Japanese product. And while that disparity was subsequently greatly reduced by increased American emphasis on quality control, it has never been entirely eliminated—as witness the fact that in both 1984 and 1985 the Pentagon felt compelled to crack down on major U.S. manufacturers for inadequate testing of semiconductors supplied to military contractors.

On the relatively rare occasions when they will openly admit to having any quality problem vis-à-vis their Japanese competitors, American businessmen are likely to argue that it's just a cost-benefit question; to aim at "zero defects" as many Japanese manufacturers do is, so conventional U.S. wisdom has it, simply a prescription for raising your costs to uncompetitively high levels.

In reality, of course, that need not always be the case. In a comparative study of American and Japanese manufacturers of air conditioners that he published in 1983, Prof. David A. Garvin of the Harvard Business School reported that the highest-quality U.S. manufacturer spent three times as much money satisfying warranty claims as the average Japanese manufacturer—and the lowest-quality American producer spent nearly nine times as much. To put it a little differently, the extra money the Japanese spent building higher quality into their air conditioners came to only about half what the Americans spent on fixing defective units.

Even more to the point, selling lower-quality goods on the strength of lower pricing is rarely a realistic option for an American company doing business in Japan. "Max Factor's lowest-cost manufacturer is our English operation," Victor Harris told me. "They produce millions and millions of units so their unit cost is unbeatable as far as we're concerned. For that reason, we've tried bringing in English-made containers for use in this market from time to time. But it just doesn't work because the quality isn't there. The cost is beautiful, but we just can't sell the stuff. So we make all our containers here in Japan—which is expensive because of the perfection required. And that, in turn, means that we can't export a lot from here. But we really don't have any choice in the matter."

The point Victor Harris was making, of course, was that in Japan building high quality into one's products is not just another device in the businessman's bag of competitive tricks; more often than not it is a sine qua non for corporate survival. Just how true that is was driven home to me sharply when Yotaro Kobayashi of Fuji Xerox relived a crucial half decade in his company's history. "Throughout the sixties and the first couple of years of the seventies," he recalled, "we were on top of the world. We dominated the market here and our customers all said Fuji Xerox products were the best of their kind—expensive, yes, but worth the money. Then at the end of 1973 the oil crisis hit and the subsequent increases in costs of all kinds made the market extremely cost-sensitive—so much so, in fact, that many of our customers opted for our competitors' products simply because they offered a lower-cost alternative. And when people began doing that they found out that many of the cheaper and so-called inferior products weren't actually that bad. So by 1974 and 1975 many customers who had left Fuji Xerox saying 'We'll come back when things improve' were telling us 'We've always thought you gave value for money, but look what your competitors are doing. We're paying 30 percent to 40 percent less for their machines, yet they produce almost as good a copy and sometimes better. If you want us to return, you'll have to do a much better job.' "

This, of course, is a message a number of companies in the United States have also heard in recent years; directly or indirectly, potential customers, both foreign and domestic, have delivered the same kind of warning to manufacturers in a variety of American industries. All too often, the response of the American manufacturers has been either angry denial of the criticism or a resort to highly publicized but relatively perfunctory gestures toward improving product reliability. As anyone who has done business in Japan will testify, however, such attempts at sleight of hand rarely pay off there—and so the reaction at Fuji Xerox was sober introspection.

"We came to the conclusion," Kobayashi recalled, "that unless we did something drastic we would cease to exist in the marketplace. So we began a quest for something new. That was what inspired our adoption of the principle of TQC—total quality control. Then we focused our attention on coming up with a really good product—one which our customers would not hesitate to tell themselves and everybody else was the best available. We came out with such a product—the 3500 [photocopier]—in 1978. It was drastically different in terms of cost performance and established a new industry standard in Japan. It became a great success and two years after we introduced it we won the Deming Award."

The Deming awards, as anyone with even a cursory interest in the contemporary Japanese economy quickly learns, are named after W. Edwards Deming, an American statistician who more or less single-handedly sold Japanese industry on the importance of rigid quality control and thereby became one of the most revered figures in Japan's business pantheon. Established in 1951 and given annually ever since for outstanding industrial achievement through the use of statistical quality-control techniques, the Deming awards are pursued by Japanese-based corporations with almost the intensity of Sir Gawain pursuing the Holy Grail. And there is, I believe, an implicit message for any American enterprise that hopes to succeed in Japan in the emphasis which Yotaro Kobayashi placed on capturing the award: when he wanted to find one capsule phrase to sum up his company's competitive resurgence, the president of Fuji Xerox did not cite a boom in sales or increased return on investment but, rather, public recognition of a notable improvement in product quality.

When it comes to consumer goods, the Japanese are obsessed not only with product quality but also with the way the product is packaged. "What this market requires," Mark Popiel of Dodwell once remarked to me, "is almost overpackaging."

My own guess is that the premium Japanese consumers place upon packaging that often strikes Westerners as unduly elaborate and expensive is just another manifestation of the deep concern with aesthetic style and manner of presentation that has always characterized Japanese culture; at a traditional formal dinner in Japan, for example, the appeal that the arrangement of the food makes to the eye and the ritual involved in serving it are no less important than its taste. In any case, whatever the cause, Japanese instinctively tend to regard ugly or merely utilitarian packaging as the hallmark of an inferior product.

So far as the American company which hopes to sell consumer goods in Japan is concerned, all this has one obvious implication: packaging which may have proved acceptable in other world markets often will not work in Japan. And this may well be the case even though the product the package contains is identical to that sold in other markets and is of high quality even by Japanese standards. Thus, while all the razor blades Schick sells so successfully in Japan are imported, the packaging for them is designed and made in Japan with heavy input from the marketing specialists at Hattori-Seiko.

This process, as Max Factor's experience with British-made cosmetics containers attests, can rule out seemingly attractive economies of scale and add heavily to costs. But any attempt to economize on packaging in Japan is dangerously likely to backfire—sometimes in unforeseeable ways. In his book *From Bonsai to Levi's,* George Fields cites the case of a foreign manufacturer who, with all apparent logic, decided he could use the same packaging everywhere in Asia by the simple device of including instructions in English, Chinese and Japanese. But while this worked reasonably well elsewhere in Asia, it didn't work in Japan. The reason, Fields explained, was that Japanese tend to regard other Asian societies with condescension and the fact that the product carried instructions in Chinese immediately downgraded it in their eyes.

Another obvious temptation for the cost-conscious American purveyor of consumer goods in Japan is to try to "Japanize" packaging that has been successful in the United States simply by translating whatever wording it contains into Japanese. But this, too, has risks, not all of them immediately obvious to the layman. The visual impact of English type, to start with, is so different from that of Japanese ideographs that a package design conceived with one of these forms of writing in mind may prove ill-suited to the other. Then there is the fact that much of the labeling used in Japan isn't actually written in ideographs but in phonetic symbols—and Japanese, improbable as it may seem, rejoices in not just one but two phonetic syllabaries, each of which carries somewhat different overtones, conscious and subconscious. And even when it comes to what might appear more basic aspects of packaging such as the use of color and fragrance, Japanese sometimes react quite differently from Americans. According to the late Mark Zimmerman of Sterling Drug, for example, they regard the color yellow and the smell of lemons as unsuitable in toiletries. (Lemon fragance, however, is fine for anything to do with dish- or clothes-washing.)

Given all these complications, it is clearly only natural that some of the most flourishing American exporters of consumer goods to Japan as well as American-owned firms that manufacture there rely heavily upon local expertise in dealing with these packaging problems. And while that does inevitably lead to increased costs in many cases, the bread thus spread upon the waters can be returned manyfold—a point dramatically demonstrated by an experience that Mark Popiel of Dodwell is fond of recounting. Some years ago, according to Popiel, Dodwell introduced into Japan a Belgian product consisting of ground coffee beans packaged together with a plastic cup and a filter—a kind of handy-dandy kit designed to make it possible to brew real coffee in the office, say, with a minimum of fuss and equipment. Though it was less than a runaway success, the coffee kit sold well enough that within eighteen months a competitive Japanese product appeared on the market. At that point, Popiel recalls with a small smile, Dodwell drew upon the wisdom it had acquired in long years of experience in

Japan: it put its product into a new and considerably fancier package, increased its price—and watched its sales really take off.

Important as they are, high-quality products and superior packaging by themselves will not ensure commercial success in Japan. Far more than Americans or Europeans, Japanese are also sticklers for good service—and good service, particularly in the eyes of an industrial or commercial organization in Japan, begins with prompt and accurate delivery of any goods it has contracted to purchase. In the experience of Holger Wittich, a German entrepreneur who carved out his own niche in the Japanese business world by importing foreign porcelain and glassware, this is too seldom understood by American suppliers. Some of the American firms with which he deals, Wittich told a Japanese reporter in early 1985, see it as no great cause for excitement if the invoice they send with a shipment doesn't quite match the number of items actually sent. "If we complain," Wittich went on, "their reaction is apt to be 'Oh, it's only a few pieces difference.' But that doesn't work in Japan. Here, if you say you're shipping 101 pieces, it's really got to be 101 pieces."

What's more, the 101 pieces have to arrive exactly on the date specified. "God help you if you don't deliver by the right day," said Harry Cooper of APV K.D. a few years ago. "Then you are really in trouble." Simply to be sure of meeting delivery dates, Cooper added, his company, a supplier of equipment to the food and beverage industries, invariably stockpiled a large amount of its products in Japan.

Again, this rigid insistence on keeping to precise delivery schedules sometimes strikes uninitiated Americans as arbitrary, if not downright persnickety. But, in reality, it is a function of the fact that major Japanese corporations typically keep inventories of all kinds as small as possible and rely instead on elaborately detailed scheduling. "When they decide on a project," said Cooper, "they plan ahead on how and when they are going to launch the project even before they have built the manufacturing plant. They plan the day the product is going to come out of the plant, the day it goes to the distributors and the day it goes out to the retail stores." And an executive of Emerson Japan Ltd. made the same point in a somewhat different way. "You have to keep tabs on the customer's production schedule," he said, "because in Japan there aren't any warehouses for the assembly lines."

To a degree, this inflexibility on delivery schedules constitutes a built-in handicap for American companies exporting industrial equipment to Japan: inevitably, their lead time tends to be longer and somewhat more unpredictable than that of their Japanese competitors. But this is a problem which Peter Katsuno of Teledyne appears to believe can be compensated for by judicious hand-holding. "Our customers," he told me, "want to be reassured that a product coming from so far away won't be either too late, which would throw off their production schedule, or too early, which would force them to readjust their payment schedules. So from time to time, they'll call up and ask 'How far have you progressed on that order?' And they aren't really satisfied when we tell them it's on schedule; they want to know more: 'Have you melted ingots yet? Is it in the forging stage, the machining stage or what?' Well, we're conscious of their anxiety and their need so we make every effort to keep them well informed."

Like nearly all executives of established U.S. affiliates in Japan, Katsuno also emphasizes that making the sale and delivering a satisfactory product on time is often only the prelude to winning the loyalty of a Japanese customer. Both individual consumers and great corporations in Japan expect and get a degree of after-sale service rarely found any longer in Europe or the United States. As of 1985, for example, anyone who ordered a part from the BMW service operation in Tokyo before 3 P.M. was guaranteed delivery the next day. I should be surprised if that proved true everywhere in Germany—and I can testify from personal experience that it is far easier to get prompt repairs in Tokyo on certain electronic gadgets manufactured by the American subsidiaries of Japanese corporations than it is in New York.

"The fact is," Peter Katsuno admitted to me, "that Japanese companies do provide a lot of service so we really have to match them. . . . It's in our interest to be flexible. If the warranty has just run out when the customer needs assistance and you tell them 'Sorry, the warranty is up,' you may never get any follow-up business. In fact, we have had cases where people used the machine improperly, in which case it is outside the warranty. But even then we have sometimes had to provide something so that the customer doesn't bear the full brunt of repair costs."

Like expensive packaging, this kind of service obviously adds significantly to a manufacturer's costs. But in some cases at least American subsidiaries or affiliates in Japan have actually found it more effective to compete on the basis of outstanding service rather than lower cost to the customer. One particularly striking example of this phenomenon is the Japanese subsidiary of Connecticut's Loctite Corporation. Though its annual volume was still only about $10 million a year, Nihon Loctite grew with remarkable rapidity in the mid-1980s and as of 1985 the company held 50 percent of the Japanese market for adhesives used in the assembly of automotive engines and was making growing inroads into the market for industrial adhesives in the electronics field.

The chief explanation for this, according to Robert Krieble, the spare, laconic New Englander who heads Nihon Loctite's American parent, lies in Loctite's heavy emphasis on what might be called pre-sale service. "Japanese products in our field are good," Krieble told me in his home in Connecticut one afternoon in 1985. "There are only a few areas in which we could honestly claim significant superiority in product terms. But what we do have is superior knowledge: we understand where and how to use adhesives beneficially in the assembly of parts better than anyone else in the world."

This, as Krieble sees it, gives Loctite a crucial edge over its Japanese rivals. "Their idea of competition," he said, "is to cut price. What we concentrate on in our industrial business, by contrast, is engineering development. Our salesmen go to a potential customer and say 'Here's what you can do with adhesives in your particular situation' and then they work with the customer's advanced-development people on just how best to do it." Krieble paused for a second, chuckled and summed up Loctite's basic sales technique. "We give know-how away," he said. "And when the customer agrees that we've solved his problem, then we charge like hell for our product."

Like Nihon Loctite, many other American affiliates in Japan do not employ price-cutting as their primary competitive tool—largely because there is often no way they can hope to do so. Meeting Japan's stiff standards of quality, packaging and service is obviously an expensive proposition and its effects in driving up costs are reinforced by the workings of Japan's swollen distribution system. On average, each retail sale that is made in Japan is preceded by twice as many wholesale transactions as it would be in the United States and each additional link in the distribution chain inevitably means an additional markup.

There are, however, certain compensations for the American exporter or investor in Japan who is prepared to incur these additional costs. Except in the dwindling number of industries where the Japanese still practice overt protectionism, meeting the demands of the Japanese marketplace generally counteracts any stigma that might stem from sheer foreignness. Though he has very vocal reservations about some of the treatment accorded U.S. companies in Japan, Herbert Hayde of Burroughs Japan told me flatly: "If you service your customer base in this country, you won't lose it—provided, of course, that you continue to supply a product that has good performance and price. In our industry, they don't buy a Japanese product over an American one unless you fail on those points."

The other great compensation for the higher costs imposed by the demands of Japanese customers is that, very broadly speaking, those costs are covered by the higher prices Japanese are prepared to pay for what they buy. In general, as anyone who has ever lived in Japan will unhappily attest, the price of consumer goods there is substantially higher than in Europe or the United States. And this is a state of affairs to which the Japanese public seems surprisingly resigned—so resigned, in fact, that avid bargain-hunting is far less characteristic of Japanese than of Americans. "The market here," Sam Maugeri of Warner-Lambert Japan once pointed out to me, "is markedly less price sensitive than it is at home."

Like most generalizations, that one has to be quickly qualified. In many respects, the Japanese market can be very price sensitive. When it comes to products such as toilet paper or detergents, where brand differentiation and loyalty are relatively slight, the Japanese housewife will often shave her supermarket bill by buying the "economy size" package or simply whatever brand is cheapest. Discounting of cameras and consumer electronic devices has become so accepted that it is now the principal industry of the Akihabara district of Tokyo. And large differences in price between products perceived as being of somewhat comparable quality can also bring out the thrifty strain in Japanese. Most amateur photographers in Japan, for example, have high respect for the quality and reliability of Kodak film, but except on special occasions tend in practice to settle for Fuji Photo film. This pattern of behavior, Kodak's Albert Sieg believes, stems back to a period when extremely high Japanese tariffs on imported film forced Kodak to charge much more for its wares than Fuji Photo did.

What really stimulates resistance in Japanese buyers, however, is not so much high prices as frequent changes in price. "The Japanese consumer is conditioned to higher prices, but he rejects large or constant price increases," Dodwell's Mark Popiel told me. "You just can't keep raising prices in Japan the way American or British supermarkets do." And that is even more true of industrial customers than of individual consumers—which constitutes a special hazard for any U.S. firm exporting to Japan in a period of fluctuating exchange rates or a high rate of inflation in the United States. "Frequent price changes is one complaint we often get from customers at such times," said Teledyne's Peter Katsuno a few years ago. "When the exchange rate fluctuates by so much we have to sit down with our customers and explain it."

As Katsuno's comment implied, American subsidiaries and affiliates in Japan that sell primarily to industrial concerns have learned that they must justify their prices to their customers with a candor and degree of detail rarely required in the West. But even the pricing of consumer goods, as Sterling Drug's Mark Zimmerman pointed out in *How to Do Business with the Japanese,* is a more complex matter in Japan than it normally is in the United States. Marketing people in Japan, Zimmerman wrote, "spend as much time discussing the right price for an article as they do on the product or its promotion. The price has to be *what the consumer would expect to pay.*"

Determining what the consumer would expect to pay can, of course, be difficult—particularly in the case of a highly innovative product. Here again, though, there are compensations for the risk and effort involved. "Once the price level is set for a particular type of product," Mark Popiel observed to me, "consumers here accept it more easily than consumers elsewhere." Indeed, once the price has been established, it can sometimes be just as dangerous to lower it as to raise it. "It confuses the market when you compete on price," Masao Sasaki of Hattori-Seiko said when we were discussing the pricing of Schick razor blades. "Small cuts in price

don't influence people much and would actually have bad reper-
cussions on the image of the company and its product." In the
mind of the Japanese consumer, in short, high price is often taken
as de facto evidence of high quality.

That, of course, is true to some extent in every country, but the
extraordinary degree to which it is sometimes carried in Japan was
epitomized for me by a conversation I had with Victor Harris of
Max Factor. "In the cosmetics industry here," Harris said, "prices
are twice what they are for comparable items in the States—and
it's very important to have the brand which is the highest priced in
its field. We're constantly in a kind of reverse price competition
with Shiseido and Kanebo to have the most expensive brands. The
cheapest lipstick we sell here is $15 or more a copy. Our SK2—our
entry in the biotechnical field if you will—is around $70 for a
three-ounce bottle and we can't make it fast enough. It's insane.

"Of course," Harris went on, "since price is equated with quality, there are no cut-rate sales: if you have a 50 percent–off sale,
you won't sell a single item. On the other hand, you can't raise
prices on a brand here either. So what you do is discontinue it and
bring out something new at a higher price."

Admittedly, the pricing practices that prevail in the cosmetics
industry in Japan are rather special, just as they are in the cosmetics business in the United States. But the instinctive association of
price with quality in Japan often extends to products totally lacking in the necromantic overtones possessed by beauty aids. Schick
products, as Sam Maugeri happily informed me, regularly sell for
about 25 percent more than comparable items manufactured by
Feather, Schick's principal Japanese competitor. And even in a
field as prosaic as the soft-drink industry the same psychology has
been observed. "When we first began to compete here," Weldon
Johnson of Coca-Cola Japan recounted, "the government in-
structed us that we must charge five yen a bottle more than Japanese brands. Since they sold for ¥30 a bottle in those days, that
meant we had to charge ¥35 a bottle and at first we saw that as
a tremendous hurdle. But the Japanese public assumed that the
extra five yen meant our product was better so our sales boomed."

Both Schick and Coca-Cola, moreover, have benefited not only
from their perceived quality but from another phenomenon described to me by Mark Popiel of Dodwell. "Once a brand starts
taking off in Japan," said Popiel, "it develops a momentum of its

own. . . . I think this is partly a function of the group mentality of Japanese. Once a brand has achieved the kind of dominance that Coca-Cola or, say, Nestlé has, it becomes almost self-perpetuating because the Japanese like to be seen drinking or eating whatever everyone else is drinking or eating." And that, of course, means that besides enjoying large unit sales the dominant brand in a particular field can hope for an uncommon degree of invulnerability to price competition.

10 Competition and Co-existence

Japan is a very competitive society and we have a very competitive economy.

—Yoriko Kawaguchi,
Ministry of International
Trade and Industry

When the average American sees a statement like Mrs. Kawaguchi's, his reaction is apt to be "So what else is new?" The squadrons of Toyotas, Nissans and Hondas cruising American highways, the countless Japanese VCRs that grace American family rooms and, of course, such much-publicized events as Hitachi's efforts to spy out IBM trade secrets have long since strongly impressed upon the American consciousness the fact that the Japanese are potent and sometimes ruthless business competitors.

But not perhaps strongly enough. For according to a number of the Americans who do business in Japan itself, anyone who has competed with Japanese firms only in American or European markets has led a relatively benign and sheltered existence.

Consider for example the case of Nike, the Oregon-based running shoe and sports apparel empire. As I noted earlier, Nike's founder, Phil Knight, put in nearly a decade as a U.S. distributor for Japan's Asics Tiger and in that process became an enthusiast for certain aspects of Japanese management. What's more, by the time Nike went into a joint venture in Japan in 1981, the company had competed effectively with Asics Tiger as well as several other foreign firms in a number of markets. Yet even with all that background Gary Kurtz, the chief executive officer of Nike Japan, admitted to me in 1985: "I think to some extent we underestimated the competitive environment here."

One of the things that make competition in Japan particularly stiff is that there is so much more of it there than in most places. The Japanese economy produces new companies in almost the same profusion that a female salmon produces spawn—and the attrition rate in both cases is similar. In 1980, for example, about 14,000 Japanese companies went bankrupt; that was nearly 13 percent higher than the comparable figure for the United States even though this country had twice as many corporations as Japan overall. And by 1984 the number of corporate bankruptcies in Japan had soared to 20,841, involving total liabilities of nearly $14.5 billion.

Out of this economic Darwinian process, however, there emerge enough tough survivors to assure the Japanese consumer of a vast diversity of choice. "Bear in mind that there are only half as many of us Japanese as of you Americans," I was once reminded by my friend Jiro Tokuyama, who heads the Nomura School of Advanced Management. "Yet there are more than ninety different brands of color TV sold in this country and more than thirty different manufacturers of personal computers. That's a big strength for our economy, but it makes it hard for outside companies to break into the market."

The seemingly reckless determination of Japanese corporations to go head-to-head with their competitors almost regardless of profit margins also has another consequence: it can make it difficult for a foreign subsidiary or affiliate to hang on to significant market share in Japan even when it originally created the market for the product in question. As we have seen, it is only a matter of time—and generally not very much time—until any product or service that wins the approval of Japanese consumers, whether it be cancer insurance or Fox's bagels, finds itself facing Japanese competition. And the days when the primary Japanese competitive tool was simply to produce a cheaper imitation of a Western product are long gone.

There is, in fact, a certain analogy between the way contemporary Japanese industry approaches product development and the way that it approaches capital investment. In their book *Restoring Our Competitive Edge,* professors Robert Hayes of Harvard and Steven Wheelwright of Stanford make the point that while the phrase "capital investment" tends to be interpreted by Americans to mean the construction of new plants, what it more often means to Japanese is the upgrading of machinery that they already have. In 1980, for example, only 25 percent of U.S. capital investment was spent on improving the performance of existing machinery but some 60 percent of Japanese capital investment went for that purpose.

This, according to Hayes and Wheelwright, has important consequences: because Japanese workers are so often involved in the upgrading of their machinery, they receive a kind of natural retraining, which means that capital investment in Japan results not only in improved manufacturing processes but in better-performing workers and higher product quality as well.

In somewhat similar fashion, when Japanese firms set out to make a competitive version of a product originally developed by somebody else, they generally follow a kind of incremental strategy. Here is how the process is described by Masanori Moritani, senior researcher for the Nomura Research Institute, in his book *Japanese Technology:*

> One of the characteristics of competition in Japan is the establishment of small distinctions between one's own product and similar products made by other manufacturers. These tend to be minor improvements in convenience, function, miniaturization and the like. . . . Thus five, six or even as many as 10 companies may be producing virtually identical products, but upon close examination you will find a number of small innovations in each. Since each firm is rapidly making such improvements in its goods, the cumulative effect is immense. In two or three years the product can be completely transformed.

Partly because so many of them have witnessed this phenomenon, some U.S. companies and joint ventures operating in Japan have come to a significant conclusion: the mere fact that they may possess superior technology does not offer them any surefire protection against their Japanese competitors. One executive who admits that his company has learned this lesson the hard way is Albert Sieg of Kodak Japan. "When we brought the pocket camera to this country, it changed the Japanese camera market in concept," Sieg recalled in early 1985. "Until then, Japanese camera makers had been pushing very strongly single-lens reflex cameras—large complicated devices. Their original reaction to the pocket camera was that it was a toy that the Japanese consumer would not be interested in. But when we were successful with the pocket camera, they sensed that there was after all a need for this kind of simpler apparatus among people—particularly younger people—who were more interested in getting pictures than in the equipment they used to get them. So they hit on a strategy to which, unfortunately, we were not as sensitive as we should have been. That was the development of the simple-to-use 35mm camera—and we let them get the upper hand in that."

There is, Sieg pointed out, what might be called a silver-haloid lining to that cloud: the new cameras have greatly increased the demand for costly 35mm film and it is from film rather than hardware that Kodak derives the greater part of its profits. Nonetheless, he said, the way in which Kodak had been outflanked by its Japanese competitors in this instance had taught the company that "we have to add more value to our product through marketing rather than just a technology push or pull. . . . We believe we will continue to have the edge over everybody in technology, but we've learned that we'll have to bring it to the marketplace faster than we have ever done before."

The commonest complaint voiced by American businessmen when they seek the exclusion of a particular Japanese product from the U.S. market is that the Japanese are not only fierce competitors but unscrupulous ones. And even though it does not constitute the fundamental explanation for Japan's economic successes, this is not an allegation that can simply be dismissed out of hand: those who make it can cite too many open-and-shut cases to support their point.

The most notable of these in recent years, of course, was the 1982 "sting" in which executives of Hitachi Ltd. offered to pay a phony consulting firm staffed by FBI agents and IBM security personnel more than $600,000 in an attempt to get hold of proprietary information on IBM software. For Hitachi, one of Japan's three or four largest companies, it was not only a humiliating revelation of technological inferiority to IBM to be caught at this game but a highly expensive one to boot: besides paying some

$44,000 in fines, Hitachi had to negotiate a settlement with IBM that will ultimately cost it an estimated $300 million.

While it was unusually large in scope and uncommonly well publicized, the Hitachi case nonetheless reflects a no-holds-barred approach to competition that is by no means unfamiliar to U.S. companies or affiliates doing business in Japan. In 1982, by his account, Mark Zimmerman of Sterling Drug was approached by representatives of a Japanese company who asked that his head office in New York stop buying a particular chemical from a European supplier and start buying it from their company instead. When told that this was impossible, Zimmerman later wrote, the Japanese threatened that "they would make a slight technical modification to the chemical to avoid patent-law prosecution and sell it at rock-bottom prices to Japanese imitator companies who would then price my company out of the market."

In this instance, the Japanese company was ultimately unable to make good on its threat for legal reasons, but not all such stories end so happily. In the mid-1970s, for example, International Playtex Inc. decided on the strength of its enormous success in the United States to start manufacturing brassieres and pantyhose in Japan for sale on the local market. But according to Victor Harris of Max Factor (which is subordinate to IPI in the Beatrice conglomerate hierarchy), Playtex executives overlooked a key point: "They forgot to find out that the business here is totally controlled by Wacoal—and Wacoal just called all of its retailers and said 'You take one Playtex brassiere and we're pulling our line.' So Playtex couldn't get one piece of merchandise into a store; not one brassiere did they sell."

When he told me that tale early in 1985, Harris clearly saw nothing too remarkable about it. "IPI is a fine, successful organization," he said, "and the boss tells that story on himself. But now, they're asking me if I can find them a distributor powerful enough to cope with Wacoal. All I can tell them is: 'There *isn't* anybody powerful enough to cope with Wacoal.'"

In the United States where companies regularly invoke—and get—court rulings in such matters, Harris's statement might seem extraordinary. But things are different in Japan as anyone doing business there can testify.

Perhaps the best illustration of this difference is to be found in the angry insistence of so many American businessmen that their

Japanese competitors "dump" goods in the United States by selling them below the cost of production. Here again the most clamorous such charge in recent memory involved Hitachi Ltd. At a farewell dinner held in his honor in Tokyo in mid-1985, outgoing Undersecretary of Commerce Lionel Olmer indulged in a shocking breach of Japanese manners—and some would say of American manners as well—by presenting his hosts with a copy of a memo allegedly circulated among distributors of Hitachi semiconductors in the United States. Openly aimed at Hitachi's chief competitors, both American and Japanese, in the production of so-called EPROM (erasable programmable read-only memory) chips, the memo urged the U.S. distributors: "Quote 10 percent below their price. If they requote, go [down] another 10 percent. Don't quit till you win." What's more, the memo added, no matter how sharply they cut prices, the distributors could count on a 25 percent profit.

Clearly abashed by the ensuing uproar in the United States, Hitachi promptly declared that the offending memo, reportedly drafted by someone in the San Jose, California, marketing office of the company's American subsidiary, in no way reflected the policy of Hitachi America Ltd. That may well have been the case, but in one sense it was begging the issue. For the fact was that in the period in question all semiconducter manufacturers had badly overestimated the demand for EPROM chips and as a result the market was awash in excess production. And in such situations, no matter what constraints American law and custom may impose upon them in the United States, Japanese companies see nothing intrinsically unfair in seeking to maximize their long-term market share by selling goods below the average cost of production in the industry. Indeed, as the next chapter will make plain, this is a widely practiced industrial strategy in Japan and one that carries no particular moral stigma there.

Inherent in the different approaches to pricing in the United States and Japan is a significant philosophical point. There are certain forms of economic competition such as industrial espionage and commercial bribery which, although they crop up with greater or lesser frequency in every country, are at least for public purposes more or less universally conceded to be unethical. But there are other business practices which, while held in some societies to be grossly unfair, are seen elsewhere as quite acceptable.

And while American businessmen who operate in a purely domestic context may be in a position to ignore this particular facet of cultural relativism, those who have any involvement in the Japanese marketplace emphatically are not.

This fact was dramatically driven home a few years ago to my friend Inger Elliott, an erstwhile photojournalist who founded a New York–based company called China Seas that does a thriving business in Indonesian batiks and other decorator fabrics. Eager to find a prestige outlet for her wares in Japan, Inger negotiated a contract with a major Japanese department store chain which specified, among other things, that her firm was to register the China Seas trademark in Japan. When she tried to do so, however, she discovered that the Japanese retailer had itself registered the trademark in Japan well before the agreement between it and China Seas was signed. Worse yet, she learned that in Japan the first person to apply for a trademark is generally awarded it—even though he may never have used it commercially and it is the recognized symbol of a foreign company.

Like any true American, Inger first thought of taking the matter to court, but after consulting people with some experience in Japan she finally decided upon another course: she wrote a very polite letter to the Japanese retailer lamenting the loss of face she would suffer if she were unable to register her trademark as the contract required. Within a very short time, an apologetic telex came in from Tokyo announcing that the Japanese company certainly had no intention of causing Mrs. Elliott to lose face and had therefore withdrawn its own application for the China Seas trademark.

Here again, however, the annals of American business in Japan include many similar stories with less happy outcomes. In the early 1970s when lawyers for McDonald's went into Japan's national patent office to apply for trademarks they discovered that just one day earlier a Japanese food distribution company had registered the world-famed golden arches as its own commercial symbol. By resorting to interminable negotiation and litigation, McDonald's Japan was able to go ahead and use the golden arches anyway, but as of the time this book was being written the question of who legally owned that trademark in Japan was still undecided.

Ostensibly, McDonald's should not have had so much trouble: under Japanese law, the foreign owner of a trademark can in theory prevent its unauthorized registration by somebody else if the trademark is well known in Japan and its use by a Japanese concern would create confusion in the minds of consumers. But the existence of those conditions is often hard to prove, with the result that a number of U.S. firms ranging from General Electric to Coca-Cola have found themselves obliged to buy back their own trademarks or trademarks confusingly similar to their own. And to forestall this kind of eventuality, experienced U.S. ventures in Japan often register a particular trademark for use with all sorts of products only marginally related to their basic business: as of 1983, for example, Max Factor had all its major brand names and symbols registered for ten different classes of goods, including medical products.

On one level, the problems U.S. firms have with trademarks in Japan is clearly a function of the differences between American and Japanese law on the subject. But a society's laws, broadly speaking, tend to reflect its cultural predispositions and that would seem to apply in this instance. Unquestionably, there have been cases in which Japanese have quite deliberately registered well-known foreign trademarks in order to be able to shake down in one way or another the companies associated with those trademarks when they sought to do business in Japan. But more often the seemingly unethical behavior of Japanese with regard to trademarks stems from a less sinister cause. As George O'Haver, an in-house lawyer for Coca-Cola Japan, told the *New York Times* in April 1983: "The Japanese people have not really been tuned into the concept of industrial trademark property. . . . If you have a mark like ours that is commonly identified as a part of Western culture, they think they can use it to decorate anything."

Alien as Americans often find the Japanese attitude toward trademarks, however, the Japanese view of contracts offers an even sharper example of differences in business behavior stemming from different cultural roots. Somewhat ironically, the most scathing denunciation of the Japanese position on contracts that I have ever heard from an executive of a U.S. affiliate in Japan was voiced not by an American but by Den Fujita of McDonald's Japan. Though McDonald's in the United States is a franchise operation, more than 85 percent of the McDonald's stores in Japan were company-owned as of the beginning of 1985 and Fujita minced no words in explaining why. "People in this country don't know what a contract is," he told me with obvious indignation. "In America once you sign a contract people keep their word. In this country they break it easily; here people don't mind breaking a promise."

Among the people who run U.S. subsidiaries and joint ventures in Japan, however, Fujita's view seems to be a minority one. Kentucky Fried Chicken Japan has operated with conspicuous success on a franchise basis and so has Seven-Eleven Japan. And Walt Disney's Jim Cora expressed an opinion fairly common among American businessmen in Japan when he told me that one of the pleasures of doing business there was that "you don't have to put everything in writing."

Nonetheless, if only to appease their parent companies and stay on the right side of U.S. law, American affiliates in Japan are as a practical matter obliged to make extensive use of written contracts. And this can easily become a major source of cross-cultural confusion. Looking back on his five years in Japan with Sterling Drug, Mark Zimmerman wrote: "I do not remember one incident when [our Japanese partners] ever referred me to a contract in order to persuade me to take a certain action that they thought was necessary. On the other hand, I was frequently obliged to remind the Japanese side that through oversight they were acting in violation of a contract. They just don't read contracts after they are signed and filed!"

The fact that Japanese businessmen often sign contracts without bothering to read them carefully is easy enough to explain: they don't attach the same importance to a contract that Western businessmen do. When they are operating in Europe or the United States, Japanese executives have long since learned to do as the Caucasians do and take legalisms seriously. But among themselves they operate either without contracts or with minimal ones because they regard it as foolish to try to make binding written provisions to govern the behavior of individuals or institutions in an inherently unknowable future. By Japanese lights, a contract should be open to flexible interpretation so that if circumstances change significantly the relationship between the parties to the contract can be readjusted to assure that none of them suffers unduly.

Under certain conditions, this relativistic view of contractual obligations can lead Japanese companies to behave more justly in the ultimate sense than most Western companies would under similar circumstances. As I recounted in my book *The Japanese Mind,* an American mining operator of my acquaintance once made a contract to supply iron ore to a Japanese company and, when the terms of trade shifted radically, found himself losing money on every shipment. With no legal escape from the contract open to him, he had resigned himself to bankruptcy when, to his amazement, the Japanese—with whom he had a long-standing association—unilaterally upped the agreed-upon price enough to assure him a profit.

At the same time, however, the not-so-binding contract favored in Japan can pose serious potential hazards to a U.S. enterprise operating in the Japanese context. As Teledyne's Peter Katsuno pointed out, a Japanese customer can be forever alienated if he is refused something to which he feels he is morally entitled simply because he signed a contract specifically denying him such benefits. And it is the consensus among American and Japanese executives with whom I have discussed the matter that any joint venture in which the American partner continually invokes the letter of the legal agreements involved is almost inevitably headed for disaster.

Often, in fact, the longer an American businessman has worked in Japan the more inclined he is to shun the more egregious trappings of U.S. legalism. Some years ago, David Gregg recalled for an interviewer his initial experience as president of Control Data Japan. "When I came over," Gregg said, "we wanted to set up a new business and we understood that there was much red tape involved. So I did what almost any Western businessman would do—got a lawyer. It was only afterward that I found out that it was not traditional to do business with a lawyer, even when dealing with the government. . . . What I accomplished was to delay the whole project by about six months and spend a lot of money on unnecessary fees."

No matter what his personal inclinations, however, any executive of a U.S. affiliate in Japan must try somehow to reconcile Japanese business customs and law with the demands of American business customs and law—and that can mean walking a very fine line. Sheldon Weinig recalls that when he asked a Japanese with whom he had developed a solid and mutually beneficial relationship to sign a contract with him, the Japanese took it as a sign of mistrust and was extremely upset. "I explained to him that it didn't change things between us but that for the purposes of the American company I simply had to have something on paper," Weinig told me. "In the end, he went along, but I don't know whether he will ever totally forgive me."

What Dr. Weinig recognized is a principle that is accepted by every successful U.S. affiliate in Japan that has come to my attention—namely that business relations in Japan, even the relations between companies, come down to personal relations based on mutual faith. The Japanese do not live by any abstract moral code such as the Ten Commandments. Morality, as they see it, lies in not disappointing the expectations of those with whom they live and work and in serving to the best of their capacity the group with which they are identified.

It is the supreme importance of personal relationships and group loyalties—together with the fact that competition in Japan essentially takes place between groups rather than individuals—that explains why Japanese corporations sometimes indulge in behavior which appears to Westerners unpardonably aggressive or even downright unethical. The other side of the coin, however, is that those same characteristics, properly harnessed and exploited, have on numerous occasions proved extremely helpful to American business interests in Japan.

When he talks with newcomers to Japan, my friend Dean Jiro Tokuyama of the Nomura School of Advanced Management almost invariably stresses one point: for most of its history Japan has been a land of such limited economic resources and opportunities that completely unrestrained competition would have constituted a pre-nuclear form of mutual assured destruction. To guard against that and to establish some rational basis for sharing such scant wealth as they had the Japanese very early in their existence began to bond into mutual-support groups whose members protected each other's interests against outsiders and developed elaborate rules governing their own mutual relations. It is this fact, I believe, that in large part accounts for the strong group-orientation of contemporary Japanese. And just as individual Japanese bond into groups, Japanese institutions bond into still larger groups. "Our competitiveness co-exists with a willingness to work together in adjusting to change," a perceptive MITI official named Masahisa Naitoh once wrote. "To the Japanese way of thinking it is acceptable and natural for companies to cooperate in order to cope with common problems."

The most widely known example of this tendency toward corporate cooperation in Japan is undoubtedly the existence of what foreigners still sometimes refer to as the *zaibatsu*. In fact, the true *zaibatsu*—enormous economic empires totally controlled by a single holding company and/or family—were broken up by the U.S. Occupation authorities after World War II and have never reappeared in anything like their original form. Instead, they have gradually been replaced at the center of Japanese economic life by six major industrial groups—which are more loosely linked corporate confederations ranging in size from the DKB (for Dai-Ichi Kangyo Bank) group of some 90 companies to the Mitsubishi group, which has more than 150 member companies.

The complexity of these confederations is truly mind-boggling; the 1984/85 edition of the indispensable reference book on the subject, Dodwell Marketing Consultants' *Industrial Groupings In Japan*, runs to 568 pages. Yet in essence all of them operate essentially the same way. Each group is made up of a potent agglomeration of companies engaged in virtually every imaginable form of business activity—manufacturing, banking, insurance, trading, real estate, transportation, etc., etc. The only formal ties between the member companies of a particular group, however, lies in the crossholding of shares. In other words, any company in the Mitsui group will include among its stockholders one or more other Mitsui companies. These stockholdings are not necessarily very large; even in the Sumitomo group, where the figure is highest, only 21.4 percent of the total shares of member companies were crossheld as of 1985. But with the crossholding of shares, of course, goes interlocking directorates and all that that implies in the way of conjoined interests.

Perhaps even more important than any legal link, however, is an informal one: each of the six major industrial groups has established, generally under an innocuous name such as the White Water Club or the Second Friday Conference, a council composed of the presidents of the group's leading companies. Ostensibly, these councils have no authority over the group's member companies and exist only to foster friendship and the exchange of information among the presidents. Since no minutes of presidential council meetings are ever published, it is difficult to prove that they are, in fact, anything more than high-level kaffeeklatsches. Nonetheless it is widely assumed that in addition to protestations of friendship the discussion extends to such matters as key personnel appointments in member companies, intragroup financing, problems in government relations, joint investment in new industries and co-operation in research and development.

It also seems clear that the influence of the presidential councils extends even beyond the confines of their member companies. Just below the six major industrial groups on Japan's economic totem pole are a dozen or more so-called independent groups, most of which center around a single large manufacturer such as Nissan Motors or Nippon Steel. Though often quite large—the Nippon Steel group includes about 180 companies—these agglomerations are usually focused on no more than half a dozen industries and sometimes essentially on just one. This means that in matters outside their normal scope they tend to turn to one of the major industrial groups for assistance and hence become in some degree subject to its influence.

In the eyes of many Americans, the mere existence of all these mutual support groups in Japan constitutes an invisible barrier to penetration of the Japanese marketplace by U.S. companies and their Japanese affiliates. On the face of things, that would seem logical and there clearly is at least some truth to the frequently voiced charge that Japanese companies prefer when possible to buy whatever they need from other companies belonging to the same industrial group. Such statistical data as exist on this practice, however, suggest that it is considerably less widespread than foreigners sometimes allege and in any case it does not invariably work to the disadvantage of U.S. interests in Japan.

The reason for that is that it is entirely possible for a firm with strong American ties to become part of a Japanese mutual support group and many U.S. affiliates in Japan have successfully done so. To cite that most obvious case, a joint venture between a U.S. company and a Japanese company that belongs to one of the big industrial groups can reasonably hope to be taken under the group's wing. And while it may not have the same influence in the group's councils that a purely Japanese company would, the joint venture can nonetheless enjoy some of the important advantages of group membership.

To begin with, affiliation with an established industrial group in

Japan can in certain circumstances be the key to getting into the Japanese market at all. The Japanese life insurance industry, for example, is closely supervised by Japan's Ministry of Finance, which protects the viability of existing companies so zealously that as of the mid-1970s, when Allstate came along, no new life insurance company had been licensed to do business in Japan for more than half a century. Whether the Sears, Roebuck subsidiary could have negotiated this bureaucratic obstacle course purely on its own is arguable. Wisely, however, it decided not to try to do so. Instead, it aligned itself with the Seibu Group, a collection of some ninety-five companies which had its origins in a department store chain but now engages in activities as diverse as the development of planned communities and the manufacture of organic fertilizer. Headed by the dynamic Seiji Tsutsumi, a onetime student radical who is thoroughly conversant with Japan's corridors of power, Seibu was able in the relatively short space of a year and a half to wangle out of the Ministry of Finance a license for a joint venture called Seibu Allstate Life Insurance Company—or SALIFE for short.

Besides opening doors in Japanese government offices, linking up with an existing corporate group in Japan can help a U.S. firm get launched there in another important respect: raising money. Because interest rates in Japan have traditionally been lower than in the United States and because operating primarily on borrowed money is perfectly acceptable there, many American firms have preferred to keep their initial capital investment in a Japanese venture low and to rely heavily upon loans from Japanese banks. And while affiliation with a group is by no means a precondition for borrowing money in Japan, it can make that process significantly easier.

This is so because each of Japan's six major industrial groups has a leading bank as one of its core members. As a result, when any company linked with one of these groups embarks on a joint venture with an American firm, the joint venture almost automatically acquires a degree of creditworthiness with the group's banking network—a fact which can be of particular importance to a new and untested enterprise. As I mentioned earlier, Nike's access to bank loans was assured by its partnership with Nissho Iwai, a trading company with ties to two of the six major industrial groups, and Mitsubishi Corporation, the trading company for the

Mitsubishi Group, performed the same service for Kentucky Fried Chicken Japan. Because Mitsubishi Corporation was half-partner in his venture, Kentucky Fried Chicken's Loy Weston by his own account managed at one point to leverage a paltry $200,000 in paid-in capital up to $8 million. "If Kentucky Fried Chicken Japan hadn't worked," he told an interviewer in 1984, "I'd be in jail now."

For U.S. companies that wish to manufacture in Japan or to do significant sourcing there, linking up with a Japanese industrial group has yet another lure. As President Takeo Shiina of IBM Japan noted in 1984: "Access to . . . technologically developed sources of supply is a powerful hidden advantage to foreign investors willing to research and identify local suppliers." And in a group context, this research process can sometimes be speeded up. Through its Japanese partner in a joint venture, the American company involved can try to tap the collective wisdom of the group, each of whose manufacturing members typically will have captive subcontractors of its own as well as an informed appraisal of its competitors' suppliers.

Useful as it has been to some of them, however, involvement with a Japanese industrial group is obviously not a suitable—or even available—option for every American venture in Japan. And it is by no means the only form of fruitful cooperation with Japanese industry open to American investors. By careful cultivation of institutional and personal relationships, even wholly owned U.S. subsidiaries in Japan can gradually build their own informal mutual support groups—and a number have. Thus, Takeo Shiina's IBM has over the years developed a network of suppliers that now includes more than a thousand Japanese firms. And more recently by enlisting independent Japanese companies as distributors and entering a series of joint ventures—including a highly significant one with giant Nippon Telegraph and Telephone to create the kind of complex telecommunications system known as a "value added network"—IBM Japan appears to have embarked on a conscious effort to broaden its mutual support base.

For a smaller, wholly American-owned company that cannot hope to operate on the scale of an IBM, the nucleus of a support network is often as near as its bank. Where most Americans find any talk of "your friendly neighborhood banker" cause for hollow laughter, bankers in Japan do, in fact, seek to play an active and positive role in the affairs of their business clients—so much so that when he first arrived in Japan Mark Zimmerman was amazed by the treatment he and Sterling Drug received from the local branch of the Sumitomo Bank. "Their services, " he wrote, "included helping us to locate a new office (through Sumitomo Real Estate), leasing a computer (through Sumitomo Leasing), researching an acquisition possibility . . . and accompanying me as a go-between to introduce me to potential business partners. One of the assistant managers was so excited about my company and its growth prospects in Japan that on his daily rounds for the bank he would help line up sales opportunities for our industrial chemicals. Thanks to him, we were able to get several important contracts."

Besides taking advantage of the supportiveness of Japanese bankers, there is an even more obvious way for an out-and-out U.S. subsidiary to pursue acceptance by the Japanese community—namely, to take what would be almost an instinctive step if it were operating in the United States and join the trade association or associations that speak for its particular industry. But in a survey that it took in 1982, the American Chamber of Commerce in Japan (itself a support group whose role will be considered in a later chapter) discovered considerable ambivalence about the wisdom of this approach. Of 169 U.S. firms polled by the ACCJ fewer than two-thirds belonged to the Japanese trade associations related to their business and less than half believed that it was in their interest to join such associations.

In part, these attitudes obviously stemmed from a feeling of being unwelcome. Only thirteen of the firms polled claimed that they had actually been denied membership in a Japanese trade association but another twenty-four had never tried to join one because they expected to be turned down. And the perception was widespread that even if an American firm was granted membership in an association, its representatives would be largely or totally excluded from one of the most important functions of such groups in Japan—which is to formulate recommendations to the Japanese government on the framing of standards and regulations for the industry in question.

Though the situation is now changing somewhat, this is a suspicion that has often proved justified in the past. At least one senior executive of a U.S. firm long established in Japan, however, believes that American concern about being excluded from trade association policy-making is often a self-fulfilling prophecy. Though he declined to be identified for fear of making trouble for his parent firm in the United States, this old Japan hand argued that an American firm that is prepared to play by local rules can derive benefits from association membership in Japan that could not be duplicated in the United States. "In our early years here," he said, "we were a very active participant in the associations in our industry. We sat down with our major Japanese competitors and mapped out strategies—things such as we won't take your employees if you don't take ours, none of us will shave prices or create any fuss and we'll approach the government together when we have a problem. It all worked beautifully: we had respect for each other and we established some long-standing personal and business relationships."

That said, my informant cheerfully added, "Of course, some of the things we did might not be 100 percent legal back home."

11 The Long and Short of It

On first meeting, Victor Harris of Max Factor seems almost the archetype of the California-bred executive—informal, irreverent and, judging from a casual and unselfconscious reference to his family's nine automobiles, completely at ease with the lavish materialism of the brave new society beyond the Rockies. Yet in at least two important respects, Harris differs sharply from most American managers, whether they hail from California or Connecticut. Where the great majority of senior American executives have had only limited exposure to international business if any at all, Harris has spent his entire career in the management of Max Factor's foreign operations. And where more and more contemporary U.S. managers are hired guns who move nimbly from one corporation to the next as personal interest seems to dictate, Harris has strong emotional ties to his company: his father before him worked for Max Factor and, among other things, opened the company's first branch in Japan.

It was scarcely surprising then that when I discussed his company's affairs with him in early 1985, Harris at first expressed what sounded like unalloyed pleasure in the accomplishments of Max Factor in Japan. It was, he informed me, the biggest foreign company in the retail cosmetics field in Japan—and only three Japanese firms outstripped it in their home market. "We do very well here," he assured me. "In fact, we do more business here than we do in the United States."

Yet as Harris talked on it quickly became clear that, profitable though Max Factor might be in Japan, it hadn't done nearly as well there as he thought it could have done. "Right now," he told me, "we have a 5 percent share of the market. But in the good years our share was closer to 10 percent. Don't get me wrong: in overall volume our business has gone up, but it hasn't kept pace with the growth of the market. Our Japanese competitors have grown faster than we have . . . much faster. So far as retail goes, I'd guess Shiseido now has 45 percent of the market, Kanebo 25 percent and Kosei perhaps 15 percent."

Why, I asked, had the Japanese been able to grow so much faster? "Because they didn't have the same corporate restrictions on them that we did," Harris replied bluntly. "The Factor family sold out to Norton Simon in 1973 and now, of course, we are part of Beatrice, a still larger group. That isn't all bad, but once we became part of a group there were changes in our ability to be competitive and aggressive here. The years since 1973 haven't been as good for us."

As Harris himself tacitly conceded, however, Max Factor's problems in Japan run deeper than just being part of a conglomerate. "For the last three or four years," he told me, "the cosmetics market here has been flat. No one's sales have been going up. And all the American companies here have reacted to that the way our organization has. Our bosses say to us: 'Hey, your costs are going up and you can't fire people. You'd better pull back—cut your advertising etc., etc.' "

Sighing, Harris went on: "The Japanese say: 'Nuts to that!' What they tell themselves is this: 'Five years down the road when the cosmetics business is going ahead again, we want our share of market to be 55 percent instead of the 45 percent it is now. We can't increase the total market right now, but we can take share away from Factor and Rubinstein and Lauder and here's what we'll have to spend in the next three or four years to do that.' And that's exactly what they're doing, pounding away harder than ever. They're spending more and dominate every advertising medium; they're putting vast money into R&D and product development; they're taking fabulous care of their retailers.

"Where's all this getting them?" asked Harris rhetorically. "I'll tell you where. The 13 percent share of the market that the foreign companies now hold between them all will sooner or later become 10 percent and then 8 percent. And in the end, if the Americans don't wise up, it may disappear altogether—because you can't exist in the cosmetics business here without good market share; the retailers won't handle you."

The constraints that Max Factor's American owners have placed upon its efforts to grow in the Japanese market epitomize what may well be the single most serious handicap faced by American affiliates in Japan. That handicap is the addiction of so much of U.S. corporate management to business strategies based on what Kentucky Fried Chicken's Loy Weston has described as "quarteritis."

By quarteritis, of course, Weston refers to what most managers of publicly owned corporations in the United States perceive as the overriding importance of showing increased earnings in their company's next quarterly report. The conventional wisdom is that American managers are forced into this frame of mind by the nature of corporate financing in the United States—the fact that American companies have traditionally relied heavily upon equity investment and so, at least for public consumption, must make it their prime purpose to serve the best interests of their stockholders. But this explanation takes for granted that what is in the stockholders' best interest is obvious, whereas in reality all that is obvious is what the majority of American stockholders *think* is in their best interest. And that, of course, is quick profits. As President Albert Sieg of Kodak Japan pointedly reminded me: "Most people in the U.S. buy your stock for a six-months' capital gain, not for long-term growth."

Almost inevitably, this means that any given set of corporate managers in the United States is rated above all on its success in running up its company's shares—and the best way to do that is by maximizing short-term profits and fattening dividends. This, as Kodak's Sieg also reminded me, often leads the chief executives of U.S. corporations to take the same line with their company's Japanese affiliates that they do with its domestic divisions. "What many of them tend to say," Sieg noted, "is 'Don't talk to me about three or four years from now; tell me what your next quarterly report is going to look like.' "

Unfortunately, however effective this approach may be in an American context, it is totally alien to the Japanese way of doing business. Publicly owned Japanese corporations aren't even required to publish quarterly reports and their managers are not greatly concerned with short-term fluctuations in stock prices. Here again, the conventional wisdom sees this primarily as a consequence of the prevailing method of corporate financing. Because

Japanese companies operate so heavily on borrowed money, it is said, their executives must pay special heed to the bankers who lend them the money—and who characteristically take the long view. And even when it comes to dealing with stockholders, the ones whose views matter most to a Japanese company are the other corporations that have invested in its shares and that are primarily interested in its long-range prospects.

There is, I think, considerable truth to these explanations. It is probably significant, too, that Japanese executives, unlike their American counterparts, are seldom given substantial stock options—which means that they have no personal incentive to run their company's stock up at the fastest possible pace. Nonetheless, I believe that Albert Sieg is right when he says: "The Japanese businessman is just as cognizant of his stockholder as the American businessman. But the Japanese businessman thinks that if he makes sure the business is healthy and that it will prosper in the long term, the stockholders are going to do fine." And it is of central importance that Japanese stockholders, individual as well as institutional, generally seem to share that view.

To the harried chief executive in Chicago or the Silicon Valley, it may well seem that all this is of little more than academic interest—that it has at best only marginal relevance to his day-to-day struggles with his Japanese competitors. But, as Max Factor's experience suggests, that is a delusion. To begin with, the radical difference in the way Japanese and American executives view their obligations to stockholders produces radical differences in their strategic objectives. "There was a survey a while back in which Japanese and American executives were asked to list their primary corporate objectives," consultant James Abegglen told me in January 1985. "The Japanese cited market share, return on investment and development of new products, in that order. Share prices was way down on their list—at about the same level that improvement of working conditions was for Americans. But the Americans put share prices first, followed by return on investment and then market share."*

---

* There is an additional difference on this score that Abegglen didn't mention. In measuring a company's financial performance, most Japanese executives, unlike

Inevitably, these differences in strategic goals frequently lead Japanese and American companies to react to an identical business problem or opportunity in almost diametrically opposed ways. And nowhere is this more evident than on investment policy. "The big problem American companies have here," Abegglen told me, "is that they don't invest enough to make their Japanese operations competitive."

When he said that, I was forcibly reminded of a story recounted to me by the late Yoshiya Ariyoshi who for a number of years headed NYK (for Nippon Yusen Kabushiki Kaisha), Japan's biggest shipping line. For a Japanese businessman of his generation, Ariyoshi was both uncommonly cosmopolitan and uncommonly blunt and one crisp October morning in 1980 he began to inveigh against what he regarded as the indefensible shortsightedness of U.S. industry. "Back in the late 1960s," he said, "a man named Stanley Powell who was then running the Matson Line proposed to me that Matson and NYK start a joint venture in containerships. I knew Powell to be a very able fellow: when Alexander Baldwin, the big Hawaiian company that owned Matson, put him in as president of the line it had been running in the red for years; he got it back in the black. I also knew that successful operation of containerships took a lot of know-how and that Matson had invented certain ways to cut loading time drastically. So a joint venture seemed like a good idea and I agreed to become his partner.

"The trouble came when I told him that because the capital outlay for ships, containers, computer systems and so forth would be very heavy our joint venture couldn't hope to show a profit until its third year in business. As I saw it, we'd lose money the first year, break even the second and then move into the black.

"Because of the importance of getting into what was then a new technology, the idea of waiting three years for a profit didn't worry anybody at NYK at all. But Powell said to me: 'No, I have to start making money the first year. Otherwise, Alexander Baldwin won't agree to invest and my future might be jeopardized.'

---

their American counterparts, do not use return on investment as their yardstick. Instead, they make return on sales their gauge and often are content so long as both sales and operating margins increase, even though the ratio between them—which is what constitutes return on sales—may actually be decreasing.

"Well, that was the end of the joint venture. Here at NYK we went ahead and contracted with Mitsui Shipbuilding for our own containership. It was the first one ever built in Japan, but they got it to us in 300 days—just ten months from design to delivery. Meantime, Matson applied for a U.S. government subsidy to help finance their containerships and because of all the red tape involved it took four years before they got their first one."

And what about Stanley Powell, I inquired. Did he make his instant profit when he finally got into the business? "No," said Mr. Ariyoshi a little sadly. "In the end, he was fired."

It would be nice to think that Mr. Ariyoshi's tale was just an isolated anecdote. Unhappily, however, variations on the same theme still abound—some of the most notable involving the application of robots and other numerically controlled tools. As a result of massive investment in technology largely developed in the United States, Japanese industry now has in service several times as many robots as does America's far bigger industrial establishment. And this is merely the newest phase of a long-standing drive by major Japanese corporations to reduce the amount of human labor that goes into their products through heavy spending on automation—a drive so successful, to cite just one example, that it now takes substantially fewer man-hours of work to produce a car in Japan than it does in Detroit.

At first blush, it might seem odd that the Japanese are willing to spend so much to reduce their labor costs when hourly wages for manufacturing workers in Japan are already substantially lower by and large than those that U.S. workers command. But on closer examination it makes eminent sense. Because machines make fewer mistakes than humans do, automation reduces the number of defects in Japanese products—which obviously enhances the sales appeal of those products. Even more important, cutting unit production costs through automation helps Japanese companies achieve their primary goal of expanding their market share—particularly in industries where they can pursue something known as the "learning-curve strategy."

The learning-curve strategy—which as a formal concept was pioneered by America's Boston Consulting Group—applies only to products which are sold in great quantity or are clearly destined to be sold in great quantity at some point in the future. It rests essentially on a simple rule of thumb: every time the market for such a product doubles, economies of scale will quite substantially reduce the cost of producing it. When this happens, a company—or at least a U.S. company—that was fortunate enough to be among the first to market the product will be inclined to go on selling it at its original price and thereby increase its profit margin. The resulting increase in short-term profits, however, almost inevitably will cost the company some of its market share since other companies that are prepared to accept slimmer profit margins will come into the field and acquire a certain amount of business by selling the product at a price that reflects the drop in manufacturing costs. And if the potential size of the market appears very large, there is a risk that some hungry latecomer will seek to capture most of the anticipated growth in it by "pricing forward"—that is, by asking a very low price based not upon current production costs but on the level to which costs will fall when total sales volume in the industry reaches something close to its maximum size.

Pricing forward is clearly a risky and expensive device: a company that indulges in it will lose money on each item it sells until the day arrives—if it ever does—when the market finally becomes big enough that manufacturing costs actually fall to the level the company has projected they will. Nonetheless, Japanese companies are often willing to pay this price because, as Albert Sieg once remarked, they are convinced that "if you have the largest share of the market you can't help but make money in the long run."

They are so convinced of that, in fact, that they cannot conceive why a rationally run corporation would operate on any other assumption. Even President Haruo Okinobu of Yamatake-Honeywell, for all his American education and strong ties with U.S. business, was adamant when I raised the subject with him. "Look," he said in the patient tone of a man explaining one of the more obvious facts of life to a slightly backward child, "it's like this: when a market is not mature, you go after market share. Then, when it becomes mature, you go after profit."

The difference between the basic business strategy commonly employed by U.S. companies and the one preferred by their Japanese competitors has perhaps been most clearly revealed in recent years in the semiconductor industry. It was, of course, U.S. technology that created semiconductors, those wafer-thin microchips that store whatever information any computer possesses and execute the commands that it receives from the software applied to it. Given this technological lead, many people still foresaw no serious challenge to U.S. supremacy in the field as late as 1980 when by far the biggest-selling semiconductor was the 16K RAM—a storage or memory chip capable of containing slightly more than 16,000 separate pieces of information. And on the surface of things, the assumption of continuing American dominance seemed reasonable: of the $940 million worth of 16K RAMs sold in the United States that year, 60 percent were U.S.–made. And even in Japan, the world's second largest market for semiconductors, sales of chips imported from the United States or manufactured by the local subsidiaries of U.S. companies were brisk.

Already, however, there were portents which anyone who sought to look beneath the surface could hardly fail to find unsettling. In October, 1980, Dr. Koji Kobayashi, chief executive officer of NEC, the giant communications company that has emerged as one of Japan's three top computer makers, matter-of-factly told me: "We went into the semiconductor business fifteen years ago and have invested very big money in it."

A rugged, self-assured man and normally quick to laugh, Dr. Kobayashi clearly found the semiconductor business no laughing matter. "It's a complicated industry," he said slowly. "You have to operate on the learning-curve principle and we have been trying to do that." He hesitated for a moment and then added prophetically: "In the United States, there is too much pioneering spirit you might say. There are too many companies making semiconductors and most of them are too small. If you have forty companies in the field, thirty-nine of them are likely to go bankrupt eventually because in a learning-curve situation you can't make a profit without big production."

At the time, I must confess, I didn't give sufficient weight to Kobayashi's comment. Along with all the small U.S. semiconductor companies, I reflected, there were also some very big ones—companies that were just as aware of the learning-curve formula as NEC and that, like it, aimed from the start at extremely large-scale production.

What I wasn't allowing for was the impact of quarteritis on even the biggest U.S. companies. A few days after I spoke with Kobayashi, however, that was spelled out for me by Jerry Cowan, a mustachioed Arkansas-born electronics engineer who had married a Japanese girl and established his own semiconductor sales company in Japan. "What the Japanese semiconductor manufacturers have done," Cowan explained, "is to automate as a way of achieving better quality. Because it reduces the percentage of defective chips you make, automation in the end reduces your production costs. But it also requires heavy initial investment and the U.S. manufacturers haven't been willing to make that kind of investment. Instead, they decided to have most of the final stage of chips production done by hand in low-wage places like Mexico or, more often, Southeast Asia. That's much cheaper in the short run, but because of human error it gives you a far higher defect rate—which means that in the long run it is actually more costly to make chips that way than in an automated plant."

With a pessimism that at that time found little echo in the United States, Cowan went on to point out that along with higher quality and lower costs, the Japanese had another card up their sleeves—faster product development. By the fall of 1980 when he and I spoke it was already clear that the 16K RAM chip was ultimately destined to be superseded by the 64K RAM chip, which instead of 16,000-odd pieces of information could store more than 65,000. In fact, Cowan noted, several Japanese manufacturers already had 64K RAMs in production. By contrast, only one U.S. company—Texas Instruments—was then producing them.

Inevitably, getting to market with large quantities of the new chips ahead of most of their American competitors won the Japanese semiconductor makers new business: by 1984, the year that sales of 64K RAMs hit their peak, Japanese factories were supplying about 60 percent of those purchased on the U.S. "merchant market."*

This, of course, was a major setback for American producers of

---

* The merchant market, in effect, is the number of chips sold for use by somebody other than their manufacturers. Use of the term arose because the total demand for semiconductors is not fully reflected by the number sold on the open market. In the United States, for example, both AT&T and IBM are major semiconductor producers but the bulk of their output goes into their own computers rather than being offered for sale.

memory chips—but the worst was yet to come. Treading hot on the heels of the 64K RAM came the 256K RAM, a chip able to accommodate more than 260,000 pieces of information. By June 1985 at least three Japanese companies were reportedly making 3 million to 4 million of these a month—and once again the only American firm producing in comparable quantity was Texas Instruments.

Since the 256K RAMs were at first vastly more expensive than the 64K RAMs, the logical assumption was that it would take time before semiconductor users switched to them en masse—time that the American chip makers could use to play catch-up. In fact, that might well have been the case had it not been for a massive error in judgment on the part of both Japanese and American manufacturers. Runaway sales of personal computers in 1983 convinced all semiconductor producers that this relatively new market for their wares was going to experience huge and rapid growth. Accordingly, they began churning out memory chips in unprecedented volume and the personal computer makers, anticipating a great speed-up in their operations, proceeded to assemble large semiconductor stockpiles.

The trouble was that everyone had misread the market. In 1985, a year when personal computer sales had been expected to double, they actually increased by less than a third. Predictably, the computer makers began to live off their inventory of memory chips and drastically reduced their purchases of new ones. And with that the price-cutting by chip makers desperate to dispose of their current production began: even the new 256K RAMs, which had been initially priced at about $45 apiece, fell to $3 or less.

For Japanese semiconductor manufacturers, this was a serious blow: it meant that they were losing money on every chip that they sold and that more customers than expected quickly switched to 256K RAMs, on which the manufacturers' loss was largest. All of the major Japanese producers, however, were divisions or subdivisions of huge diversified corporations that could cover their losses on semiconductors out of profits on everything from computers to VCRs. Thus armored—and unshaken in their conviction that market dominance ultimately pays off—they continued to manufacture and ship.

By contrast, some of the best-known U.S. suppliers of memory chips were purely and simply semiconductor manufacturers with no other profitable lines of business to tide them over. And even some diversified U.S. corporations that had the capability of underwriting large short-term losses on their semiconductor operations were deterred from doing so by concern for this year's bottom line and fear of an adverse impact on stock prices.

The upshot was that late 1985 saw a rash of plant closings and mass layoffs by American semiconductor companies. It also saw most of them abandon any plans to go into production of 256K RAMs—a state of affairs that left their Japanese competitors holding more than 90 percent of the U.S. merchant market for such chips. "The battle for the RAM memory market is over," proclaimed San Francisco securities analyst John Lazlo in mid-1985. "The Japanese have won."

In reality, the defeat suffered by the American semiconductor industry was not quite as cataclysmic as the pronouncements of its spokesmen or a casual reading of the U.S. media might have suggested. Loudly expressed fears that control of the merchant market for memory chips would give the Japanese a major technological advantage seemed exaggerated: both AT&T and IBM remained strong in the field and during 1985 both unveiled prototypes of a "megachip" capable of storing no less than a million pieces of information. Beyond that, random-access memory chips even in the peak sales year of 1984 accounted for only about one-eighth of the total market in semiconductors. And in logic chips, the microprocessors that carry out instructions and are the heart of a computer, American companies as of 1985 still held a large lead: 64 percent of the world market as opposed to 27 percent for their Japanese competitors.

Despite all these mitigating factors, however, there was no way of blinking the fact that Japanese industry had captured from American industry a market amounting to $3 billion worldwide in 1984 and had done so by following its standard strategy of making heavy initial investment and buying market share with low prices. All of which prompted John P. Stern, the top representative of the American Electronics Association in Tokyo, to ask in the spring of 1985: "Isn't it time for U.S. industry to think up measures to cope with that?"

The answer to John Stern's plaintive question is that measures to cope with the long-term strategies pursued by Japanese industry do not have to be invented from scratch. They already exist—and the American enterprises that have achieved sustained success in Japan have generally done so precisely because they were flexible enough to employ techniques that too many executives in the United States itself dismiss out of hand as impractical.

The adjustments in strategic approach required to compete on equal terms with Japanese firms in their home market have probably come easiest to American companies that have gone into joint ventures in Japan. The reason for this is that almost invariably the Japanese partner in such a venture will either rule out the short-term approach favored by most U.S. companies or at least insist that it be considerably moderated.

On occasion, in fact, American executives of a joint-venture company in Japan have been known to use the Japanese partner as a kind of stalking horse in their dealings with their U.S. parent. In a 1984 interview in the *Journal of Japanese Trade and Industry,* Loy Weston of Kentucky Fried Chicken commented: "When the home office wants you to do something dumb . . . you can tell them that your joint-venture partner doesn't like the idea—even though you've probably never even told your partner about it because he *would* think it was dumb. I've punched that ticket so often it looks like a lace curtain."

More often, however, if the joint venture offers enough advantages, the U.S. partner will consciously accede to the Japanese partner's insistence that long-term growth take precedence over short-term profit-taking. At Ajinomoto General Foods, for example, Director Kunihiko Fukuda told me: "When our joint venture was formed the partners agreed not to pursue short-term return. So for our first ten years we invested heavily in capital assets, training, and so forth—and paid no dividend at all." Similarly, when the Seibu organization and Allstate established SALIFE, they agreed upon a plan which assumed that it would take ten years before the enterprises broke even on a cumulative basis. (In the event, that goal was reached in nine years.)

In short, the most obvious way for a U.S. affiliate in Japan to counter the long-term strategy of its Japanese competitors is to adopt precisely the same strategy itself. When Haruo Okinobu of Yamatake-Honeywell so patiently explained market share strategy to me, he was not just generalizing; he was talking about the way he ran his own company. "We're prepared to wait longer for a payout than Honeywell in the U.S.," he said. "In the sixties and seventies, we went after market share; now [in the 1980s] we're going after profit."

As Okinobu's comment implies, it is obviously difficult for a purely American company operating under the censorious scrutiny of U.S. securities analysts who think that "long term" means "next year" to insulate a wholly owned subsidiary in Japan from short-term pressures. But contrary to the insistence of some U.S. businessmen, it is not impossible to do so even if you don't have a Japanese partner on whom to lay off the responsibility. "If you look at IBM or Coca-Cola—those American subsidiaries that have done well over a period of years—you'll see that they didn't come up with quick results," Yotaro Kobayashi of Fuji Xerox reminded me. Indeed, according to Coca-Cola's Weldon Johnson, his company had been in Japan "for ten to twelve years" before it began to make a profit. And Coca-Cola's patience was far from unique: five full years after Schick invaded Japan, its razor blades had captured less than 5 percent of the Japanese market while its major Japanese competitor still held close to 80 percent.

By no means have all American companies that have tried to establish themselves in Japan displayed such willingness to make a down payment on future prosperity by foregoing instant gratification. In recent years, however, the long-term approach has won some prestigious converts among U.S. firms with a long-standing Japanese presence. One such has been Eastman Kodak which in 1984 significantly restructured its operations in Japan and as of early 1985 was still engaged in a thoroughgoing review of its opportunities there. "I'm not under pressure to turn a bigger profit this year or next year," President Albert Sieg of Kodak Japan told me at that time. "I *am* under pressure to develop a strategy that looks as if it will improve our position here."

How fruitful such an approach can be has been amply demonstrated by the experience of Johnson & Johnson Japan. Though J&J products were first sold in Japan in the 1930s and the company has had a corporate presence of one kind or another there since 1961, it was only in 1979 that James Burke, chairman of the parent company, decided to make the Japanese market his top priority outside the United States. "He bought the idea that one has to wait longer for a payout here," Kneale Ashworth of J&J Japan told me six years later. "He said, 'I want growth in Japan.'

And, of course, when you have a growth strategy, you have to be a bit patient." But in J&J's case, it turned out, not excessively so: by 1985, the company's patience had been rewarded not only with growth but with what Ashworth happily described as "lots of money."

Rich as the ultimate rewards may be, however, the adoption of a growth strategy by an American subsidiary in Japan more often than not involves a certain amount of self-control and flexibility on the part of its parent company in the United States. "It is important," said Fuji Xerox's Kobayashi, "that it be made plain that changes of personnel at headquarters won't automatically bring changes of policy in Japan." This, in essence, can require giving the Japanese subsidiary a status different from that of the parent company's U.S. subsidiaries or divisions—a proposition that some U.S. chief executive officers find difficult to swallow. But there are also U.S. companies so pragmatic that they are prepared to give their Japanese subsidiaries a status not only different from that of their American divisions but different from that of their other overseas operations as well. This, for example, is true of Teledyne Japan. "This is not a profit center in the strict sense," Peter Katsuno of Teledyne Japan admitted to me. "In certain cases we are prepared to give up our own profit or to conduct business at a much lower level of profit in order to help our manufacturing divisions sell their products in this country."

Teledyne Japan, in other words, is above all a sales and marketing operation. And in establishing it as such, Teledyne has capitalized on a strength more common among U.S. companies than their Japanese rivals and one that a number of Americans doing business in Japan believe can sometimes nullify the classic Japanese business strategy. The addiction that Japanese companies have to buying market share, so the argument runs, tends to render them vulnerable in situations where, for one reason or another, that tactic is ineffective and more sophisticated techniques are required to win customers. When I asked Loctite's Robert Krieble how his company had managed to take business away from its Japanese competitors, his immediate reply was: "Marketing; they just aren't as good at marketing as we are." And when I put the same question to Warner-Lambert's Sam Maugeri I got a virtually identical answer: "We do a better job of marketing; that's essentially it."

Marketing, in fact, is a field in which, on at least one notable occasion, Japanese industry has demonstrated that it, too, can be afflicted by an inability to adapt quickly to new challenges. In this case the victims were Japan's pharmaceutical companies which had traditionally sold the vitamin pills that they manufactured through drugstores. Legally, however, vitamin pills are not classified as drugs by the Japanese government and in 1975 Shaklee Japan, a subsidiary of the San Francisco company of the same name, took advantage of that fact to begin peddling its vitamins direct to consumers by means of door-to-door salesmen. Fearful of alienating the distributors they relied on to handle their prescription drugs, the Japanese pharmaceutical companies hesitated to follow suit. The upshot was that, within a decade, Shaklee Japan had captured a major share of the vitamin pill market and boasted sales of vitamins and health foods amounting to more than $100 million a year.

As I noted in an earlier chapter, there are a fair number of American executives who believe that one of the prime benefits of doing business in Japan is learning lessons that make it easier to compete with the Japanese everywhere else in the world including the United States itself. Some of these lessons—the ones most frequently discussed in the U.S. media—involve essentially tactical matters such as inventory management and improvements in manufacturing technology. But potentially at least intelligent borrowing from the Japanese in the field of basic business strategies may offer even greater rewards.

The skeptics—and there are many of them—who argue that this particular kind of cross-cultural transfer simply is not practical would do well to study the recent history of Xerox Corporation. By the late 1970s, the Rochester, New York, giant had lost more than half the U.S. market for plain paper photocopiers—a market that it had originally created. Copiers made by companies such as Canon, Ricoh and Sharp were flooding into the United States and the Japanese advance seemed as irresistible as it had been earlier in consumer electronics. "We were horrified to discover that the Japanese were selling their small machines for what it cost us to make ours," Xerox chairman David T. Kearns recalled in an interview with the *New York Times* in late 1985.

Unlike U.S. steel and auto companies, however, Xerox refused to concede that it could not compete with the Japanese on equal terms. With the assistance of Fuji Xerox in Tokyo, it began to monitor the operations of its Japanese competitors in painstaking detail. While much of U.S. industry continued to scorn the Japanese reliance on "reverse engineering," Xerox openly adopted it and disassembled competitive copiers for piece-by-piece study—and when it discovered that the Japanese were making their machines better and cheaper by increased use of plastics it was not too proud to do likewise. It also adopted a number of other Japanese practices: it worked more closely with its suppliers, pushed to develop new products and get them to market more quickly than in the past and launched an all-out drive to reduce the number of defective components it produced.

Probably the single most important step Xerox took, however, was in the realm of long-term strategy: between 1980 and 1985 it spent nearly $100 million to automate its manufacturing and materials handling operations. By so doing, it managed in that same period to cut in half both the number of people that it employed in manufacturing and the cost of producing its copiers.

The result of all this is that at least where office photocopiers are concerned Xerox is once more very much back in contention. "We have come far enough," Kearns said in late 1985, "to know that we can continue to manufacture a substantial part of our machines in the United States and compete on a worldwide basis." And his view was supported by more disinterested parties such as Leonard A. Schlesinger, a onetime member of the Harvard Business School faculty who made a detailed study of the Xerox resurgence. "Xerox," said Schlesinger, "is one of the first American companies in an industry targeted by the Japanese to stem the inroads being made by Japanese companies."

For practitioners of "quarteritis," there might also be food for thought in another aspect of the Xerox experience. Though the misadventures of an insurance subsidiary caused Xerox to post an overall loss in the third quarter of 1985, its stock for most of that period traded at prices close to its fifty-two-week high. The apparent reason: the stock market attached less importance to Xerox's immediate financial troubles than it did to the significant upward trend visible in the company's profits on copiers and other information-processing devices.

12 Of Barriers and Bureaucrats

Not long ago a reporter for the *New York Times* came in to see me, sat himself down on that couch over there, flipped open his notebook and said: "Tell me about non-tariff barriers that Johnson & Johnson faces here in Japan." When I told him we didn't face any, he said: "I beg your pardon." So I said again: "We don't face any non-tariff barriers. We've got lots of problems but that isn't one of them." With that, he shut his notebook and got up to leave. I was a bit surprised and asked him: "Don't you want to hear the good news?" He said: "No, I just want to hear about non-tariff barriers"—and away he went.

—Kneale Ashworth,
January 1985

In his obsession with non-tariff barriers, the reporter who walked out on Kneale Ashworth reflected an assumption that has become an article of faith with a great many Americans. Whenever a particular sector of U.S. industry or agriculture is unable to sell its products in Japan—or to sell them in as great a quantity as it would like—it is a foregone conclusion that the cry of "unfair trade" will be raised. And if in response the Japanese point out that their tariff rate (2.8 percent in 1982) is actually lower than that prevailing in the United States (3.2 percent), their protestations are contemptuously brushed aside. For tariff rates, so the majority of American businessmen, bureaucrats and politicians believe, are no longer a meaningful issue in Japanese-American trade relations; the central problem as Japan's critics see it is that the Japanese government stubbornly continues to protect Japan's domestic industries through a seemingly inexhaustible array of non-tariff restrictions ranging from outright import quotas to arcane testing regulations artfully devised to exclude foreign products.

In reality, as I have argued earlier, this accusation is today largely erroneous and dangerously misleading. The fact that it is so widely credited in the United States, however, is understandable—and when Japanese officials, as they often do, react to it with a show of injured innocence they are being more than a little disingenuous. For in the 1960s and early 1970s when free trade was still an almost unchallenged pillar of U.S. economic policy, the Japanese government fought relentlessly to keep Japan's domestic market essentially the private preserve of Japanese industry and agriculture. By resorting to every protective device known to man, including high tariffs, Japan's leaders successfully created a kind of hothouse atmosphere in which one Japanese industry after another was able to attain world-class competitiveness with startling speed.

To recall this history, moreover, is not merely to rake up the dead past. For even though Japan can legitimately claim that its markets nowadays are just about as open as anyone else's, the aftereffects of past protectionism continue in many instances to haunt American companies with Japanese interests. Consider, for example, the case of Kodak which in the years immediately following World War II dominated the film market in Japan with products shipped in from the United States. To put an end to that situation, the Japanese government imposed tariffs of 20 percent and more on imported film and as a result, in the words of Kodak Japan president Albert Sieg, "our Japanese competition was basically able to buy the market." By 1985, to be sure, the tariff on film had been reduced to a bearable 5 percent, but by then the horse had been stolen. "What we live with today," Sieg told me, "is a residual of an unfair trade advantage. We are never going to be able to achieve the level in this market that we could have achieved if trade had been free all along."

In hindsight it is tempting to argue that Kodak might have forestalled the rise of Fuji Photo Film, its main Japanese competitor, by establishing its own film-manufacturing facilities in Japan. But even that tactic would not necessarily have prevented ultimate erosion of Kodak's dominance—or so at least the history of IBM Japan suggests.

In 1960, when IBM was still without serious rival in the field of computer technology, Japan's Ministry of Trade and Industry agreed to allow the company's Japanese subsidiary certain important rights only on condition that IBM disclose its computer patents to seven selected Japanese firms. Then for several years therafter, according to the testimony of former IBM Japan president Sanae Itagaki, the company "acceded to the [Japanese] government's demand to delay the manufacture of computers in Japan to enable the domestic makers to catch up." Given these and other forms of government assistance, it is scarcely surprising that in the early 1980s Fujitsu and NEC actually managed to outstrip IBM in computer sales in Japan and were beginning to offer it competition elsewhere in the world.

Inevitably, this kind of discrimination against foreign enterprise in the past still shapes the way in which many Americans perceive Japan's current trade policies. And despite the extensive dismantling of trade barriers that has occurred in Japan since the mid-1970s, the negative impressions created by earlier Japanese protectionism continue to be reinforced by awkward economic diplomacy. "The Japanese," James Abegglen told me flatly, "are foolishly tough negotiators when it comes to trade questions."

To be more precise, the Japanese have been, as I see it, dangerously ineffective in trade negotiations. Partly because it is so difficult and so time-consuming to achieve a consensus among the various Japanese government agencies and private interests involved in any trade questions, Japan's trade negotiators have fallen into a pattern of self-defeating behavior. On issue after issue ranging from beef and citrus fruit to metal baseball bats and telecommunication equipment they have initially dug in their heels and insisted that American demands were either unreasonable or impossible to meet. Then, as U.S. pressure continued and mounted in intensity, the need for action of some kind became apparent to all interested parties in Japan and concessions were made—often very substantial ones. By the time the concessions were offered, however, either American tempers had grown so frayed or so many new issues had moved to center stage that the Japanese got little or no credit for their action. Indeed, even when it turns out, as it did in the case of metal baseball bats, that the Americans have raised a tempest about a matter of no real commercial importance, it is a perception of Japanese intransigence rather than American mis-judgment that lingers in the public mind in the United States.

Besides contributing to inept diplomacy, the curiously decen-tralized nature of governmental and political power in Japan has other unfortunate consequences as well. For both historical and cultural reasons, the Japanese bureaucracy is even less responsive to the wishes of the nation's political leaders than its American counterpart. One result of this, as I noted earlier, is that policies announced in all good faith by the prime minister or senior mem-bers of his cabinet are not infrequently vitiated in practice by the on-the-spot decisions of relatively minor officials. Sometimes, as in the case of the customs officer who held up delivery of the Amer-ican Club's paddle-tennis rackets, this reflects the psychological legacy of years of protectionism. Often, however, it represents nothing more than bureaucratic pettifoggery. "Government offi-cials everywhere can be characterized as animals that are fond of feeding on red tape," former MITI vice-minister Naohiro Amaya once remarked to me. "It is my impression, though, that Japanese officials—especially lower-ranking ones—are more that way than others."

Whatever the reason for an obviously discriminatory bureau-cratic decision, a foreign enterprise that has been victimized in this way can sometimes get the action reversed by appealing to higher authority or to the Office of the Trade Ombudsman, an agency created by the Japanese government in 1982 specially for the pur-pose of settling such grievances. The Ombudsman's office, how-ever, still does not possess enough clout with other government agencies to be as effective as it ought to be. And not infrequently by the time an obviously unfair decision is reversed the commercial opportunity originally perceived by foreign suppliers has disap-peared or significantly diminished. In 1983, for example, Johnson & Johnson wanted to introduce to the Japanese market medical imaging devices that sold for up to $2 million apiece but was unable to do so because the Ministry of Health refused to accept foreign test data on medical machines. Some eighteen months later, as one of a series of measures designed to appease U.S. wrath over the trade balance, Prime Minister Yasuhiro Nakasone announced the reversal of that policy. By then, however, Japan's Toshiba had developed similar machines of its own.

Sometimes, too, the diffusion of power in Japan becomes so

systemic that it poses a virtually insurmountable problem for foreign enterprises. This, according to a senior MITI official of my acquaintance, proved to be the situation when J. C. Penney became interested in the possibility of opening stores in Japan. Though this idea encountered no opposition from the Japanese government, Penney executives reportedly abandoned it after they discovered that in any Japanese community the local merchants' association can veto the establishment of new stores above a certain size. This is a right that was originally granted the merchants' associations as a means of ensuring that Japan's own supermarket chains and discount stores would not drive too many of the country's myriad small shopkeepers out of business and thereby swell the unemployment rolls. The conscious purpose of endowing a private-interest group with such authority was not, in other words, to exclude foreign competition. Yet in the J. C. Penney case, at least, that appears to have been the practical effect. And there is an abundance of other political and economic constraints through which—sometimes by inadvertence but sometimes quite intentionally—foreign enterprises are still placed at a disadvantage in Japan.

From the point of view of a doctrinaire free trader, then, the behavior of the Japanese over most of the years since the end of the U.S. Occupation can be summed up by a paraphrase of the Anglican Prayer of General Confession: they did many things that they ought not to have done and left undone many things that they ought to have done. And even in the last decade Japan's trade policies, while no less liberal than those of most other industrial nations, have continued in a number of areas to be marred by vestigial protectionism.

Given these facts, it might seem reasonable to assume that the executives of American subsidiaries and affiliates in Japan—the people out on the firing line, so to speak—would be bubbling over with horror stories about the roadblocks put in their way by the Japanese government. In my experience, however, the noisiest outcries about "unfair" Japanese trade practices emanate from quite different sources: (1) American companies that display little or no interest in doing business in Japan but have lost market share here at home to Japanese competitors, and (2) U.S. companies whose efforts to break into the Japanese market have been ill-considered or relatively perfunctory—or both. And all too often the charges leveled against the Japanese by such companies remind me of an encounter that I had with an American businessman at the "Made in U.S.A." trade fair in Nagoya in early 1985. A manufacturer of log homes, this gentleman complained at length about his inability to extract from Japanese authorities information as to how potential customers in Japan could get building permits for his structures. After commiserating with him on that score, I asked what led him to believe there might be a market for log homes in Japan anyway. "Oh," he said, "I know the Finns and West Germans have sold them here." I reflected on that for a moment and then, out of what I suppose must be characterized as cowardice, decided not to inquire whether Finnish and German log homes could be erected in Japan without building permits.

If this had been an isolated case, it would be of no importance. But the reality is that a great many American complaints about Japan's non-tariff barriers actually reflect lack of enterprise or competitiveness on the part of the protesting company rather than any insuperable obstacles to its success raised by the Japanese government. Far more significant than this kind of scapegoating, in my view, is the fact that among the men who head U.S. ventures in Japan these days there is little disposition to indulge in blanket denunciation of the way the Japanese authorities treat American companies or their affiliates. Indeed, in 1983 when the Study Group on Direct Foreign Investment in Japan asked 285 foreign affiliates there to rank their five biggest problems, government regulation and interference came next to last on the list, just barely ahead of the problem of communication with parent companies abroad.

In part, the relative equanimity with which the managers of U.S. affiliates in Japan regard the Japanese government reflects a resigned awareness that businessmen everywhere—emphatically including Japanese businessmen in the United States—have to live with pervasive and often unfairly restrictive government regulation. "I sometimes think Japan is overcriticized for trade barriers," Nike Japan's Gary Kurtz said to me. "I don't notice a whole bunch of problems here that aren't common in America."

Beyond that, executives who have served with American ventures in Japan over a substantial period of time are keenly aware that Japan is one of the few countries in the world that have offered foreign enterprise more rather than less access to their markets in the last few years. "Ten years ago," Kneale Ashworth told me, "I would have said that licensing and other regulatory devices were used as non-tariff barriers here. But regulatory difficulties have diminished greatly since then. At the highest levels, people are making a big effort to cut red tape."

Even in cases where government regulations do create difficulties for them, moreover, American executives working in Japan often decline to cry "foul." When I quizzed Victor Harris of Max Factor Japan on the subject, he said: "There's only one area in which we have a problem with Japanese government regulations. There are a number of preservatives and colors that we can use in the United States that we aren't allowed to use here. In such cases, we have to reformulate—and sometimes reformulation isn't possible because that particular ingredient is what makes the product work. But I don't think even that specially penalizes foreign companies. We don't run up against any non-tariff barriers per se."

To my surprise, in view of what I had read in the American media about Japanese discrimination against foreign pharmaceutical products, President Sam Maugeri of Warner-Lambert Japan took essentially the same position as Victor Harris. "So far as we're concerned," he said, "if you're talking about non-tariff barriers, they would have to be in the pharmaceutical area. It's extremely complex and a great many tests have to be repeated here because the Japanese won't accept clinical data from abroad. That's because the Ministry of Health takes the stand that Japanese are different from Westerners in terms of size and that there may be other differences as well—possibly in the metabolic yield of products, for example."

Maugeri hesitated for a moment and then went on: "But, you know, that's not an unreasonable position in my opinion—especially from a dosage standpoint. Japanese *are* smaller and you might almost expect a 10 to 15 percent reduction in dosage right off the bat. Besides, certain products aren't tolerated as well by Orientals as by Westerners; aspirin, for example, has a high incidence of side effects among Japanese. Maybe the Ministry of Health goes overboard; maybe it should say: 'You have to do at least confirmatory studies in Japan with Japanese subjects, but we'll accept the overall safety data developed in the U.S.' Still, it's not a bad policy as it stands. And in general, so far as government regulations go, I'd say foreign companies are now treated no differently than local companies."

By no means every chief executive officer of U.S. ventures in Japan will concede that he enjoys the "level playing field" that protectionist U.S. politicians piously insist is all they ask of Japanese trade policy. But a surprising number do—and, where our protectionist politicians frequently resort to the "fairness" ploy when their actual purpose is to obtain special advantages for U.S. enterprise, a level playing field genuinely is all that most American firms with extensive operations in Japan feel entitled to expect. As a rule, too, the executives of such companies are careful to be sure of their ground before raising complaints of inequitable treatment by the Japanese authorities. Like many American businessmen in Tokyo, Sam Maugeri is distressed by what he calls "insufficient transparency" in Japan's governmental processes. "Everything is done behind closed doors," he said. "Then, all of a sudden, you get a decision handed down." Even in the case of this thoroughly legitimate grievance, however, Maugeri was quick to add: "Of course, that's a problem for Japanese companies, too."

By the same token, many executives of U.S. companies in Japan find it both unrealistic and unreasonable to argue—as American government officials and academics sometimes do—that certain basic aspects of Japanese culture and economic life should be modified to suit American convenience. When a U.S. manufacturer of telecommunications equipment expressed outrage that Nippon Telegraph and Telephone had declined to accept a proposal because its specifications were not in the metric system, little sympathy was expressed in the American business community in Tokyo. "After all," said an executive of another U.S. telecommunications firm, "NTT wouldn't accept a proposal with non-metric specs from a Japanese firm either." And I encountered a similar reaction when I raised a proposition that has grown increasingly popular with many U.S. critics of Japanese trade policy—namely that the complex and inefficient Japanese distribution system in itself constitutes a non-tariff barrier against U.S. products. "Distribution here is an enormous difficulty," conceded Johnson & Johnson's Kneale Ashworth. "But I just don't see it as a non-tariff barrier. You have to remember that the president of Lion, our major Japanese competitor, says the same things about his wholesalers that I say about ours."

Given the fact that they are peculiarly vulnerable to the actions of the Japanese government, it might seem strange that managers of American subsidiaries and joint ventures in Japan are in general less critical of Japanese trade and economic policies than many businessmen and officials back in the United States. There is, however, an obvious explanation for that: the U.S. affiliates that have survived and prospered in Japan have done so in part precisely because over the years they have developed techniques for dealing successfully with Japan's economic bureaucracy.

These techniques, of course, vary from industry to industry and from company to company. But a very basic one which cuts across industry lines involves the adoption of a creative rather than defeatist approach to government regulations. Not infrequently, U.S. ventures in Japan have been able to achieve their goals by scrupulously adhering to the letter of a regulation while ignoring its intent. In the early 1960s, for example, many U.S. firms declined to go into business in Japan out of unwillingness to accept a Japanese partner. As I noted in an earlier chapter, however, Johnson & Johnson in 1961 managed to launch a venture without Japanese participation by interpreting the phrase "local partner" to cover a British-owned trading company domiciled in Japan. And more recently, as we have also seen, Seibu and Allstate in their joint insurance ventures have found a way to use essentially the same sales organization for both life and casualty insurance without violating a Ministry of Finance regulation that prohibits the issuance of both these forms of insurance by a single company.

Circumvention of irksome restrictions, moreover, is not the only form of creativity U.S. firms in Japan have displayed where government regulations are concerned; on occasion, differences in U.S. and Japanese regulatory practices have created major opportunities for American businesses alert enough to spot them. It is highly doubtful, for example, that the American Family Life Assurance Company could have grown in Japan with such extraordinary speed if, as it does in the United States, it had relied primarily on individual agents to sell its cancer insurance policies. What really put American Family over the top in Japan was its decision to sell initially chiefly through so-called corporate agencies—the subsidiaries that many big Japanese companies establish to handle fringe benefits for their employees.

Under this arrangement, the corporate agency for a particular company actually serves as an agent for American Family. It lines up twenty or more customers for cancer insurance among the employees of its parent company, sells them the insurance at a group rate and arranges for their premiums to be met through payroll deductions. In the United States, so I was told by Yoshiki Otake, a top executive of the Japanese branch of American Family, such activity would be regarded as involving a conflict of interest on the part of the employer and as a result it would be illegal. Under Japanese law, however, it is perfectly permissible—and as of 1985 policies sold by corporate agencies accounted for 90 percent of all the cancer insurance American Family had written in Japan.

Important as skillful navigation through Japanese's regulatory maze is, however, success in dealing with the Japanese government has one thing in common with success in private dealings in Japan: establishing mutual trust and a sense of shared interests is a more effective tool than any legal stratagem, however shrewd. In recognition of that, a number of U.S. subsidiaries and affiliates in Japan have made a point of demonstrating their determination to be good corporate citizens of Japan. Thus, in discussions with the Ministry of Finance, Seibu Allstate Life Insurance discovered that ministry officials were increasingly concerned by the fact that insurance in Japan was chiefly sold by relatively inexpert female agents, often widows or housewives working part-time. By launching a program to train highly professional male agents, the company not only served its own interest but won brownie points with its regulators.

In somewhat more indirect fashion, Coca-Cola Japan has also succeeded in combining self-interest and good citizenship. In certain areas of Japan *mikan*, or tangerines, are an important cash crop, but in Coca-Cola's early years in the country Japanese growers were producing *mikan* in quantities far larger than the market could absorb. Using technology developed by its Minute Maid subsidiary in the United States, Coca-Cola helped farmers' cooperatives to produce higher-grade tangerine juice and began to market it. Today, Coca-Cola Japan is the largest commercial user of locally produced fruit juices and, as a result, is persona grata with the country's politically potent farm lobby.

Such efforts, to be sure, have not always won over Japanese officialdom—especially where what appears to be a critical Japanese economic interest is at stake. Despite its thoroughgoing efforts to "Japanize" itself and the numerous concessions it has made to Japanese interests, IBM Japan has remained in an ambivalent status so far as the Japanese government is concerned. "Sometimes they say we're a Japanese company, but sometimes they still say we're a U.S. company," a senior executive of IBM Japan told me in mid-1982. "It seems to depend on their convenience and what the issue is."

In other cases, however, persistence in wooing Japanese officialdom has paid off handsomely—even in fields such as the petroleum industry where the Japanese government actively sought to restrict foreign participation. Here an outstanding example is Exxon, which has both a wholly owned marketing subsidiary and joint-venture marketing and refining companies in Japan. Speaking at the Japan Society of New York in March 1984, Masamoto Yashiro, executive vice-president of Esso Eastern, remarked: "The turning point for us came during the oil crisis of 1973. At that time, the Ministry of International Trade and Industry was especially eager to hear Exxon's views on the world energy outlook. Exxon, in turn, was open, forthcoming—and above all objective—in the analysis we provided the government. As a result of our increased credibility in the eyes of MITI, our standing in government circles has grown greatly and our views are taken more seriously than before. As evidence of this new relationship, in 1975 I was the first representative of a firm to be named to a MITI-sponsored industrial policy committee—the Petroleum Deliberation Council. And Exxon representatives have since participated in various other private industry councils, further proof that American companies can exert effective influence even in government circles."

The experiences cited by Exxon's Yashiro almost inevitably raise a key question: By what means *can* American business most effectively make its influence felt and its voice heard in Japanese governmental circles?

When they are confronted with that question in concrete terms, the instinctive response of many American businessmen, particularly those with little experience in Japan, is to holler for help from Washington. And there is no question but that over a period of time pressure brought to bear upon the government of Japan by the government of the United States often achieves a great deal. By hammering away year after year at the Japanese over their restrictive quotas on beef and citrus fruit imports, for example, U.S. trade negotiators gradually extracted enough enlargement of those quotas so that the issue has now been largely defused. More recently, persistent protests from U.S. officials finally elicited from the Japanese an offer to abandon regulations that in effect froze U.S.–made car telephones, telephone pagers, two-way radios and portable computers out of the Japanese market. And in the dying days of 1985 continuing U.S. insistence that Japan must open up its capital markets produced another Japanese volte-face. Until then no foreign securities firm had ever held a seat on the Tokyo Stock Exchange and in late 1984 when Merrill Lynch tried to buy the only seat to come up for sale in a long time, it was outbid—from sheer economic xenophobia, some charged—by a Japanese firm. Less than twelve months later, however, the Tokyo Stock Exchange increased its membership from eighty-three to ninety-three seats and earmarked six of them for selected British and American firms, of which one, appropriately enough, was Merrill Lynch.

As I intimated earlier in this chapter, pressure from Washington tends to be particularly effective in dealing with the diffusion of political power in Japan. Though rivalry between governmental agencies is a familiar enough phenomenon in the United States, it pales alongside that which is endemic in Tokyo where the inevitable battles over turf are rendered even more bitter by the resentment that more plebian ministries cherish toward elite institutions such as MITI, the Finance Ministry and the Foreign Ministry, which recruit their officials from the top graduates of the top universities. The absurd proportions which such feuding can attain was most forcefully driven home to me one morning early in 1985 when I remarked to a friend at MITI that he looked very tired. "I am," he replied. "I was up all night trying to get the Ministry of Post and Telecommunications to talk to us." Upon further inquiry, I discovered that in a fit of bureaucratic pique all officials of Post and Telecommunications had quite literally started refusing to accept any phone calls from their colleagues at MITI and that it had taken the personal intervention of a senior cabinet minister to restore communications.

Where this kind of intramural feuding or even a substantive disagreement between its various arms hamstrings the Japanese governmental machine, the weight of the American government can on occasion tip the balance. In the matter of mobile telephones and radio gear, for instance, the Foreign Ministry was able to overcome the intransigence of the Post and Telecommunications Ministry by invoking the specter of American retaliation against Japanese telephone equipment. And by stressing the fact that it had become a serious political issue with the United States, the Finance Ministry was able to chivy the clubby Tokyo Stock Exchange not only into creating new seats but into reserving more of them for foreign firms than the exchange's governors had originally wanted to do.

For U.S. enterprises in Japan, however, invoking the assistance of the U.S. government carries a bit of the same downside risk that calling in close air support does for an embattled infantry unit: you can never be totally sure in advance where the "friendly" ordnance is going to hit or whom it is going to hurt worst. On occasion, in fact, U.S. trade negotiators have actually done a disservice to groups that they were trying to help. This, to judge from the comments of John Stern, the director of the American Electronics Association's Tokyo office, was the upshot when the Nakasone government was induced to bring pressure on Japanese companies to buy U.S.–made semiconductors rather than readily available, high-quality Japanese chips. The psychological impact of that action, Stern suggested unhappily, was not unlike one sometimes created by affirmative action hiring programs in the United States. "It creates the impression that our chips aren't very good," he told a *Fortune* magazine reporter.

More often yet, U.S. negotiators are too indiscriminate in their protests to the Japanese: they weaken their credibility in important matters where they have a legitimate grievance such as impediments to exports of U.S. forest products to Japan by putting undue weight on trivial issues such as testing standards for metal baseball bats—a product which cannot conceivably have significant impact on the overall trade balance. And much too frequently U.S. government complaints to the Japanese are quite simply hypocritical. Thus, at the very time when American representatives were raising the loudest uproar over Japanese import quotas on citrus fruit and beef, no fewer than forty-four U.S. state governments had adopted "agricultural restrictions" that barred imports of Japanese tangerines, and federal regulations limited U.S. beef imports to 8 percent of domestic consumption. (By contrast, the Japanese were then importing 30 percent of the beef they consumed.)

Not surprisingly, these and even more egregious instances of a "do as I say not as I do" approach on the part of the U.S. government are perceived by the Japanese as naked power plays rather than a reflection of any genuine dedication to free trade and that in turn tends to impel Japanese officialdom to drag its feet. Understandably, too, the reaction is much the same when American spokesmen demand controversial changes in the way the Japanese conduct their own affairs—as they did, for example, when they blithely urged that the Japanese government abolish all its standards relating to voice clarity in telephone transmissions on the grounds that consumers could decide for themselves whether a particular piece of telephone equipment performed adequately or not. And to compound their sins, U.S. trade negotiators often unveil such proposals for the first time with a blaze of publicity, having neglected to lay any groundwork for them beforehand in private discussions with Japanese officials. Here again, the result can actually be to delay achievement of the goal the United States seeks, since the failure to engage in *nemawashi,* the consensus-building process so central to Japanese culture, alarms Japanese officials and almost guarantees that their initial reaction will be negative.

For all these reasons, U.S. government efforts to assist American business in Japan are, as I have already suggested, a mixed blessing. Overall, probably the most balanced assessment of them I have heard—and one that is clearly shared by many American businessmen in Japan—was pronounced by that notably cosmopolitan Japanese, former MITI vice-director Naohiro Amaya. "In my personal opinion," Amaya said, "it's a good thing that the Americans continually insist that there's so much red tape here that must be removed. Without that kind of pressure the red tape would persist." But then, smiling at the neatness of the allusion he was about to make, he added: "At the same time, American businessmen who want to develop markets here must remember that, as Benjamin Franklin said, Heaven helps those who help themselves."

Happily, in their dealings with the Japanese government, American subsidiaries and affiliates in Japan are doing more to help themselves all the time. To be more specific, they are gradually escaping the role of unmitigated outsiders and to some extent are becoming a part of the governmental process in Japan.

One important element in this evolution has been the great weight that many U.S. ventures and affiliates have placed on the recruitment of outstanding Japanese executives. In a few cases, American companies have emulated a practice widespread among Japanese firms by capitalizing on "the descent from heaven"—the phrase commonly used in Japan to describe what occurs when a bureaucrat retires from the civil service in middle or late middle age and joins a private corporation. There are, for example, ex-government officials in the managerial ranks of American Family Life Assurance Company and, in the most notable instance that I am aware of, Texas Instruments Japan is headed by Hideo Yoshizaki, a onetime top MITI official who, among many other achievements, reportedly invented the phrase "non-tariff barriers" while serving as a Japanese representative at GATT (General Agreement on Tariffs and Trade) negotiations in Geneva.

Generally, however, retiring bureaucrats of senior rank prefer Japanese corporations to those with foreign owners and have little trouble in gratifying that preference. Accordingly, in their attempts to build personal ties inside the bureaucracy, American subsidiaries or joint-venture companies most often rely on recruiting new graduates of top universities whose college friends and classmates will be the senior civil servants of the future. This, of course, is a process which inevitably is slow to bear fruit, but a number of U.S. ventures in Japan have now been established there long enough that such efforts have begun to pay off for them. Indeed, Masamoto Yashiro of Exxon (which first began operations in Japan in 1949) credits his company's current influence in Japanese government circles not just to its handling of the 1973 oil crisis but also to its active university recruitment policy. "Over the years," he said in 1984, "these efforts have been successful and our contacts with the bureaucracy have grown considerably."

Still another way in which American subsidiaries and affiliates in Japan have succeeded in winning greater attention in Japanese government circles is by becoming more effective in making common cause with each other—by becoming, in a sense, an increasingly potent lobby inside Japan itself. In this respect, their primary instrument has been the American Chamber of Commerce in Japan, an organization whose influence and effectiveness have markedly increased over the years. In part, this is attributable simply to the growing size of the American economic presence in Japan; between 1980 and 1985 alone, the number of companies belonging to the ACCJ jumped from 485 to 585. But in part, the ACCJ's growing clout stems from heightened sophistication and greater flexibility in dealing with the Japanese government.

Perhaps the two most notable demonstrations of the ACCJ's potential recently have been in the field of information technology. The stage was set for the first of these in 1984 when MITI, in a lamentable reversion to its old protectionist habits, urged that the Japanese government adopt a new law governing copyrights on computer software. Essentially the proposed legislation would have required that any company doing business in Japan must license its proprietary software for use by Japanese companies at a price established by MITI whenever MITI deemed that this was "in the national interest." What's more, in the process of registering its software in Japan, a company would have to disclose full details concerning its construction to the Japanese government—a requirement unparalleled anywhere else in the world.

For the American computer industry, this would have been a devastating blow. Since software as of the mid-1980s was a field in which U.S. technology was still superior to Japanese technology, the net effect of MITI's proposal could have been to vitiate an important American competitive advantage. Beyond that, as President Herbert Hayde of Burroughs Japan explained to me, the margin of profit in the computer business nowadays comes primarily from software and service rather than from hardware—so that, besides threatening their competitiveness, MITI was also posing a potential threat to the ability of American computer makers to finance their future.

Soon after this potential thundercloud appeared on the horizon, the ACCJ asked the stocky, hard-driving Hayde to enlist as many of its members as possible in a High Technology Committee. Hayde plunged into the task with his customary energy and by early 1985 there were 100 companies represented on the High Technology Committee—thirty of which, including such titans as AT&T, ITT and General Electric, constituted a subcommittee on computers and technology. Keeping up a relentless and noisy drumfire of protest, the High Technology Committee took its case against

MITI's attempted software grab to the press, to Washington and to everyone in the Japanese government who would listen. And in dealing with the Japanese, the committee made a point of not confining itself to the traditional "representations at the highest level." "In situations like this," Hayde explained, "the cabinet minister isn't really the guy you want to get to; you want to get to the people who develop positions, the advisory groups that create these ideas in the first place. In the software case, for example, the names of the people credited with writing the legislation took up two full pages of paper."

In the end, all this uproar together with the protests from the U.S. government that the ACCJ was able to generate obliged MITI to abandon its plans to introduce the software copyright law into the Japanese parliament in 1985. "They still want to do it," Hayde told me in March of that year, "and I expect it will come back again in some other form sooner or later, but we're watching them." And in another somewhat similar situation, the ACCJ's lobbying efforts contributed to an even more clear-cut victory. In what Hayde described as "an obvious attempt to lock us out of the market," the Japanese government at one point proposed to limit to less than 20 percent the participation of any foreign firm in the establishment of the advanced telecommunications systems known as VANs (Value Added Networks). In the face of a campaign orchestrated by the High Technology Committee, however, Tokyo ultimately did an about-face and removed any limit on foreign participation with the result that major American firms have now embarked on joint ventures in the VAN field in Japan.

In achieving these victories, the ACCJ shrewdly used a variety of tactics, playing hardball on some occasions and being the soul of reasonableness on others. In one instance when the Japanese stalled for months about making copies of proposed ordinances available to the ACCJ, Hayde bluntly informed the cabinet minister involved that no U.S. businessman would testify before any Japanese government hearing on the matter until the ordinances were forthcoming. "They want us to testify so that they can say 'I guess this means it's okay with the American business community,'" he said. "But it's not okay and we're not going to comment until we know what we're commenting on."

Hayde sang a completely different tune, however, when, in his capacity as president of the ACCJ for 1985, he was appointed to a private citizens' council that the Japanese government had established to advise an interministerial economic committee. There was, he conceded, a distinct possibility that his appointment could prove a "sham"—a sop designed to placate the Americans without giving them any substantive role in the council's deliberations. Nonetheless, he told me, he was going to work hard at the job. "I'm hopeful it can develop into another channel we can make use of," he said. "The respect of these people is something you have to earn. There's no sense to bringing up a whole host of complaints and meaningless crap. But I think that if we are very specific and find appropriate ways to express our views on really important bilateral trade issues, we'll gain points."

That Hayde's approach will ultimately prove the right one seems highly probable. Advisory councils and committees whose members are drawn from the private sector play an extremely important role in shaping Japanese economic legislation and regulations and as of late 1985 Americans had already been named to serve on several such committees. If the Americans capitalize on these opportunities intelligently and the trend toward American participation in quasi-governmental deliberations grows, it could, as Hayde suggests, open up important new channels of influence for U.S. business in Japan. And, at worst, the growing involvement of Americans on the scene in Japan's internal decision-making processes can serve as an early-warning system that will help to ensure that in the future the pressures which Washington brings to bear upon Tokyo are more intelligently focused and soundly based.

13 Strictly Private

From time to time on the commuter train that conveys me from exurbia into Manhattan I share a seat with an amiable gentleman in his early sixties whom I take to be a senior corporate executive. Precisely what his business is I don't know because we have never actually introduced ourselves and by silent mutual agreement refrain from inquiring about each other's personal affairs. We do, however, quite frequently exchange opinions on the state of the world inspired by something reported in the morning's *New York Times* and on one such occasion my seatmate looked up from his paper to remark: "You know, just about every day there's an article in here quoting some economist or other who says that unless we follow his particular prescription the country is headed for hell in a handbasket. I suppose that ought to worry me, but whenever I read one of these pieces it reminds me that back when Reagan was first elected the same guys were saying that he was going to wreck the economy—and what we've wound up with is the lowest inflation rate in years, more people employed than ever before and a boom in the stock market. And then I have to ask myself: if all the economic gurus were wrong then, why should I believe them now?"

My immediate reaction to that question was to take refuge in the conventional irony that, after all, nobody is perfect. And even upon considered reflection, I have been unable to come up with any more convincing defense of macroeconomic forecasting. The high degree of prestige and generous material rewards frequently enjoyed by economists are conferred upon them primarily because of a widespread assumption that their predictions are scientifically grounded and hence possess some special validity. But the reality is that the future performance of any economy depends upon so many inherently unpredictable variables—social, political and technological as well as purely economic—that the production of a reasonably accurate macroeconomic forecast is almost invariably a matter of good luck rather than good judgment.

That, of course, is a proposition that will strike many people as highly exaggerated if not downright nonsensical. Yet anyone who proclaims the efficacy of economic prediction must somehow come to terms with what happened during the oil crisis of the early 1970s. Then the conventional wisdom was that the international financial system was threatened with imminent breakdown because of massive transfers of capital to the OPEC nations caused by sudden staggering increases in crude oil prices. Convinced that disaster was just around the corner, economists proceeded to propose a variety of complex remedies, none of which was ever adopted, to avert a catastrophe that never occurred.

No less instructive, in my opinion, is an even earlier bit of history. In late 1985, under the derisive heading "Famous Last Words," the New York Times published excerpts from some newly declassified U.S. government documents dating back to the presidency of Dwight Eisenhower. One of these, drawn from the minutes of a cabinet meeting in August 1954, read as follows: "Secretary [of State John Foster] Dulles introduced lengthy consideration of the need for negotiating international trade agreements favoring Japan. He indicated that there was little future for Japanese products in the United States and that the solution lay in developing markets for Japan in presently underdeveloped areas such as Southeast Asia."

Now John Foster Dulles, to be sure, was no economist. There were, however, plenty of economists practicing their art in August 1954 and, so far as I can discover, none of them was any more prescient than Mr. Dulles in anticipating Japan's ultimate emergence as a major competitor in the American market.

I cite these failures in foresight not out of any ill will toward economists, whose predictive record is little if any worse than that of most social scientists. Rather, my intention is to sound a cautionary note concerning proposals to cure the U.S. trade deficit by radical new departures such as the creation of institutions designed to enhance the government's power to influence industrial and commercial decisions in this country. It is, I suspect, quite likely that a decade hence such proposals will turn out to be just as irrelevant as some of those advanced in the 1970s for dealing with "the petrodollar problem." I wouldn't be surprised either if, a generation from now, our present concerns over the trade deficit will appear quite as myopic to our children as those that John Foster Dulles expressed about Japan's limited export potential now look to us. To be more specific, I think it entirely possible that in due course the United States will once again find itself running a comfortable surplus in its international trade—and that this turnabout, if it occurs, will be the result not of governmental planning or guidance but of the interplay of politics, technology and market forces in ways that we cannot now foresee with any certainty.

Clearly, however, that is far from an assured prospect and at best is unlikely to materialize for some time to come. Meanwhile, there is one aspect of this country's international commerce that poses such grave urgent risks that it would be flirting with disaster to ignore it in the Micawber-like belief that something will turn up. In its economic dealings with Japan the United States must achieve a more satisfactory position and must do so relatively quickly—not so much for purely economic reasons as for political and geopolitical ones.

Economically, as I noted at the beginning of this book, Japan is only one of our problems: in 1984, for example, the elimination of our trade deficits with Canada, Taiwan and Korea—deficits which totaled more than $34 billion—would have achieved just about the same effect in dollar terms as the elimination of our $37 billion deficit with Japan. But in terms of U.S. politics it is Japan which has been cast in the villain's role and unless that perception can be altered it seems virtually inevitable that protectionist reprisals against Japan by the United States will increase both in number and in their impact on the Japanese economy.

To more and more Americans nowadays, of course, excluding or limiting sales of certain Japanese products in the United States seems a perfectly legitimate assertion of self-interest. But the truth is that, except in the most shortsighted view, such action would actually run counter to our self-interest—and not merely because it would force American consumers to pay billions of dollars more for the goods that they purchase each year. Far more disturbing, in my view, is the potential threat that this kind of economic assault on Japan would pose to our own national security.

For many years now the Japanese and American governments
have hewed to a mutually rewarding bargain with each other. Under
the terms of that bargain, Japan gives us an indispensable strategic
foothold in East Asia and in return is promised U.S. military protection if it should be attacked. Very nearly as important to the Japanese as the overt security guarantee, however, is the expectation
that the United States will continue to play the leading role in maintenance of an international economic system that enables Japan to
prosper despite its extremely limited natural resources. Almost inevitably, any major American resort to protectionism would render
the Japanese somewhat less confident of the wisdom of their national bargain with the United States. And if American protectionism were carried far enough to work significant economic hardships
on Japan, the stability of the present Japanese political establishment—and ultimately of Japanese democracy itself—could be en-
dangered.

These are risks of which relatively few people in the United
States appear to be aware. The prevailing American view, I believe,
continues to be the one that a group of U.S. senators privately
expressed to one of modern Japan's most impressive statesmen,
the late Nobuhiko Ushiba, back in 1977. "Remember, Mr. Minister," one of them said, "the United States doesn't need Japan, but
you do need us."

For better or for worse, however, the United States *does* need
Japan. More precisely, perhaps, it cannot afford to pay the price of
seriously alienating Japan. In strictly economic terms, the Pacific
Basin is rapidly becoming the most important area of the world so
far as the United States is concerned—already, in fact, our trade
with the Pacific nations exceeds that which we do with the nations
of Western Europe—and in the Pacific Basin Japan plays a pivotal
strategic and economic role. The emergence of a Japan inimical to
the United States or even merely indifferent to American concerns
would greatly diminish our power to influence events in that re-
gion. And that would not only damage American interests, it would
dangerously alter the balance of power in the entire world.

Among Americans who concern themselves with Asian affairs,
there is an influential handful that has begun to be concerned by
this possibility. At an off-the-record meeting of "Japan experts"
that I attended in late 1984, an ex-diplomat with extensive experience in the Far East declared: "Over the years we have played a

game of brinksmanship with Japan and this is becoming increasingly risky. Given the Japanese character, it is not impossible that one day the rubber band will snap—and not our way but the other way. . . . It's important to remember that Nakasone is basically an opportunist inclined toward a kind of Japanese Gaullism." And, to my surprise, a member of the Reagan Administration who was present endorsed this view, warning that it was not safe to assume that the Soviet Union, which has traditionally treated Japan with contempt, can necessarily be relied on to persist in that stupidity. "Ultimately," he said, "the Japanese could decide that their real road to security lies in negotiations with Russia."

This, however, is still very much a minority view. Among the people who shape U.S. policy toward Japan the prevailing attitude is still that expressed to me by an Asian specialist in the State Department in the early 1980s. "The Japanese aren't going to turn against us because they have nowhere else to go," he said confidently. "China and Russia don't offer the kind of markets Japan needs to maintain its high level of economic development and the Japanese are too vulnerable in terms of both resources and geography to play the Gaullist game seriously."

Those are almost incontrovertible arguments—provided one assumes that nations can be expected to act rationally. It was not, however, rational for the Japanese to attack the United States in 1941. Nonetheless, they did so, essentially because they had concluded that there was no other way in which they could shake Franklin Roosevelt's determination to end their imperialistic adventure in China through economic pressure.

Here I must emphasize that I in no way mean to imply that adoption of any of the protectionist measures so far proposed in the United States could lead to a replay of the Pacific war. But protectionism resembles drug abuse in one respect: as time goes by, larger and larger doses are required to achieve the desired effect. That, I believe, is one of the lessons to be learned from the history of the 1930s; another is that when great nations resort to "beggar thy neighbor" trading policies, the inevitable result is a contraction of the whole world economy—which, in turn, creates fertile soil for the growth of political extremism and international conflict. And in the nuclear age no country, however powerful, can afford to take that kind of gamble.

For all these reasons, I believe it is imperative that the present

American drift toward the adoption of protectionist policies against Japan be halted as soon as possible. And it seems equally clear to me that, realistically speaking, this goal can only be achieved if the American public is presented with what it regards as convincing evidence that the United States has turned the tide in its economic dealings with Japan and that in the future the profit from such dealings will be more equitably divided between the two countries.

To convince the majority of Americans that such a turnabout has actually occurred will, I suspect, require at least some degree of change in the public's perception of what is truly important in the economic relationships between countries. There is, however, no blinking the fact that it will also require change in the realities of the situation: there must be measurable increases in the amount of money that U.S. business earns in Japan and less rapid growth in Japanese exports to the United States.

So far as I can see, there is no insuperable reason why these objectives should not be accomplished without resort to protectionism on the part of the United States. To be sure, they could be accomplished more quickly and completely given certain changes in policy by the American and Japanese governments—and, as I noted in an earlier chapter, some of the policy changes that would be most useful are not likely to be made soon, if they are made at all. It is my conviction, however, that even without any dramatic new departures in governmental policies, American private enterprise can, in the years immediately ahead, significantly increase the profits it derives from doing business in Japan and thereby serve not only its own interests but the national interests of the United States.

When I suggest that U.S. business can make a major contribution to improving our national economic position vis-à-vis Japan—and can do so without any major new forms of assistance from Washington—I am, of course, making certain assumptions. One of these is that U.S. trade negotiators will continue to press hard for freer access for U.S. goods in fields where Japan still does engage in overt or disguised protectionism and where American industry has a reasonable prospect of being able to compete successfully in the Japanese market. A corollary to this is the assumption that, however grudgingly, Japan will make substantial concessions to such pressures where they are soundly based and rationally presented. This I believe to be an odds-on probability not only because it would be consistent with the way the Japanese government has behaved for some years past but also because, as a Japanese diplomat of my acquaintance told me in late 1985: "There's no one of any stature in my country who doesn't dread the possibility of our getting into an economic shootout with the United States."

My third assumption—which I make somewhat more hesitantly—is that in the foreseeable future the Japanese yen will never again be allowed to rise to the absurdly overvalued level of 261 to the dollar that it hit in March 1985 and that, as a result, the United States will enjoy better terms of trade with Japan.

This admittedly is not a prediction that can be made with absolute certainty, partly because of the unpredictability of U.S. and Japanese government policies on this score. The exchange rate that obtains as I write this—about 170 yen to the dollar—is in considerable measure the result of the intervention in the currency markets undertaken by both the American and Japanese governments beginning in September 1985. With total of $100 billion to $150 billion sloshing through world currency markets on any given day, it is questionable whether governments, which have nothing like such sums available in their exchange reserves, can over the long term be confident of successfully manipulating exchange values simply by dumping or buying up a particular currency. Even more to the point, it is unreasonable to expect that Washington and Tokyo will always see eye-to-eye on what the yen-dollar exchange rate should be and act in concert to achieve it: no Japanese government, for example, could safely ignore the domestic political consequences that would ensue if the Japanese economy were hit by a serious recession caused by the fact that the yen had grown so strong as to drastically reduce Japan's ability to import and export.

On balance, however, the odds seem good that the dollar will remain "low" in relation to the yen for some time to come. But it is important to bear in mind that even a cheaper dollar offers no instant cure-all for the U.S. trade balance. Foreign trade contracts and lead times on export deliveries tend to be long and the markets that U.S. industry and agriculture lost to foreign competitors in the years of the excessively strong dollar will not be regained overnight. According to many foreign trade analysts, in fact, unless its value takes a further and unexpectedly precipitous fall, the "cheaper" dollar is unlikely to have a significantly favorable impact on U.S. trade with Japan until well into 1987.

Still, between the progressive elimination of Japan's surviving trade barriers and a more favorable exchange rate it seems clear that U.S. exporters ought to find the Japanese market a more benign and attractive one in the years immediately ahead than they did in the first half of the 1980s. Japanese concessions, past and future, to U.S. demands for freer access for U.S. products in a number of areas already targeted by U.S. trade negotiators should offer lucrative new opportunities to American manufacturers of cigarettes, paper, plywood, pharmaceuticals, medical equipment, telecommunications equipment and industrial electronic gear. At the same time, lower dollar prices should help to halt the decline that has taken place since 1980 in the competitiveness of U.S. agricultural products and increase the appeal to Japanese buyers of such things as U.S. chemicals and wood pulp.

It would be a grievous mistake, however, for American businessmen to assume that a more favorable exchange rate and Japanese trade concessions by themselves will automatically produce these results—or that significant increases in exports to Japan can be achieved only in products singled out for special attention by government trade representatives. Even in fields where constraining trade barriers are eliminated, U.S. companies that may thereby be inspired to launch a serious effort to export to Japan will have to emulate the meticulous attention to quality, service, intelligent marketing and effective distribution that underlie the past successes in the Japanese market of firms such as Warner-Lambert, Burroughs and Teledyne. And instead of relying entirely on traditional export processes, some of the would-be new exporters would surely be well advised to consider imaginative devices such as the consortium arrangement under which America's Smith Kline and Japan's Fujisawa Research Labs exchanged proprietary drugs for distribution in each other's countries.

Given sufficient aggressiveness and, in some cases, greater efforts to enhance the competitiveness of their products, it should also be possible for a considerable number of U.S. companies that do not now export to Japan to do so successfully even in fields where trade barriers have not been the limiting factor. To offer an industry-by-industry survey of such potential markets or detailed proposals for exploiting them is well outside the scope of this book. But, like Den Fujita of McDonald's Japan, I am totally persuaded that U.S. manufacturers of goods ranging from do-it-yourself products to auto parts could find profitable new niches in Japan if they would do some or all of the following things:

1. Make a serious study of the Japanese market with particular emphasis on Japan's changing economic and social patterns
2. Tailor their wares to Japanese tastes and requirements
3. Move as swiftly to exploit opportunities in the Japanese market as Japanese firms do to exploit opportunities in ours
4. Keep a much closer eye on Japan's increasingly innovative technology and, where feasible, borrow from it assiduously.

The mere fact that the United States has it within its power to sell more goods to Japan does not, of course, by itself assure an easing of Japanese-American economic tensions. So long as the attention of the American public remains exclusively focused on our merchandise trade deficit with the Japanese, it will be of key importance not only that U.S. exports to Japan increase in the years immediately ahead but that they increase at a faster rate than Japanese exports to the United States.

This raises the question of just how much U.S. business can reasonably expect to expand its imports to Japan under existing conditions—to which the only honest answer is that nobody really knows. As of early 1985, the U.S. Department of Commerce estimated that if Japan eliminated all its remaining barriers against U.S. products, American exports to Japan might increase by $17 billion a year. And in a letter to the *New York Times* in August 1985 the department's chief economist, Robert Ortner, edged a little further out on the limb suggesting that with totally unrestricted access to Japanese markets U.S. exports might rise by as much as $20 billion a year.

This was heady stuff: if a turnaround of such magnitude had occurred in 1985, for example, it would have cut our $50 billion trade deficit with Japan to $30 billion—or nearly 20 percent less than the deficit for 1984. Outside the Commerce Department, however, the prevailing view among trade experts was that Ortner and his colleagues were indulging in wishful thinking. Most other government economists doubted that the disappearance of all trade barriers would increase U.S. exports to Japan by more than $8 to $10 billion. And in a highly detailed 1985 study of the matter, C. Fred Bergsten and William R. Cline of the non-partisan Institute for International Economics implicitly dismissed even that figure as too high. The actual reduction in the trade deficit produced by complete Japanese liberalization, they argued, would be no more than $5 to $6 billion—a sum which, as a New York–based Japanese businessman of my acquaintance gloomily observed, "would have about the same effect on your Congress that a ten-cent tip does on a Manhattan taxi driver."

All of these estimates, however, rested on limited assumptions: they did not make any allowance for the potential impact of a cheaper dollar on Japan's imports and exports. Yet by the end of 1985 the U.S. prices of certain Japanese products—notably semiconductors, machine tools and automobiles—had already risen as a result of altered exchange rates, and while the increases were not yet substantial enough to curtail noticeably U.S. purchases of those products, some Japanese manufacturers nonetheless saw them as disturbing portents of a looming decline in the competitiveness of Japanese goods in the American market.

Another factor which none of the prognosticators took into account—understandably since it was totally unquantifiable—was the drive for increased competitiveness at home and abroad visible in certain sectors of U.S. industry. But here again there were certain hopeful signs: a growing number of American companies were responding to the Japanese challenge with determined efforts to cut costs and raise productivity, often through the use of manufacturing technologies and methods taken over from the Japanese themselves. Admittedly some of the most notable of these efforts, such as those launched by Xerox, Armco Inc. and Ford Motor Company, would do nothing to increase U.S. exports to Japan, but they were nonetheless calculated to have a favorable impact on the trade balance by impeding Japanese capture of even greater shares of the American market.

To assess with any precision the interaction of all these forces and their net effect upon Japanese-American trade is clearly impossible—which serves to demonstrate once again the inherent limitations of economic forecasting. Nonetheless, there would seem to be enough trends favorable to U.S. enterprise currently visible to make it reasonable to believe that if American businessmen take intelligent advantage of their export opportunities our trade deficit with Japan can be reduced very perceptibly by 1987. And while that alone will not silence the Japan-bashers, there are still other opportunities which, if properly exploited and adequately explained to the American people, could serve to diminish the pressure for protectionism.

Some of the brightest prospects for U.S. business in Japan stem from a reality to which I have alluded before—which is that the so-called trade balance is a highly imperfect gauge of the actual economic dealings between two countries. Reflecting only exchanges of physical goods, the merchandise trade balance totally ignores the increasingly important international commerce in nontangibles: the sale of licensing and royalty agreements, the provision of transportation, financial and consulting services and a host of other business activities involving ideas and know-how rather than concrete products. Yet a dollar extracted from foreign tourists or earned by the sale of insurance abroad is worth just as much as one earned by the export of beef or widgets and contributes directly or indirectly to the creation of jobs in the country that provides the service in question. And since the role of the service industries looms ever larger in the Japanese economy as well as in our own, the prospects for greater U.S. penetration of the Japanese market in this area are, I believe, particularly promising.

One reason why this is so is that Japanese service industries, while growing rapidly in size and sophistication, remain in many instances less highly developed than their American counterparts and, as a result, are more vulnerable to competition than Japan's manufacturing industries. And while U.S. companies have already taken advantage of this situation in fields such as insurance and computer software, there are a number of others ranging from direct mail advertising to hospital management where U.S. expertise has not yet been fully exploited in Japan.

Another advantage enjoyed by U.S. service entrepreneurs lies in the perennial Japanese fascination with U.S. culture and the United States itself. Again it is beyond my scope to offer any blueprint for capitalizing more heavily on this phenomenon, but the possibilities run all the way from expanded production of dubbed American films for video tape rentals to more aggressive tourist promotion. (In 1984, Japanese tourists spent nearly $1 billion more in the United States than American tourists did in Japan, but one travel industry expert has argued that even this figure could be substantially increased if the U.S. government would budget a relatively modest amount to attract more Japanese visitors—something, say, like the $15 million a year that the government of the Bahamas spends to lure American tourists.)

Perhaps the most important opportunities for greatly expanded U.S. service sales, however, are being created by the internationalization of the Japanese banking and financial systems. With the barriers to full foreign participation in these fields progressively falling, major U.S. financial institutions are moving eagerly to exploit Japan's huge pool of savings in every possible way. As of the end of 1985, for example, Citibank was rumored to be considering the purchase of a Japanese bank with 101 local branches—and while that transaction did not in the end take place, a major American venture into retail banking in Japan seems probable sooner or later. It also seems clear that in the reasonably near future American firms will play an important role in such lucrative activities as the management of Japan's ballooning pension funds and the underwriting of securities.

In short, there seems every reason to assume that, in addition to boosting its merchandise exports, the United States can considerably increase its service sales in Japan in the years immediately ahead—and thus reduce still further the real gap in bilateral trade between the two countries. And on top of that, it seems safe to assume that the investments made by U.S. companies in Japan will produce a steadily growing flow of profits back to this country. (With the exception of money earned through banking operations, such "repatriated profits" are not reflected in either the merchandise or service trade statistics; yet, again, a dollar of repatriated profit is worth just as much as a dollar earned by exporting.)

Just how much and how quickly our national income from investments in Japan increases, however, will depend directly on the degree of vision and enterprise that American businessmen display in seeking a larger foothold in the Japanese economy in years to come. On that score, paradoxically, the past U.S. record leaves much to be desired, yet nonetheless offers grounds for optimism.

For most of the forty years since the end of World War II, the foreign investments made by American industry have been primarily inspired by three considerations: U.S. energy and raw material requirements, the relative ease of doing business in the developed economies of Western Europe and the low labor costs available in the underdeveloped nations. This meant that Japan, which was not particularly attractive on any of these counts, got the short end of the stick. In 1982, American investments in Japan amounted to only about 3 percent of our total private investment overseas—a figure equaled, ludicrously enough, by U.S. investment in Belgium, which has an economy less than one-tenth the size of Japan's. And as late as March 1984 more than 40 percent of the 200 American manufacturing and mining companies ranked highest in sales by *Fortune* magazine still had no major operations in Japan.

All this undeniably betrays a deplorable shortsightedness on the part of too many U.S. corporate managers in the past. Yet there is encouragement to be found in the remarkable penetration of the Japanese economy that U.S. industry has achieved with the relatively modest assets that it has so far committed in Japan: in 1984, according to McKinsey & Company's Kenichi Ohmae, just 200 American companies grossed more than $44 billion in direct manufacturing and sales operations in Japan. And even more encouraging is the evidence that U.S. businessmen in growing numbers are responding to the pull of Japan's unequaled economic dynamism. Since 1982, according to Mrs. Yoriko Kawaguchi, who heads the foreign investment division of the Ministry of International Trade and Industry, direct U.S. investment in Japan has been increasing at a rate of about 20 percent a year and in 1983 alone it ran to more than $420 million.

Much of this growing flow of money has gone into start-up operations: by MITI's reckoning, nearly a score of new manufacturing facilities were built in Japan in 1982 and 1983 by U.S.–controlled corporations. By the mid-1980s, however, a considerable share of it was being spent on the purchase of substantial interests in existing Japanese corporations by firms such as Merck, Goodyear and Colgate-Palmolive. Either way, not all of these new ventures can be expected to succeed and at best it is likely to be some years before the more recent of them begin to return significant profits to their U.S. parents. There are, however, U.S. investments of somewhat longer standing—some $700 million worth between 1975 and 1980—that should start paying off soon. And for U.S. firms long established in Japan, such as Coca-Cola, IBM and McDonald's, profit prospects have already been brightened by an exchange rate that means their yen earnings now translate into more dollars than was the case in the early 1980s.

Even if all the favorable omens now visible are borne out and American business simultaneously expands its exports, service sales and investment earnings in Japan, the results will almost certainly fail to satisfy economic primitives in the United States. In early 1985 a MITI official who is highly knowledgeable about the U.S. economy and whose judgments I have found consistently accurate over a period of years flatly told me: "Provided anything approaching free trade between the U.S. and Japan is allowed to continue, you will go on running with a trade deficit with us as far ahead as I can see." And in their 1985 study of the subject, Bergsten and Cline of the Institute for International Economics reached essentially the same conclusion: even at a time when Japan and the United States were in "global equilibrium," they suggested, it would be normal for the Japanese to have a trade surplus with the United States of $15 to $17 billion a year.

Disturbing as it may initially sound, however, this is not in reality a prospect that ought to worry anyone. A merchandise trade deficit of that size with Japan would do the U.S. economy no harm—particularly if it were partially offset by a positive American balance in service trade with the Japanese. Or, to be more precise, such a trade deficit with Japan would be entirely acceptable provided we were not at the same time running deficits with all our other major trading partners.

How long it may take the United States to get onto this kind of economic footing with Japan is a matter of speculation and it would be utterly deceptive to argue that such a footing can ever be achieved exclusively through the efforts of U.S. private enterprise. But it is by no means unrealistic to assert that greater activity in Japan by U.S. business can rather quickly produce real progress in that direction—enough progress so that with intelligent political management the pressures for more and more protectionism can be successfully repelled.

This, however, assumes that when progress has, in fact, been made it will be generally perceived as such. And to ensure that may well require a conscious effort at public education by those who shape our economic thinking: bureaucrats, economists, journalists and, just conceivably, even our more enlightened politicians. To tolerate a national debate that focuses on our merchandise trade balance with a single nation to the near exclusion of all other components of our international economic relations represents a failure in responsibility on the part of our political and intellectual leaders—a failure which should at the very least be redeemed by some rethinking of the haphazard and piecemeal way in which the relevant statistics are now presented to the public by government agencies.

This, of course, is not to say that any amount of public education or more sophisticated economic reporting can compensate for unpalatable realities. The contribution that U.S. private enterprise might make even under present circumstances to an easing of our economic problems with Japan is very great indeed. But it is virtually certain to fall short of what is needed to achieve the ultimate goal—which clearly mut be the establishment of a sound long-term equilibrium between Japan and the United States. To accomplish that, in my view, significant changes in government policies will have to be made in both Tokyo and Washington.

14 Who's Us?

In the waning days of 1985 some of the more original thinkers in the Japanese foreign ministry came up with a neat scheme for solving their country's economic problems with the United States. All that was needed, they told each other delightedly, was a new world oil crisis. That would send Japan's bill for imported energy soaring and automatically wipe out its troublesome trade surplus.

"It's only a joke," one Foreign Office man carefully explained when he passed this nugget along to the *Wall Street Journal's* E. S. Browning. "But there is some truth in it." This, unfortunately, is also the best that can be said for many of the proposed policy changes that Americans have urged upon the Japanese government in recent years.

Outraged by what they see as Japan's economic misbehavior, U.S. spokesmen, both official and self-appointed, have freely pressed the Japanese to mend their ways through adoption of an astonishing array of alleged reforms. At various times and with varying degrees of intensity, they have suggested that Japan greatly increase its military spending, launch a Marshall Plan for China, adopt a comprehensive system of export quotas, earmark a fixed share of the Japanese semiconductor market for U.S. manufacturers and stiffen its antitrust laws in such a way as to prevent the coordinated restructuring of depressed industries.

Most of these proposals—and the list I have given constitutes only a modest sampling of them—would indeed have impact on the Japanese trade surplus with the United States. But they would also have other, highly negative consequences or, at the very least, involve serious risk of unacceptable side effects. A major increase in Japanese defense spending, for example, might possibly divert some of Japan's economic energies from overseas trade and in the short run would almost certainly produce an increase in U.S. exports of military equipment to Japan. In the longer run, however, it would surely result in the emergence of a painfully competitive Japanese armaments industry and, more serious yet, raise the danger of unpredictable changes both in Japan's domestic politics and in its international posture.

At bottom, then, too many American proposals as to how Japan should revamp its economic policies have been only half thought out—and that is because they have often rested on unsound assumptions. As Antonio Maria Costa of the Organization for European Cooperation and Development once observed: "It is certainly wrong to punish Japan for its efficiency in production." To argue, in other words, that America's problems can be cured by imposing unwise American economic practices on Japan is nonsense, both philosophically and practically. And it is equally misguided to believe, as a disturbingly large number of Americans appear to do, that both the responsibility and the remedies for the Japanese-American trade imbalance lie solely in Japan's hands.

Yet, as muddled as American thinking on this subject has often been, it has been basically right on one count: there are still important steps which the Japanese could take to assist American enterprise and which in their own national interest they should take with as little delay as possible.

One of these would be to give higher priority—the highest possible priority, in fact—to eliminating resistance within the Japanese bureaucracy to trade liberalization and the internationalization of Japan's economy. As things now stand, Japan's civil servants still possess both too much latitude in interpreting economic policy and too much power to shape economic legislation and regulations. In recent years, some of the bureaucrats in Tokyo whom I esteem most highly have complained to me of growing political interference in the operation of their ministries. Much as it may outrage my mandarin friends, however, I am convinced that what is called for now is an even stronger assertion of control over governmental operations by Japan's elected political leaders.

Specifically, the politicians should make it plain—perhaps by a few well-publicized punitive actions—that bureaucrats who wage a private war against foreign imports or who devise gimmicks such as the Software Protection Act in order to deprive foreign enterprises of competitive strength will find their careers blighted. Restrictive measures such as those which curb the activities of U.S. lawyers in Japan or permit "advisers" from Japanese private industry to rig the product standards imposed by the Japanese government on their American competitors must be swept away. It should be axiomatic that in any particular industry American-owned businesses in Japan will unquestioningly be accorded the same privileges enjoyed by their Japanese-owned counterparts in the United States. By the same token, it should be routine rather than exceptional for managers of American-owned enterprises in Japan to be consulted by government economic agencies on all levels. (To argue, as I have heard MITI officials do, that only Japanese citizens can be permitted to participate in the regulatory deliberations of Japanese ministries is legally inaccurate according to Japan's own Supreme Court and, in any case, contrasts unpleasantly with the freedom of access which representatives of Japanese business have to federal, state and local bodies in the United States.)

If they hope to make such notable changes in the mind-set of the bureaucracy, however, Japan's political leaders must first make it unmistakably plain that they are genuinely prepared to live with the consequences of stronger American competition. It would obviously be indulging in fantasy to think that any Japanese government will willingly pay the political cost of measures that threaten major long-term damage to the national economy. In the past, however, Japan's Liberal Democratic rulers have been lamentably quick to cave in to premature—and frequently exaggerated—yelps of economic distress from special-interest groups. In one striking instance of this, the Nakasone government at the end of 1985 unveiled plans to subsidize smaller exporters whose foreign orders had fallen because of the increased cost of the yen on foreign exchange markets. Politically expedient as it may have been, this move not only runs counter to the purpose of strengthening the yen in the first place but served to reinforce foreign criticism that Japan is guilty of "export mania."

The latter is a charge that Japanese government spokesmen denied for many years. The Japanese economy, they insisted, is not truly export-driven and as evidence they cited the fact that Japan derives a far smaller share of its gross national product from exports than do Britain and West Germany—or, for that matter, any of the major industrialized nations except the United States. Statistically, this is true enough, but in this case, as in so many matters, the raw statistics are deceptive: a number of key Japanese industries are in fact characterized by an excessive preoccupation with export markets and it is these industries that play the greatest role in shaping economic relations between Japan and its foreign trading partners.

To be fair, however, the undue reliance of important elements of Japanese business on foreign sales is at least in part a natural consequence of an obsession with "fiscal prudence" on the part of Japan's politicians and bureaucrats. American and European observers have long argued that the best way to reduce overblown Japanese trade surpluses lies in more rapid expansion of Japan's domestic economy and a general increase in the Japanese standard of living that would produce greater demand for imported goods. There are, moreover, obvious measures by means of which the Japanese government could stimulate such expansion. Some of the Japanese capital that now goes overseas could be lured into domestic investment by revising tax laws which currently make it more lucrative to put money abroad than to keep it at home. Consumer spending could be stimulated through greatly increased—and badly needed—government investment in infrastructure and housing as well as through creation of more extensive and easily accessible consumer credit facilities. And a major step toward higher living standards might be achieved by a drive to reduce the great disparity between the wages paid by Japan's large corporations and those prevailing in the myriad smaller enterprises which employ two-thirds or more of all Japanese workers.

Most of these ideas have, in fact, long been discussed in Japan and support for them seems to be gradually growing. In early 1986, in fact, in a ground-breaking report to Prime Minister Yasuhiro Nakasone, a panel of distinguished private citizens headed by a former governor of the Bank of Japan strongly urged "a historical transformation" of the Japanese economy into one primarily fueled by domestic demand.

How soon there will be any meaningful action on this score, however, is hard to predict. Revealingly, a program allegedly designed to increase domestic consumption that Nakasone unveiled with great fanfare in the spring of 1986 proved to involve no additional expenditure of government funds whatsoever. Basically, in other words, the prime minister seemed to be trying to do the trick with mirrors and the reason why was clear: he, like most other Japanese leaders, was afraid to fly in the face of a commitment to reduced government spending that became one of the sacred cows of Japanese politics at the end of the 1970s.

To justify their parsimony, which was powerfully pressed upon them by the cautious bureaucrats of the Ministry of Finance, Japan's politicians have pointed out that for years the Japanese government ran budget deficits which were even larger in relation to the gross national product than those of the United States. The comparison, however, is misleading, for where the U.S. government has increasingly been driven to borrow abroad to finance its deficits the Japanese government has been able to do so by tapping domestic savings. Unlike the United States, in other words, Japan has it within its power to live better without going into hock to foreigners.

To be sure, the political consensus that produced the drive for smaller government in Japan will not be easy to reverse nor would it be reasonable to ask Japanese politicians to show more courage than their American brothers in resisting the demands of special interests for insulation against foreign competition. Yet there seems no question that by gratifying the evident desire of younger Japanese for more of the good things of life, Japan's leaders could at the same time reduce the risk of an economic breach with the United States. And those are incentives which skillful politicians should be able to employ to their own advantage.

As the history of Japanese-American relations over the last fifteen years makes plain, there is one great drawback to dwelling on the things Japan could do to alleviate the economic problems between our two countries: it encourages Americans to overlook the fact that those problems are in large part of our own making and to obscure the urgent need for the United States itself to revise a wide range of government policies bearing on our commerce with Japan.

It is, I believe, improbable that the U.S. government by its own unaided efforts can fully and permanently remedy the present Japanese-American imbalance—or at least not as long as so many Americans persist in regarding our trade gap with Japan as a primary cause of our international economic difficulties rather than the most conspicuous symptom of them. In the long run, it seems highly unlikely that the United States can deal successfully with Japan on any enduring basis unless we Americans come to grips with the basic causes of the growing instability of our economic position worldwide. And that will happen only if we are prepared to swallow a good deal of painful medicine ranging from much more stringent long-term control of government spending to abandonment of the national illusion that our wages and living standards can forever increase while our comparative industrial productivity steadily declines.

All this, however, does not mean that nothing but a national economic reformation can ease our present tensions with the Japanese. Well short of that, there are specific and thoroughly feasible measures open to the U.S. government that would considerably enhance the ability of U.S. private enterprise to compete successfully in Japan.

Some of the measures to which I refer are ones whose sole purpose so far as U.S. interests are concerned would be to strengthen our hand vis-à-vis the Japanese. These include:

- The permanent stationing of high-level U.S. trade negotiators in Tokyo and the development of a support system that equips them with the most accurate possible data and realistic objectives. Given the great importance of personal relationships in Japan, frequent changes in the composition of U.S. trade negotiation teams is counterproductive. It is also counterproductive when the Japanese can legitimately complain, as they did during the 1985 trade negotiations, that U.S. trade representatives are unfamiliar with the provisions of Japanese economic regulations and have no specific proposals as to how they might be changed to American advantage.
- The mounting of a campaign to pressure the nations of Western Europe into relaxing some of their more indefensible barriers against Japanese imports. (Italy, for example, currently permits the importation of only 3,000 Japanese cars a year.) There is no valid reason why European industry should enjoy a greater degree of protection from Japanese competition than American industry, and the possibility of increased sales in Europe might at least in some degree diminish the concentration of Japanese exporters on the U.S. market.

• Federal financial and administrative support for wider and quicker dissemination of Japanese scientific and technological research in English translation. Thanks primarily to the efforts of Sen. Max Baucus of Montana, Congress has already made a modest move in this direction, but there is urgent need for more ambitious efforts including a crash program to train competent scientific translators. Contrary to complacent Western predictions in years past, Japan is emerging as a major source of technological and scientific innovation, and to keep abreast of its Japanese competitors U.S. industry must have greater access to Japanese technical literature.

• Repeal of the laws that bar oil exports from Alaska's North Slope and earmark most of the timber grown on federal lands for American sawmills in order to assure them of a low-cost supply of raw material. In both these cases, Japan would be the logical customer if the United States allowed free trade, and the potential increase in American exports would be of startling proportions: in early 1985 Murray Weidenbaum, a former chairman of President Reagan's Council of Economic Advisers, estimated that sales of these two commodities alone could reduce the U.S. trade deficit with Japan by as much as $20 billion a year.

Though Dr. Weidenbaum's estimate seems to me a reasonable one, I know of no way to reduce to dollar terms the impact that adoption of all the measures proposed above would have on U.S. commerce with Japan. Over time, however, it would surely be substantial. And there are still other possibilities for useful action by the U.S. government—steps that would assist American business in its dealings everywhere abroad but would be particularly valuable in our dealings with the Japanese.

One of these steps would be to stop restricting the exports of a wide variety of high-technology products to non-Communist countries on the grounds that they may be diverted to the Soviet Union. Neither the historical record nor the ever-increasing might of the Soviet military machine offers any reason to think that such behavior significantly enhances our national security—and it does spur the efforts of nations such as Japan that have well-developed high-technology capabilities of their own to replace potential high-technology imports from the United States with devices of their own manufacture.

Another such step would be active encouragement by Washington of joint research and development ventures between competing firms in the same industry. Here, as in the dissemination of Japanese research materials, Congress has already taken helpful steps. What is still needed, however, is a switch from cautious legal toleration of such consortia to positive promotion of them. The point here is not that it might be clever to emulate the Japanese government in its much-ballyhooed "fifth generation computer" project. Rather it is that Japan's great diversified corporations with their immense resources are in many cases now spending more on research and development than any one of their U.S. competitors can afford—or thinks it can afford. Indeed, according to one Tokyo businessman with sources in both companies, America's Hewlett-Packard budgeted less for all its R&D in 1984 than Japan's NEC spent on its single biggest project. Part of the answer to the growing R&D gap between Japanese and American industry doubtless lies in greater readiness to invest in the future on the part of U.S. corporations. Another part of it, though, would seem to lie in more pooling of their research capabilities—and given the Caesar's wife approach to any form of cooperation between competitors that has so long prevailed in the United States, this is unlikely to proceed as rapidly as would be desirable without official stimulation.

Recognition of the need for more R&D consortia, however, should be only the beginning of an assault on a more basic problem: the damaging effects on the global economic strength of the United States of antitrust and regulatory policies conceived in an era when the American market was essentially self-contained and foreign competition of only marginal concern. The toughest competition faced by U.S. industry in Japan—and, in many cases, the most effective competition it faces from Japanese-owned enterprises in the United States itself—comes from very large firms that are growing ever larger. Under these circumstances, as Secretary of Commerce Malcolm Baldridge has insistently pointed out, the section of the Clayton Antitrust Act that forbids mergers or acquisitions that "may" substantially reduce competition or might, at some undetermined point in time, "tend to" create a domestic monopoly puts American enterprise at a clear disadvantage world-wide.

No less damaging is the freedom of U.S. courts and regulatory agencies to reinterpret the antitrust laws pretty much as they see fit to do at any given moment. Whether the break-up of AT&T will ultimately provide Americans with cheaper or better telecommunications is a highly problematic question. There is no question, however, about its international impact: it simultaneously opened the U.S. telecommunications market to foreign competition and impaired the ability of one of the strongest U.S. industrial enterprises to compete in foreign markets. To be sure, the AT&T case was unique in certain respects. Nonetheless, there seems little hope of avoiding more such self-inflicted damage to our competitiveness abroad unless we adopt laws that make it mandatory for our judges and trustbusters to consider the international as well as the domestic consequences of their rulings.

None of the governmental initiatives that I have just described would by itself make a decisive difference in the ability of the United States to cope with the Japanese challenge and some of them run counter to widely held beliefs and deeply entrenched special interests in this country. Yet anyone inclined to dismiss them out of hand would do well to recall that in our dealings with Japan over the past generation our chief national liabilities have been outmoded patterns of thought and mistaken assumptions about the degree of comfortable inefficiency that we could safely afford.

Politics, as its practitioners never tire of saying, is the art of the possible, and it would be folly to hope that at any time in the foreseeable future either Japanese or American leaders will reckon it possible to push through all the policy changes that would make for a healthier economic relationship between the two countries. But it does not seem unreasonable to think some of them can be accomplished—and there is at least one natural force for improvement in the status quo upon which both the Japanese and American governments can capitalize relatively painlessly. Important as it is for U.S. business to increase its stake in the Japanese economy, it is also very much in American as well as Japanese interests to see a continuing growth in private Japanese investment in the United States.

At first glance, this might seem to be a matter that requires no governmental attention. As of the end of 1981, by the reckoning of Kenichi Ohmae of McKinsey & Company, subsidiaries and affiliates of U.S. corporations produced some $20 billion worth of goods in Japan while Japanese-owned enterprises turned out only a bit over $5 billion worth of products in the United States. Since then, however, that balance has been changing as more and more Japanese companies have rushed to acquire a U.S. base. In 1983 alone, Japan's Ministry of International Trade and Industry has reported, direct Japanese investment in the United States amounted to $2.5 billion—or roughly seven times new American investment in Japan that year. And in 1984 Japanese investors for the first time put more money in the United States than did the nationals of any other foreign nation—a development which, according to Commerce Department figures, boosted total direct Japanese investment in this country to just under $15 billion.

This, much as the fact may surprise some of our more demagogic politicians, still amounted to less than 40 percent of the $38 billion worth of investments that British interests held in the United States at the same point. Nonetheless, the sudden surge in Japanese investment here and the high degree of coverage given it by the media have inevitably raised some American hackles. Early in 1985, fearful of what he believes will be their deadening effect on research and development in this country, CIA director William Casey denounced Japanese investments in the U.S. computer industry as "Trojan horses." Not long afterward Colorado's governor Richard Lamm expressed concern about Japanese access to U.S. technology and threw in a warning that Americans might be facing "economic colonialism." Meantime, spokesmen for organized labor waxed indignant over the unabashed efforts of some—though by no means all—Japanese companies to keep unions out of their American plants. And not a few American businessmen, horrified to realize that competition from Japanese-owned companies in the United States could not be suppressed by a simple resort to tariffs or trade barriers, charged that the Japanese were simply exploiting the American market by assembling their products here instead of in Japan.

By far the most sensitive of the charges raised by American opponents of Japanese investment in the United States, however, was the allegation that it fostered an unacceptable degree of foreign interference in the domestic affairs of the United States. Sen. Frank Murkowski of Alaska put it most bluntly: "Once they own your assets, they own you." Less simplistically, other observers complained of the massive scope of Japanese efforts to influence American politicians and public opinion: according to Justice Department figures, the Japanese government and Japanese corporate interests spent nearly $20 million on lobbying, public relations and legal services in the United States in 1984—and that did not include what by some estimates was an even greater amount of spending that did not have to be reported to the Justice Department because it was done on behalf of companies which, while Japanese-owned, were legally American.

On the last of these counts the Japanese did, in fact, appear somewhat vulnerable. Though Japanese business clearly has as much moral right to protect its interests in the United States as American business has to protect its interests in Japan, there was blatancy and insensitivity about such things as PAC contributions to congressional campaigns by Japanese-owned companies ($1 million in 1984) that could only prove politically counterproductive in the long run. And while there might be little the Japanese government could do directly to curb ill-advised muscle-flexing by Japanese industry, it could scarcely be questioned that some indirect governmental suasion on the point would be desirable and, in some degree at least, effective.

Both politically and economically, the Japanese government would also be well advised to seek ways to change the mix of Japanese investment in the United States. Much too large a percentage of the Japanese capital flowing into the United States in recent years has been used to purchase U.S. government securities—in other words, to buy a share of the U.S. national debt. In 1984, in fact, nearly a quarter of the $25.5 billion in notes, bills and bonds that the U.S. Treasury sold to foreigners was bought by Japanese and that represented far more than they invested in the private sector of the American economy that year.

It is entirely probable, as Federal Reserve Board chairman Paul Volcker warned in 1984, that such massive foreign underwriting of our national debt is "unsustainable" over time. But so long as it continues it constitutes a temptation to the U.S. government to go on living beyond its means through mortgaging abroad an increasing share of the wealth that will be created in this country in years ahead. This is a temptation that the Japanese government could help to remove by adopting tax and other measures that would make U.S. government securities less attractive to Japanese capital and investment in American business more so.

At bottom, however, the responsibility for achieving a more productive pattern of Japanese investment in the United States rests with our own political leaders. To do this they should eliminate the tax break that the Treasury currently gives to foreign buyers of U.S. government paper and, infinitely more important, they must demonstrate a sustained resolve to keep our federal budget deficits at a level sustainable out of domestic savings. But even as they dampen the Japanese ardor for T-bills, they must resist all calls for restrictions on Japanese investment in manufacturing, sales and service operations in the United States. For all such investments in greater or lesser degree help to strengthen the U.S. economy and to diminish the possibilities of any national confrontation between Japan and the United States.

At the simplest level, this is so because each time a Japanese company decides to manufacture some of its products in the United States rather than bring them in from Japan, there is a positive effect on America's balance of trade. In broader, balance-of-payment terms, of course, the curtailment of the Japanese company's export earnings is in some degree offset by profits earned in the United States and sent back to Japan. But because of the excessive attention focused on the trade balance, anything that serves to reduce U.S. imports from Japan or inhibit their growth also helps to inhibit the spread of protectionist sentiment in this country.

The real value of continuing Japanese investment in U.S.–based enterprises is far more than just a matter of economic sleight of hand, however. When a new Japanese-owned factory opens in the United States it creates more jobs for Americans both directly and indirectly. The automobile assembly plant that Mazda Motors began to build in Flat Rock, Michigan, in May 1985 will one day employ some 5,000 U.S workers. But on top of that it will assist Minneapolis-Honeywell Inc., which won the contract to build the plant's computerized control system, in carving out a new niche for itself in factory automation and will create more business for enterprises ranging from local restaurants to manufacturers of safety glass.

The Mazda venture in Michigan, of course, is merely one rather modest example of a nationwide phenomenon. As of the beginning of 1985, according to the Washington-based Japan Economic Institute, some 340 companies owned or controlled by Japanese interests operated plants in the United States, employing nearly 100,000 Americans. And even that figure is deceptively small since it does not include auto salesmen, bank clerks and a host of service personnel whose jobs are directly dependent on Japanese-owned enterprises in this country nor the incalculable number of Americans ranging from video cassette rental clerks to motorcycle repairmen who indirectly owe their employment to products of Japanese origin now being manufactured in the United States.

What makes it all the harder to assess the full impact of Japanese investment on the U.S. labor market is that in addition to creating new jobs it has also preserved some that would otherwise have disappeared. In Connecticut's perennially depressed Naugatuck River Valley, not far from the hardscrabble little town where I was born, some 200 jobs were saved in early 1984 when the Nippon Densan Corporation bought up a money-losing motor fan factory and announced plans to spend $3 million automating it. More notable yet, Japan's Sanyo took over a TV assembly plant in Arkansas which had been teetering on the edge of bankruptcy and, using essentially the same work force and equipment as its unsuccessful American owners had, quite rapidly converted it to profitability.

The Sanyo performance in Arkansas highlights yet another beneficial aspect of Japanese investment in U.S. industry: its role in spurring America's domestic manufacturers to achieve increased productivity and to pay greater attention to the quality of their wares. In some cases this process, beneficial as it is in terms of our national interest, has been painful for those subjected to it: in fields such as TV and appliance production, competition from Japanese-owned plants in this country has left American-owned firms in the industry with no alternative but to shape up or go out of business. In other notable instances, however, the process has been entirely benign—the fruit of management skills which Japanese industry has supplied in join ventures with U.S. corporations.

One of these skills lies in effective uses of labor. Broadly speaking, Japanese managers tend to pay much more attention than American managers to giving their workers a sense of self-esteem and involvement. (Soon after Nippon Densan bought its Connecticut plant, one veteran of the assembly line there remarked: "This is the first time in years that we've been made to feel we're an important part of this company.") Yet, at the same time, the Japanese perform a useful service in encouraging American industry to mount greater resistance to some of the more Luddite practices favored by organized labor in the United States. In its joint venture with General Motors to build cars in California, for example, Toyota Motors agreed that only UAW members would be employed. In return, however, it extracted a price from the union: the elimination of many of the rigid job classifications that in other American auto plants often mean that half a dozen workers stand idly around while a foreman searches for someone whose job description entitles him to finish a particular piece of work.

Exactly how great an impact such moves will ultimately have on the productivity of U.S. industry is uncertain: the long-term interaction of American labor and Japanese management practices is difficult to predict. But when it comes to the transfer of production technology from Japan to the United States the omens seem unreservedly favorable. In 1984, after Japan's second biggest steel company, Nippon Kokan, bought a half interest in Pittsburgh's National Steel, the new partnership promptly embarked on a massive investment program designed to eliminate the relative inefficiencies that have cost major U.S. steel companies so large a share of their home market. As Howard M. Love, chief executive officer of National Intergroup, explained: "We came to the conclusion that we had to compete on an international basis or we weren't going to make it. Technologically, that meant we had to leapfrog rather quickly." And, technologically, National's Japanese partner proved a fertile source of ideas, offering some 700 suggestions for improvement in productivity and manufacturing quality in a matter of months. All told, these raised National's "yield"—the ratio of finished products to steel originally melted—by almost 3 percent in the first year of joint ownership.

Whatever their other consequences, the growth of the Japanese economic presence in the United States and that of the American economic presence in Japan have had an identical effect in one respect: just as there are many thoroughly patriotic Japanese who now have a vested interest in the success of U.S. enterprise in their country, so there are more and more Americans who have a vested interest in the success of Japanese enterprise in our country.

To cite only the most obvious case in point, the Reagan Administration's decision not to insist upon fixed quotas on Japan's automobile exports to the United States in 1985 was not primarily influenced by representations from the highly paid U.S. lawyers and lobbyists employed by the Japanese automobile industry. (And it certainly was not influenced by any pressure from the Japanese government which in the end cautiously chose to retain the quotas anyway.) What actually turned the tide was a campaign against U.S.–imposed quotas mounted by the American International Automobile Dealers Association, a body that boasts prosperous and influential members in virtually every congressional district in the United States. It was developments of this kind that inspired a reflection on the competing interests currently at play in Japan and the United States voiced early in 1985 by Rep. Richard Durbin of Illinois. "It used to be 'us' versus 'them,' " Congressman Durbin said somewhat bemusedly. "Now we don't know who is 'us' and who is 'them' anymore."

This is a trend inevitably deplored by chauvinists and those who have no stomach for free competition in Japan and America alike. It is also, however, one that will enhance the economic health of both countries the stronger it gets. There is, I am convinced, no surer way to avert conflict and promote mutually fruitful cooperation between Japan and America than this: an entwinement of private interests in the two nations so thorough and complex that neither country can conceive of working hardship on the other without simultaneously doing unacceptable damage to itself.

Such entwinement of private interests will by no means constitute a universal panacea, much less provide automatic solutions to all the differences of opinion on diplomatic and strategic issues that may arise between Japanese and American leaders in the years ahead. Reducing the possibilities of serious economic confrontation, however, should make it easier to resolve such differences satisfactorily—if only by diverting to more positive purposes energies now squandered on essentially foolish squabbles.

Over the more than forty years since V-J Day, the United States has made enormous contributions, direct and indirect, to Japan's unprecedented economic flowering. And even if specific measures that Americans have urged upon the Japanese have sometimes been disingenuous or misguided, the basic American demand that Japan give full play to the creative powers of private enterprise has been sound. It will not do now, however, for the United States to forget the adage that admonishes physicians to first heal themselves. At this juncture in our history, it is not only imperative that those who shape American policy refrain from throwing up more impediments to the operations of Japanese business in the United States; it is no less vital that they do whatever they can to remove all the ill-advised constraints that American enterprise faces in its efforts to multiply the many successes it has already achieved in Japan.

Indeed, as an unabashed American nationalist dedicated to the continuing greatness and well-being of the United States, I see no other sensible course for my country to follow toward Japan. For the greatness of the United States like that of any other country depends in large measure on the strength of its economic sinews— and if there is any incontrovertible lesson to be learned from economic history it is that human communities achieve maximum material well-being for their members not through restrictionism and the vain chase after autarky but through the active encouragement of international interdependence founded on enlightened self-interest.

Appendix:
The Moneymakers—
A Ranking of U.S. Ventures
in Japan

This list, which is adapted from data published by *Diamond Weekly*, covers U.S. affiliates that reported to the Japanese authorities taxable income of $1 million or more in 1984. (Declared income for taxation in Japan is the only comparative earnings figure publicly available for all such companies and 1984 is the last year for which such statistics were obtainable at the time this book went to press.)

Because it is restricted to ventures that were 50 percent or more U.S.–owned as of 1984, the list does not include certain highly profitable companies in which the American interest, while substantial, was a minority one. Obviously, too, it does not include American-controlled ventures that had large sales in Japan in 1984 but reported little or no taxable income. Finally, the list does not cover banks, brokerage houses and certain other financial institutions, nor does it cover companies that in legal terms were simply branches of U.S. corporations.

Corporate names and ownership data reflect the situation as it was in 1984.

Rank	Name of U.S. Parent Company	Name of Japanese Affiliate (Name of Japanese Co-Owners If Any)	U.S. Ownership (in Percent)	Declared Income for Taxation in Millions of U.S. Dollars*
1	IBM	IBM Japan	100%	458.6
		IBM Japan Sales Ltd.	100%	30.0
		Systems Development	100%	2.0
2	Exxon/Mobil (see also Nos. 14 and 17)	Toa Nenryo Kogyo (Fuji Bank, Industrial Bank of Japan, others)	50%	229.9
		Tonen Petro-chemical	100%	39.0
		Kygnus Sekiyu (Nichimo Co.)	50%	2.3
3	Coca-Cola	Coca-Cola Japan	100%	115.3
4	Texas Instruments	Texas Instruments Japan	100%	99.7
		Texas Instruments (Asia)	100%	11.5
5	NCR	NCR Japan (Mitsubishi Trust & Banking, Mitsui Trust & Banking, Dai Ichi Kangyo Bank)	70%	73.9
6	Caltex	Nippon Petroleum Refining Co. (Nippon Oil Co.)	50%	46.9
		Koa Oil (Six Japanese oil and insurance companies)	50%	10.6
		Nippon Oil Staging Terminal Co. (Nippon Oil)	50%	2.7
		Caltex Oil (Japan)	100%	2.3
7	Hewlett-Packard	Yokogawa-Hewlett-Packard (Yokogawa Electric Works)	75%	53.9
8	McDonald's	McDonald's Co., Japan (Fujita & Co.)	50%	41
9	Burroughs Corp.	Burroughs Co., Ltd.	100%	40.7
10	A.M.P. Inc.	A.M.P. (Japan)	100%	36.5
11	CBS	CBS/Sony Group (Sony Corp.)	50%	20.2
		CBS/Sony Records	100%	6.5
		CBS/Sony Publishing	100%	5.1
		Epic/Sony (Sony Corp.)	50%	3.7
12	Honeywell	Yamatake-Honeywell (Fuji Bank, Yasuda Trust & Banking, others)	50%	27.9
		Yamatake Keiso (wholly owned subsid-	50%	5.8

Rank	Name of U.S. Parent Company	Name of Japanese Affiliate (Name of Japanese Co-Owners If Any)	U.S. Ownership (in Percent)	Taxation in Millions of U.S. Dollars
13	Pfizer	Pfizer Taito Co.	100%	33
14	Mobil Petroleum	Mobil Sekiyu	100%	32.6
15	3M	Sumitomo 3M Ltd. (Nippon Electric Co., Sumitomo Electric Ind.)	50%	24.3
		3M Health Care	100%	8.3
16	General Electric	Yokogawa Medical Systems (Yokogawa Electrical Works)	51%	11.4
		General Electric Technical Services	100%	9.1
		Engineering Plastic (Nagase & Co.)	51%	6.3
17	Exxon (see also No. 21)	Esso Sekiyu	100%	26.3
18	Molex Inc.	Molex-Japan	100%	25.7
19	Shaklee	Shaklee Japan	100%	25.3
20	Tektronix	Sony/Tektronix (Sony)	50%	23.2
21	Exxon Chemical	Exxon Chemical Japan	100%	12
		Japan Butyl (Japan Synthetic Rubber Co.)	50%	7.9
22	Intel	Intel Japan	100%	18.7
23	General Foods	Ajinomoto General Foods (Ajinomoto)	50%	18.6
24	Dart Industries	Japan Tupperware Co.	100%	16.7
25	Amway	Amway Japan	100%	15.8
26	DuPont	DuPont-Toray (Toray Industries)	50%	9.7
		DuPont-Mitsui Fluorochemicals (Mitsui Petro Chemicals)	50%	5.2
27	Thermco Systems	Tel-Thermco Engineering (Tokyo Electron)	50%	14.7
28	Bristol-Myers	Bristol-Myers KK	100%	8.6
		Bristol-Myers Lion (Lion Corp.)	51%	5.1
29	Stauffer Chemical	Toyo Stauffer Chemical Co. (Toyo Soda Mfg.)	50%	6.2
		Kashima Industries (Toyo Soda Mfg.)	70%	4.3
		Stauffer Japan	100%	2.8

* Rounded off to the nearest $100,000 and converted from yen at the average 1984 exchange rate of ¥237.5 to $1.

Rank	Name of U.S. Parent Company	Name of Japanese Affiliate (Name of Japanese Co-Owners If Any)	U.S. Ownership (in Percent)	Declared Income for Taxation in Millions of U.S. Dollars
30	Gulf & Western	Elco International	100%	9.4
		Sega Enterprises	100%	3.2
31	Eli Lilly	Eli Lilly Japan	100%	3
		Japan Elanco Co. (Shionogi & Co.)	50%	8.8
32	American Hospital Supply	AHS Japan	100%	5.6
		International Reagents Corp. (Midori-Juji Co.)	50%	5.6
33	Johnson & Johnson	Johnson & Johnson Medical	100%	2.9
		Johnson & Johnson K.K.	100%	2.9
		Ortho Diagnostic Systems	100%	2.5
		Janssen-Kyowa (Kyowa Hako Kogyo)	60%	2.7
34	Polaroid	Nippon Polaroid	100%	10.9
35	Engelhard	Nippon Engelhard (Sumitomo Metal Industries)	50%	10.9
36	Warner-Lambert	Warner-Lambert K.K.	100%	9.9
37	Borg-Warner	Borg-Warner K.K.	100%	2.2
		NSK Warner (Nippon Seiko)	50%	6.9
38	Smith Kline	Smith Kline & Fujisawa (Fujisawa Pharmaceutical Co.)	50%	9.1
39	Mallinckrodt	Daiichi Radio Isotope Laboratories (Daiichi Seiyaku Co., Daiichi Pure Chemicals Co.)	50%	8.9
40	TRW	Tokai TRW Co. (Individual)	90.6%	2.3
		Mitsumi TRW (Mitsumi Electric)	50%	5.7
41	Heublein	Kentucky Fried Chicken Japan (Mitsubishi Corp.)	50%	7.9
42	Rohm & Haas	Tokyo Organic Chemical Industries (Toagosei Chemical Industries, Sanyo Trading Co., Japan Organo)	50%	7.7

Rank	Name of U.S. Parent Company	Name of Japanese Affiliate (Name of Japanese Co-Owners If Any)	U.S. Ownership (in Percent)	Declared Income for Taxation in Millions of U.S. Dollars
43	Yates Industries	Furukawa Circuit Foil (Furukawa Electric)	50%	7.5
44	Monsanto	Monsanto Japan	100%	6.9
45	Lubrizol Corp.	Nippon Lubrizol Industries	100%	3.4
		Lubrizol Japan (Subsidiary of Lubrizol International SA of Venezuela)	100%	2.9
46	Martin Marietta	Nisso Master Builders Co. (Nippon Soda Co.)	50%	6
47	Warner Bros. Records	Warner-Pioneer Corp. (Pioneer Electric Corp.)	51%	5.9
48	S.C. Johnson & Son	Johnson Co. (Individual)	92%	5.6
49	General Motors Acceptance (see also No. 53)	Isuzu Motors Finance Co. (Isuzu Motors)	51%	5.5
50	Applied Materials	Applied Materials Japan	100%	5.3
51	Veeco Instruments	Nemic-Lambda (Individual)	72%	5.3
52	Digital Equipment	Nihon Digital Equipment	100%	5.2
53	General Motors	General Motors Overseas Distribution	100%	5.2
54	Cross & Trecker	Murata Warner Swasey (Murata Machinery)	50%	5.1
55	Avon	Avon Products Co.	100%	5
56	Burndy	Burndy Japan (Furukawa Electric, Sumitomo Electric)	50%	5
57	Shipley	Shipley Far East Co.	100%	4.9
58	Otis Elevator	Nippon Otis Elevator (Six Sumitomo companies)	55%	4.9
59	Ford	Ford Motor Co. Japan	100%	4.8

Rank	Name of U.S. Parent Company	Name of Japanese Affiliate (Name of Japanese Co-Owners If Any)	U.S. Ownership (in Percent)	Declared Income for Taxation in Millions of U.S. Dollars
60	The Interpublic Group	McCann-Erickson Hakuhodo (Hakuhodo)	51%	4.8
61	Richardson-Vicks	Nippon Vicks	100%	4.6
62	Data General	Nippon Data General (Kozo Keikau Engineering)	85%	4.6
63	Estee Lauder	Estee Lauder K.K.	100%	4.5
64	Montgomery Ward	Montgomery Ward	100%	4.5
65	Aluminum Co. of America	Moralco (Morimura Bros.)	75%	2.5
		Shibazaki Seisakusho (Furukawa Aluminum Co. & others)	50%	2
66	Memorex	Memorex Japan (Kanematsu-Gosho)	66%	4.4
67	Walt Disney Productions	Walt Disney Enterprises of Japan	100%	4.4
68	Raybestos Manhattan	Daikin R-M Co. (Daikin Mfg. Co.)	50%	4.4
69	Franklin Mint	Franklin Mint	100%	4.3
70	American International Underwriters	American International Underwriters Japan	100%	2.3
71	AMF	Chiyoda Consultants	100%	2
		AMF K.K.	100%	4.2
72	Nike	Nike Japan (Nissho Iwai)	51%	4.2
73	Schering	Essex Nippon	100%	4.1
74	Baskin-Robbins	B-R Japan (Fujiya Confectionary)	50%	4.1
75	Corning Glass Works	N-Cor Ltd. (NGK Insulators)	50%	4.1
76	Hercules Inc.	DIC-Hercules Chemicals (Dai Nippon Ink & Chemicals)	50%	4.1
77	Zimmer	Zimmer Japan	100%	4

Rank	Name of U.S. Parent Company	Name of Japanese Affiliate (Name of Japanese Co-Owners If Any)	U.S. Ownership (in Percent)	Declared Income for Taxation in Millions of U.S. Dollars
78	Brunswick	Nippon Brunswick (Mitsui & Co.)	50%	3.6
79	Sherwood Medical Industries	Nippon Sherwood Medical Ind. (Mitsui & Co.)	50%	3.5
80	Nordson Corp.	Nordson K.K.	100%	3.3
81	Medtronic	Medtronic Japan	100%	3.2
82	Universal Oil Products	Nikki-Universal (J.G.C. Corp.)	50%	3.2
83	Donaldson Co.	Nippon Donaldson	100%	3.1
84	Speedfarm	Speedfarm Co. (Obara Engineering Products)	50%	3.1
85	Levi Strauss	Levi Strauss Japan	100%	3
86	IMS Financial	IMS Japan	100%	3
87	Dresser Industries	Niigata Masoneilan Co. (Niigata Engineering Co.)	50%	3
88	Merck & Co.	MSD (Japan)	100%	2.9
89	Berlitz School of Languages	Berlitz School of Languages	100%	2.8
90	GTE	Kondo Sylvania (Individual)	70%	2.8
91	Diamond Shamrock (see also No. 107)	Nippon Dacro Shamrock (Nippon Oils & Fats)	50%	2.8
92	Scovill Mfg.	Scovill-Japan (Sanshin-Kosan)	50%	2.8
93	PPG Industries	Asahi-Penn Chemical Co. (Asahi Glass Co.)	50%	2.7
94	Arbor Acres Farm	Arbor Acres Japan (Mitsui & Co.)	50%	2.6
95	American Cyanamid	Lederle Japan (Takeda Chemical Industries)	50%	2.6
96	Tylan Corp.	Nippon Tylan (Individual)	50%	2.5

Rank	Name of U.S. Parent Company	Name of Japanese Affiliate (Name of Japanese Co-Owners If Any)	U.S. Ownership (in Percent)	Declared Income for Taxation in Millions of U.S. Dollars
97	Quaker Oats Co.	Kao-Quaker Co. (Kao Corp.)	50%	2.5
98	General Instrument	General Instrument Japan	100%	2.4
99	Ransburg Corp.	Ransburg Japan (Tokico Ltd.)	66.5%	2.4
100	Allergen Pharmaceuticals	Santen-Allergen Corp. (Santen Pharma-ceutical)	50%	2.3
101	Dow Corning	Dow Corning K.K.	100%	2.2
102	Emerson Electric	Emerson Japan Inc.	100%	2.2
103	Uniroyal	Unitta Co. (Nitta Industries)	50%	2.1
104	Avco Financial Services	Avco Financial Services of Japan	100%	2
105	Bee Chemical	Nippon Bee Chemical (Nippon Paint Co.)	50%	2
106	Commodore International	Commodore Japan	100%	1.9
107	Diamond Shamrock Chemical	San Nopco (Sanyo Chemical Industries)	50%	1.9
108	Phoenix Chemical	Adeka Argus Chemical (Asahi Denka Kogyo)	50%	1.8
109	Simmons Co.	Simmons Japan	100%	1.8
110	Apple Computer	Apple Computer Japan	100%	1.7
111	Millipore Ltd.	Nihon Millipore Kugyo	100%	1.7
112	Determined Productions	Determined Productions K.K.	100%	1.7
113	W. R. Grace & Co.	Grace Japan K.K.	100%	1.7
114	Scott Paper	Sanyo Scott (Sanyo-Kokusaku Pulp Co.)	50%	1.6
115	Cooper Industries	Nippon Cooper (C. Itoh & Co., Kawasaki Heavy Industries)	50%	1.6
116	Revlon	Revlon	100%	1.6

Rank	Name of U.S. Parent Company	Name of Japanese Affiliate (Name of Japanese Co-Owners If Any)	U.S. Ownership (in Percent)	Declared Income for Taxation in Millions of U.S. Dollars
117	Eaton Corp.	Sumitomo Eaton Hydraulics (Sumitomo Heavy Industries)	50%	1.6
118	Graco Inc.	Nippon Gray	50%	1.5
119	Union Carbide	Union Showa (Showa Denko)	50%	1.5
120	Teledyne	Teledyne Japan	100%	1.4
121	Cambridge Filter	Cambridge Filter Japan (Kondo Kogyo)	50%	1.4
122	Caterpillar	Caterpillar Mitsubishi (Mitsubishi Heavy Industries)	50%	1

BIBLIOGRAPHY

Cohen, Stephen D. *Uneasy Partnership: Competition and Conflict in Contemporary U.S. Japanese Trade Relations.* Cambridge, Mass.: Ballinger, 1984.

Christopher, Robert C. *The Japanese Mind: The Goliath Explained.* New York: Linden Press, 1983.

Dodwell Marketing Consultants. *Industrial Groupings in Japan.* Rev. ed. New York: International Publications Service, 1982–83.

Fields, George. *From Bonsai to Levi's.* New York: Macmillan, 1983.

Gibney, Frank. *Japan: The Fragile Superpower.* Rev. ed. New York: New American Library, 1980.

Hayes, Robert M., and Steven Wheelwright. *Restoring Our Competitive Edge: Competing through Manufacturing.* New York: John Wiley & Sons, 1984.

Lawrence, Robert Z. *Can America Compete?* Washington, D.C.: Brookings Institution, 1984.

McKinsey & Co. for the United States Japan Trade Study Group. *Japan Business: Obstacles and Opportunities.* Tokyo: President Inc., 1983.

Moritani, Masanori. *Japanese Technology: Getting the Best for the Least.* Tokyo: Simul Press, 1982.

Ohmae, Kenichi. *Triad Power: The Coming Shape of Global Competition.* New York: The Free Press, 1985.

Phillips, Kevin P. *Staying on Top: The Business Case for a National Industrial Strategy.* New York: Random House, 1984.

Vogel, Ezra F. *Japan as Number One: Lessons for America.* Cambridge, Mass.: Harvard University Press, 1979.

Zimmerman, Mark. *How to Do Business with the Japanese.* New York: Random House, 1984.

Index